The Hamlyn Concise Guide to
Soviet
Military Aircraft

The Hamlyn Concise Guide to
Soviet
Military Aircraft

Bill Sweetman

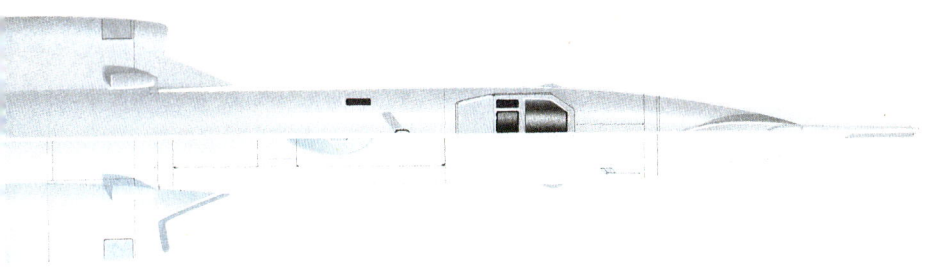

Hamlyn/Aerospace
London · New York · Sydney · Toronto

Published by
The Hamlyn Publishing Group Limited
London · New York · Sydney · Toronto
Astronaut House, Hounslow Road, Feltham,
Middlesex, England

Produced by Stan Morse
Aerospace Publishing Ltd
10, Barley Mow Passage
London W4

© Copyright Aerospace Publishing Ltd 1981

Colour profiles and line diagrams © Copyright Pilot Press Ltd

First published 1981

ISBN 0 600 34947 0 – Casebound
ISBN 0 600 34968 3 – Paperback

All correspondence concerning the content of
this volume should be addressed to Aerospace
Publishing Ltd. Trade enquiries should be addressed
to the Hamlyn Publishing Group Ltd.

Printed in England

Contents

Largest of all Soviet aircraft is the massive
Antonov An-22 turboprop freighter with its four
massive Kuznetsov engines.

Section 1
Introduction

Much of the fascination which Soviet aircraft hold for the analyst or enthusiast stems from the thick fog of secrecy with which the Soviet Union surrounds its military activities. Details which in the case of Western aircraft can be found from the nearest reference book are in Russian aircraft a matter for conjecture; frequently little more than the basic shape can be relied upon, and often not even that.

An understanding of the technical characteristics of Soviet-designed military aircraft is however essential to an appreciation of Soviet military capabilities in general, for if there is one lesson to be learned from the history of technology at war, it is that an ascendancy or disadvantage in the performance of the individual system can often outweigh a discrepancy in numbers. For many years this lesson has been held to justify the apparent numerical inferiority of NATO's forces, particularly the tactical air forces of the alliance, but more recently the validity of the argument has been called into question and the Soviet Union has shown signs of closing NATO's lead in technology.

To appreciate patterns of development in Soviet military aircraft, it is essential to bear in mind the organisation of military aviation throughout the Warsaw Pact. The term 'Soviet Air Force' is a convenient shorthand for these forces, but in fact there is no such organisation in the sense in which it is understood in the West, encompassing all activities from close support to intercontinental missiles. There are in fact three aerospace forces represented on the general staff of the Soviet Union, along with the Ground Forces and Navy. One of these forces, the RVSN, does not concern us: it is the Soviet Union's strategic missile force, armed solely with land-based missiles. Also equipped with missiles is the PVO, or Air Defence Force of the Homeland; surface-to-air missile defence of fixed targets within the Soviet Union is the responsibility of one division, the ZA-PVO, while the IA-PVO operates the Soviet Union's manned interceptors and early-warning aircraft.

Third of the aerospace forces reporting directly to the general staff is the VVS, the nearest thing to a Western air force in its structure. Support of the Ground Forces is the main role of the VVS, but it also embraces the strategic bomber force, the Long-Range Aviation or DA. Its largest division by far, however, is Frontal Aviation or FA, the tactical combat air force of the Soviet Union. FA is divided into 16 Air Armies, distributed around the Warsaw Pact states and the Soviet Union itself; each Air Army is controlled by the general staff of the district where it is based, and also embraces non-Soviet Union Warsaw Pact (NSWP) tactical air forces in that area. The third element in VVS is the transport force, or VTA, comprising a cadre of front-line tactical freighters and drawing on the resources of state airline Aeroflot in an emergency.

Another substantial force falls under Soviet Navy command: the Naval air force, AVMF, with a formidable fleet of strike and patrol aircraft backed up by an array of electronic and photographic reconnaissance aircraft. There are some indications that the Soviet Ground Forces may be following the lead of the Soviet Navy and developing its own air element, equipped with heavily armed helicopters; however, this development is not yet a confirmed fact.

The balance of priority in Soviet efforts among these diverse forces has shifted totally over the past 20 years, and this change has dominated the development of the Soviet Union's military aircraft. In the 1950s, the strategic bomber dominated the scene, and the DA and PVO enjoyed highest priority; the efforts of the industry were concomitantly diverted towards the development of bombers and interceptors. By 1960, the decision had been taken to rely on missiles as the primary strike force, and shortly afterwards it was realised that the chances of the Soviet Union becoming involved in a major conventional war were increasing. In the mid-1960s, therefore, there started the development of a number of aircraft to meet FA requirements. The PVO meanwhile began to standardise on mid-1960s interceptor designs, as the advanced Western bombers which new aircraft would be needed to counter had not materialised.

At the same time, the Soviet Navy was increasing its importance as a global instrument of power, and with the decline of the DA moved firmly into the long-range strike and reconnaissance business. As well as introducing missile-armed versions of the DA's 1950s-designed bombers, AVMF started development of aircraft designed to meet its own peculiar needs. These included a new long-range strike aircraft (the Tupolev Tu-26 [or Tu-22M] 'Backfire') and patrol aircraft (Ilyushin Il-38 'May'). The Soviet Navy also provided much of the stimulus behind early developments in vertical take-off and landing (VTOL) aircraft.

Many of these new requirements were met by radically new designs from the existing design bureaux. Originally, these design bureaux were no more than teams of engineers led by one man, and with his retirement, death or disgrace the bureau would often be dispersed. In recent years, however, this has not happened, suggesting that the bureaux have metamorphosed into large research and development organisations with facilities for building and testing prototypes, and with greater control over production than existed hitherto. In the field of commercial aircraft, there seems to be a much greater linkage between design bureaux and production locations than existed a few years ago, when production was strictly the business of the State Aircraft Factories. An interesting trend in the land of equal opportunity is that one major bureau (Tupolev) is now headed by its founder's son and

Pilots of a Soviet Frontal Aviation unit with a Mikoyan MiG-23BM 'Flogger-F' strike fighter. Most Soviet units, however, operate a more advanced derivative of the basic aircraft, the MiG-27.

another (Yakovlev) appears to be going the same way.

In most areas, the bureaux are in competition. The Mikoyan/Gurevich and Sukhoi organisations are certain to have developed and tested prototypes in nearly all categories of aircraft. For larger aircraft, such as transports, the competition presumably takes place at the design stage; the only holder of an effective monopoly appears to be Tupolev, to which bureau all large Soviet supersonic aircraft since the abortive Myasishchev M-52 have been attributed.

All elements of the Soviet forces lay great stress on ease of operation, servicing and maintenance of their aircraft, creating a strong design emphasis on simplicity and ruggedness. This has its effects on performance; for instance, the simple high-lift devices of the MiG-23/27 fighters limit their ability to carry weapons and fuel compared with contemporary Western aircraft. In fighter aircraft speed and acceleration appear to be given relatively high priority, encouraging the design of powerful aircraft with narrow cross-sections; there has never been a Soviet fighter with more internal fuel than it needed, and the besetting sin of some has been that they have too little.

As far as low-cost production goes, the Soviet Union has nothing to learn from the West, and there is little than can be said against their airframe design except that it has a tendency to conservatism which is not always in the Soviets' best interests. There has, for instance, been no Soviet equivalent of the highly effective McDonnell Douglas F-4 Phantom, the rather later Sukhoi Su-15 being far less flexible and versatile. The contemporary development of Mikoyan MiG-25, an outstanding design, showed that this conservatism is an attitude of mind rather than a reflection of weak design technology. Neither would many of the Western designers agree that the use of the basic configuration of the Tu-28 'Fiddler' in the 'Backfire' bomber was a good idea; a structurally more complex layout more like that of the Rockwell B-1 would have been more rewarding. It is also significant that in 1980 there is no sign that the Soviet Union is imminently ready to field a fighter with aerodynamics as advanced as those of the McDonnell Douglas F-15 or General Dynamics F-16, although such an aircraft has been tested.

However, it could be argued that it is not important to extract the last 10 per cent of potential from a design provided that the essential elements of the

The Sukhoi Su-15 typifies Soviet design in its evolutionary development. The latest version of the type, the Su-15VD 'Flagon-F' shown here, appeared in the mid-1970s, but the design has its roots in the late-1950s Su-9.

weapon system are present, and that the machine can be delivered to the squadrons in sufficient numbers. The re-equipment of many Frontal Aviation units with MiG-23s and MiG-27s is a case in point; the rapid production of one basic airframe has drastically altered the balance of air power in Europe to NATO's disadvantage, and the fact that the MiG could be more agile, offer better visibility or have greater endurance is of little significance beside the fact that FA is operating an aircraft of massively increased effectiveness and is moreover equipped almost entirely with such aircraft.

The MiG-23 generation has brought to Frontal Aviation a variety of systems which are completely new to the force, and vastly improved models of those which were in service in the late 1960s. The newest aircraft carry medium-range, radar-guided air-to-air missiles (AAMs) and guided air-to-surface missiles (ASMs); the MiG-23's radar is not only more powerful than that of the MiG-21, but also has look-down capability against low-flying targets; and internal electronic warfare capability is considerably improved, moreover.

On the other hand, there are or appear to be limitations to Soviet technology which can have the effect of making their aircraft seem more impressive than they really are. One of the most serious defi-

ciencies, witnessed by the Soviet Union's attempt to import high-bypass-ratio civil turbofan engines from the West and by the protracted and trouble-strewn supersonic transport programme, is in the area of high-temperature metal technology for the hot section of turbine engines. To some extent this can be overcome by accepting short lives of hot-section components such as the high-pressure turbine, but Soviet engines nevertheless appear to operate with more modest thrust/weight ratios and higher levels of specific fuel consumption than Western powerplants; together with the impact on aircraft weight that this entails, it can mean that an advanced Western aircraft may be as effective as a substantially larger Soviet machine.

Some observers have also remarked of the size of Soviet AAMs; the biggest of them, the AA-6 'Acrid' carried by the MiG-25 'Foxbat-A', is far larger even than the long-range AIM-54 Phoenix, yet the range of the MiG-25's radar is less than that of the AWG-9 used in association with the Phoenix. One theory that has been advanced is that Soviet technology in this area is not as advanced as that of the West. Again, this calls for a large carrier aircraft to perform an equivalent role.

Other areas where it can be predicted that Soviet technology is not equivalent to the West's are those which were neglected for many years. Western airborne early-warning (AEW) experience, for instance, goes back to the Project Cadillac experiments of the latter part of World War II, and takes a consistent line through the US Navy and US Air Force Lockheed EC-121 and the US Navy Grumman E-2 Hawkeye to the USAF Boeing E-3A Sentry. By contrast the Soviet designers of the Tu-126 started with no earlier experience of AEW and it is perhaps not surprising that the SUAWACS, an improved Soviet system equivalent to Sentry or the British Aerospace Nimrod AEW.3, has not yet appeared despite the fact that its arrival has been considered imminent for some years.

Airborne anti-submarine warfare (ASW) is also relatively new to the Soviet Union, whereas Western capabilities rest on 40 years' experience. While the Soviet Union will almost certainly possess similar technology in the basic sensors used for ASW, there is no substitute for experience in the areas of remote sensing and data processing, which are crucial to ASW from an aircraft.

Another area neglected for a long time was the tactical air-to-surface missile. Although the Soviet Union developed a variety of large cruise missiles for use against capital ships such as attack carriers and against land targets, Frontal Aviation strike fighters had to make do with unguided rockets and free-fall weapons until the mid-1970s. Since then, development of tactical ASMs has been pursued energetically, but not as yet to the point where such weapons can be offered for export (an indication that the Soviet Union's own forces are moving on to a newer generation of equipment) or where photographs or accurate impressions have been published. One would have thought, for example, that export customers for the strike versions of the MiG-23/27 series would have been issued by now with early Soviet ASMs such as the AS-7 'Kerry', but this has not happened.

One area of Western technology which the Soviet Union will be anxious to emulate is the compact long-range cruise missile developed by the USA. Although current Soviet cruise missiles possess considerable range, they achieve such impressive performance by brute force rather than microminiaturisation: the mere fact that tests of the latest 750-mile (1200-km) range weapon have been observed implies that it is a large weapon. The fundamental disadvantage of these weapons for use against ships is that they are large enough to be intercepted by SAMs with a reasonable chance of success, and that because of their size they cannot be launched in very large numbers. The Western cruise missile concept demands a high degree of miniaturisation in its electronics and warhead, and high efficiency from its powerplant, areas in which Soviet technology presently lags.

The Soviet Union, however, appears to lack little in the way of microwave systems technology. The resistance to jamming of even the fairly elderly 'Fox Fire' radar of the MiG-25 surprised Western analysts; the pulse-Doppler radar fitted to the late-production MiG-23s is certainly more advanced, and that associated with the AA-X-9 AAM represents another generation of development. The Soviet Union's armed forces adopt an interesting philosophy in which activities as diverse as electronic countermeasures, electronic and signals intelligence, and direct attack on enemy transmitters by missiles or ground troops are brought into a single classification: 'radio-electronic combat' or REC.

The Soviet Union devotes a very large fleet of long-range aircraft to electronic intelligence (Elint) with the aim not only of monitoring military communications but also of assessing the performance and characteristics of Western microwave systems. The formidable array of antennae featured by the Ilyushin Il-18 'Coot-A' Elint and ECM aircraft bears witness to the importance of such reconnaissance and the inputs which it brings to Soviet developments in electronic surveillance measures (ESM) and active electronic countermeasures (ECM). Soviet combat aircraft are distinguished by numerous ECM/ESM dielectrics; the installations on the MiG-23 and MiG-27 are noteworthy in that they are clearly designed into the airframe rather than added as an afterthought. Among larger aircraft, the 'Backfire' carries in its standard version an ECM suite comparable to that of a specialised ECM Tu-16.

It should be borne in mind when considering the foregoing brief assessment of Soviet technology that it applies to aircraft now in service and discussed in detail in the following pages. Detailed analysis of aircraft now under development in the Soviet Union is difficult as a result of lack of all but the most basic information about the characteristics of these types. However, it is possible to give as accurate a resumé as possible of current developments and the approximate time they are due to enter service, and it is safe to assume that the strengths and weaknesses of current Soviet technology will be reflected in their design.

The most spectacular development reported is in the field of heavy combat aircraft. In the course of Strategic Arms Limitation Talks in 1979 the Soviet Union stated that three 'new' long-range combat aircraft were under development. This somewhat bald statement in part corroborated Western intelligence leaks which also identified three lines of development. Firstly, there is a supersonic, variable-sweep strategic bomber equivalent to the Rockwell B-1. The aircraft would fully restore to the DA a place as part of a triad of airborne, land-based and submarine global-range strategic systems; currently, the DA is a somewhat wobbly leg of the Soviet triad, since its lumbering Tu-95s and scarcely faster AS-3 'Kangaroo' missiles would be hard put to it to deliver a credible attack even against the barely more youthful Convair F-106A interceptors of the USAF. Deployment of McDonnell Douglas/Northrop CF-18s in Canada will further reduce the DA's effectiveness, while the 'Backfire' lacks the unrefuelled range of a true strategic bomber. Lacking the technology needed to copy the US cruise missiles within the necessary timescale, the Soviet Union is developing a more advanced manned aircraft carrying a number of cruise missiles and outfitted with sophisticated radar, ESM and ECM.

The second reported aircraft is a subsonic ultra-long-range multi-role aircraft corresponding to the proposed fixed-winged version of the B-1. It would take over many of the missions flown by Tu-142/Tu-95s such as maritime surveillance and guidance for long-range ship-launched missiles. Armed with long-range missiles it would present a threat to targets close to defensive lines; it would also be a suitable carrier for an airborne high-energy defensive laser should such a system ever be brought to operational standard.

Third of the new types is reported to be a modified 'Backfire' with wedge inlets similar to those of the Rockwell RA-5 or MiG-25. The main effect of this modification would be to increase the maximum speed of the aircraft; possibly, the AVMF is concerned to increase the dash speed of the 'Backfire' to improve its chances of running the gauntlet through the Faroes gap, which will become increasingly dangerous as BAe Nimrods, Boeing Sentries, Grumman F-14s and Panavia Tornadoes work up in Iceland and Scotland. It is unlikely that the new 'Backfire' variant is powered by the Kolesov engine used on the Tu-144D supersonic transport, as has been suggested; the Tu-144D powerplant is a single-shaft turbojet and is optimised for supersonic speed, and its poorer specific fuel consumption would certainly penalise the range of the bomber.

Of these aircraft, only the modified 'Backfire' had attained the flight-test stage by early 1980, so it is unlikely that any of them will enter service in any numbers before 1984-5. None of them appears to correspond to either of the two developments reported in the mid-1970s (a canard delta bomber reported from the Sukhoi bureau and the RAM-H bomber version of the Tu-144), and these presumably have been abandoned. It is expected that a combination of the three types now under development will replace the entire force of Soviet heavy combat aircraft in the second half of the 1980s.

Turning to the re-equipment of the PVO air defence force, the pattern remains as it has been since the mid-1960s: flexible response to a projected threat which changes with every shift of US defence plans. The main threat at present is the cruise missile, but until 1977 Soviet efforts were orientated towards countering the B-1 bomber with its short-range missiles. With the B-1 at a relatively advanced stage of development and the possibility that the

Another massive Soviet weapon is the AS-3 'Kangaroo' missile, which may still be carried by some Tu-95s. As large as a fighter aircraft, it is probably too unwieldly to be effective against advanced defences.

USA will develop a vastly improved version of the FB-111, Soviet work in this direction has continued in case the PVO is faced with a near-term manned threat of this sort. Three main systems are thought to be at an advanced stage of development and may be deployed soon now that investment in the FA has peaked. Deployment of a new interceptor is considered as imminent. The US Annual Defence Report for 1980 states that 'it is clear that the Soviets are about to begin deploying a significant look-down, shoot-down capability in a MiG-25 version.' The missile system for this aircraft is identified as AA-X-9. It is said to have an effective range of 45 miles (72 km) and with its radar a 'four-on-four' capability; that is, the carrier aircraft can fire four missiles simultaneously at four targets. (The AWG-9/Phoenix system carried by the Grumman F-14 has a 'six-on-six' capability.) The aircraft which carries this system is identified as the 'Super MiG-25', but it seems that this aircraft has little in common with its forebear. To begin with, the Mach 3 top speed of the MiG and its poor endurance would hardly be well suited to a missile system intended to protect a large perimeter; the original MiG-25/AA-6 combination was a point-defence system, whereas AA-X-9 is unquestionably a perimeter system. One would expect the carrier aircraft to be a long-endurance two-seat aircraft and to replace the Tu-28 'Fiddler' as much as the MiG-25. A fighter in the F-14 class, known as RAM-K, has been reported (the designation indicating that the aircraft has been observed at the Ramenskoye test establishment): it is a swing-wing type and is some way from service entry. At present the most likely hypothesis is that the AA-X-9 carrier is a fighter sharing the general layout of the MiG-25 (testimony to the excellence of Belyakov's 1960 design) but with more efficient engines and, quite possibly, an aluminium structure,

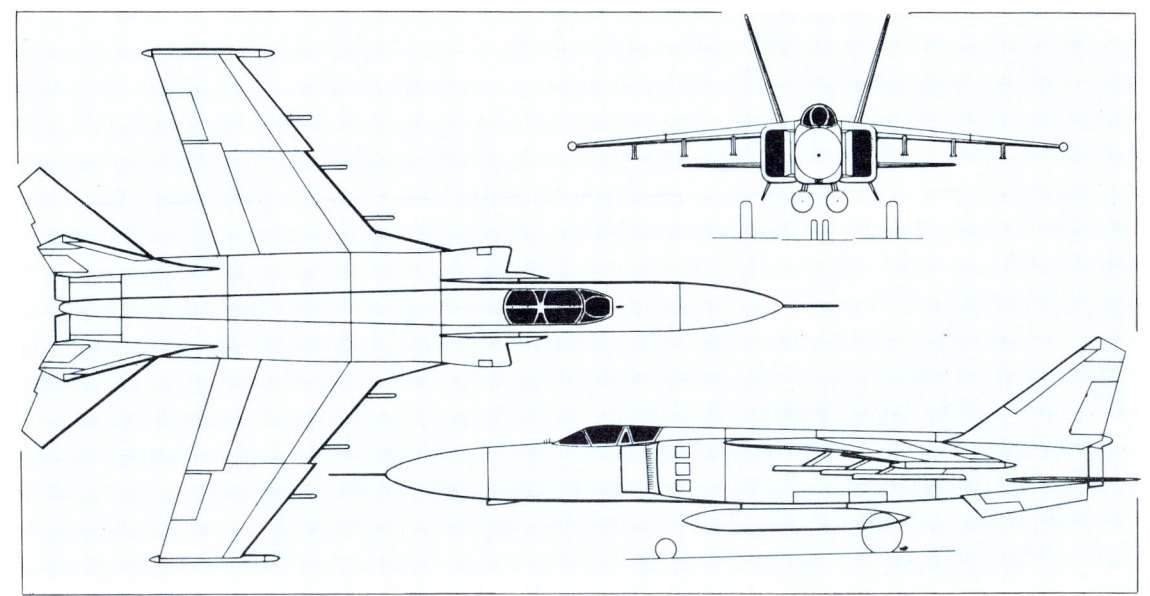

This conceptual drawing of the new interceptor referred to by US sources as the 'Super MiG-25' shows some of the similarities and differences between the new fighter and its Mach 3 forebear. The fuselage has been stretched ahead of the wing to accommodate a second seat for a weapons system operator, and has been extended aft of the wing to balance it; it is probable that the forward fuselage will have been widened to accommodate a larger radar. The span and area of the wing are increased to carry a heavier armament and external fuel. According to testimony of the defector Lieutenant Belenko, the air inlets are similar to those of the MiG-23.

reducing weight at the cost of Mach 3 capability. This would correspond to a fixed-wing, two-seat version of the RAM-K, which has also been reported.

The new 'Super MiG-25' or fixed-wing RAM-K is a two-seater carrying six AA-X-9s. Given its mission and weapon load it might be expected to be rather larger than the F-15 (68,000 lb/30,845 kg maximum take-off weight), but lacking a requirement for air-to-air combat would probably have a lower thrust/weight ratio: two Tumansky R-29s would be adequate and would appeal to Soviet conservatism.

The other major system, outside the scope of this book, is the SA-10 hypersonic SAM, which uses high speed and active homing to hit low-flying targets. Its development timescale suggests strongly that, like the AA-X-9, it is intended as a defence against manned penetrator systems rather than cruise missiles.

Both the AA-X-9/Super MiG-25 and the SA-10 would be admirably complemented by SUAWACS (Soviet Union Airborne Warning and Control System), a more advanced replacement for the Tu-126 'Moss'. This system, however, is still described as 'projected' by the US Department of Defense; that is to say, the US expects such a system to be deployed but has no knowledge of progress with development or of its characteristics. Either the Ilyushin Il-76 military transport or the Il-86 wide-body airliner could be used as a carrier for SUAWACS, as could the new long-range subsonic

combat aircraft referred to above.

The PVO's most difficult task now is to develop a counter to the cruise missile. It is difficult to say what this could be, because of the weapon's small size, its capability for defensive manoeuvring, potential for active ECM and low cost. Like the US forces, the PVO is undoubtedly working on advanced concepts such as high-energy laser weapons.

The PVO is considered likely to get its new interceptor before Frontal Aviation takes delivery of any new combat aircraft. This development is highly interesting, because the emergence of a Soviet air-superiority fighter designed for close combat and high agility has been predicted since the early 1970s. The 1980 Defense Report, however, suggests that new tactical combat aircraft will appear by the mid-1980s. Two aircraft types are reported to be under development for tactical operations. Among aircraft observed by satellite at Ramenskoye is the RAM-L, a Soviet development along the lines suggested by Northrop in the late 1960s, first published in 1971 and used for the F-17 and F-18. The RAM-L is a twin-engined single-seater, apparently slightly smaller than the Northrop fighters. Although it was detected in 1977-8 there is still no firm information as to its likely date of service entry, and it has been suggested that the Soviet Union may have decided that one-on-one air combat involving close manoeuvring is less effective than counter-air strike

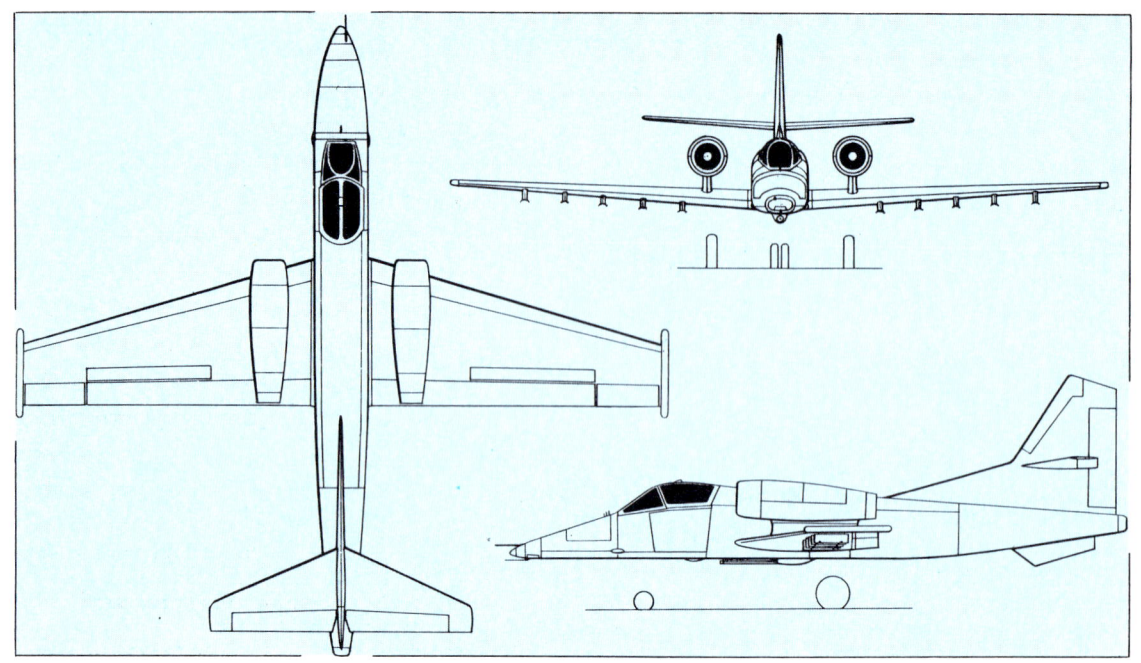

Based on an artist's impression published in the US journal *Aviation Week*, this drawing may represent the appearance of the subsonic attack described as the RAM-J. Details are conjectural, based on Soviet technology, but the aircraft does appear to have overwing engines and a mid-set tailplane, the latter being necessary to lift the tailplane out of the jet efflux. The Soviet aircraft is believed to be considerably smaller and lighter than the Fairchild A-10, weighing about 35,275 lb (16 000 kg) fully loaded compared with the 50,000 lb (22 680 kg) gross of the US aircraft. The RAM-J is the first specialised close-support aircraft tested by the Soviet Union (the country which originated the type) since the abortive Ilyushin Il-40 of the 1950s.

as a means of reducing enemy air forces. The design bureau of the RAM-L is uncertain, and the use of the designation MiG-29 is almost certainly premature.

Deployment of the RAM-J has been considered imminent for rather a long time. Detected earlier than the RAM-L, it is a somewhat smaller Soviet equivalent to the Fairchild A-10: a subsonic aircraft armed mainly with a heavy-calibre multi-barrel cannon but with provision for a large load of other weapons under its unswept wings. The RAM-J apparently differs from the A-10 in being powered by turbojets rather than turbofans: two Tumansky R-25 turbojets are reported to be mounted over the wings. Reheated versions of these engines power the Mig-21*bis* and almost certainly are fitted to the RAM-L. The RAM-K may in the long term replace the Su-17/20 in FA service.

The FA forces have now almost completed a cycle of re-equipment involving, firstly, the adoption of the MiG-23/27 as the standard fighter in place of the MiG-21; secondly, the replacement of the ageing Yak-28 by the all-weather Su-24 'Fencer'; and, thirdly, the introduction of the Mi-24 armed helicopter. However, this comes at a time when the survivability of an air force on the ground is becoming an increasing concern. In particular, British and US units

in Europe are deploying a new weapon known as JP233 which is described as having a 'devastating' effect on airfields. The Western allies know of no satisfactory counter to this weapon, and some RAF officers have suggested that it is a waste of time for NATO to develop any new battlefield aircraft which cannot be flown vertically from outside its shelter to a dispersal base. This view is not general, but the European Combat Aircraft (ECA) projected for 1992 is intended to use 1,500-ft (500-m) stretches of runway which may remain usable after an attack by a Soviet equivalent of JP233. Details of JP233 remain classified, but it is said to use a combination of runway-cratering warheads and delayed-action submunitions to prevent repair work, and to be delivered by all-weather strike aircraft. The risk which the FA runs is that of introducing a new generation of conventional take-off and landing (CTOL) aircraft just as a new generation of weapons renders them obsolete. Even the FA's vast strength in numbers and its Mi-24 may be only a cushion against such a trend.

Should the balance of air power in the central region of Europe shift decisively against the short-range CTOL combat aircraft, the FA could take advantage of AVMF research into short-take-

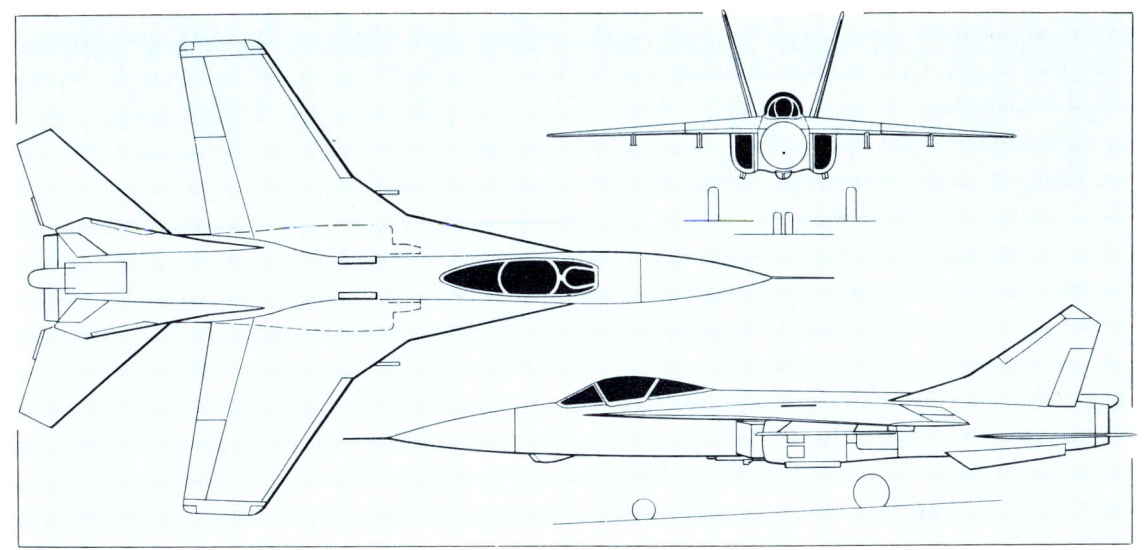

The apperance of the RAM-L, the Soviet Union's new air-to-air fighter, is less well defined even than that of the RAM-J. One source depicts it as combining a wing similar in shape to that of the McDonnell Douglas F-15 Eagle with very large leading-edge root extensions (LERXs). However, this impression, based on information provided by US sources to *Aviation Week*, assumes a more conservative layout combining a moderately swept wing (as on the MiG-25), offering low induced drag for sustained turning performance, with sharply swept root sections for post-stall controllability as on the MiG-21's delta wing; the two sections are blended into a wing of compound sweep. In thrust and weight the RAM-L appears to be in the same class as the General Dynamics F-16A.

off/vertical-landing (STOVL) aircraft. At least one combat aircraft in this category is thought to be under development. The new STOVL aircraft is believed to use a lift/cruise powerplant or powerplants without discrete lift jets. Unlike the pure-VTOL Yak-36 Forger, it will be able to make a short rolling take-off into wind from the decks of the 'Kuril'-class carriers, greatly increasing its payload and range.

The 1980 report of the US Department of Defense does not confirm US Navy intelligence leaks of mid-1979 which indicated that the Soviet Union was constructing a flat-top fixed-wing attack carrier armed with carrier-based developments of the MiG-27. The assessments of satellite information which gave rise to this report are a matter for controversy, and the development itself is surprising in view of the trends in Soviet naval policy over the past few years. The attack carrier differs from a vessel such as *Kiev* in that it is single-role ship, while *Kiev* typifies in its field the 'combination of all arms' dear to Soviet military philosophy. It could be suggested, however, that Soviet expansionism could take the Soviet Navy into areas where only a full-sized carrier could provide the support it would need to present a credible threat.

Transport capabilities in the Soviet Union's armed forces are being steadily increased with the delivery of more Il-76 freighters and the availability of wide-bodied Aeroflot Il-86s. The DA may develop a new tanker aircraft to support its new bombers, using as the basis either the Il-76 or the Il-86. On the other

hand, this role could be filled by the new subsonic multi-role aircraft. However, there are at least two major developments under way on the transport side.

A massive new helicopter identified by the NATO reporting name of 'Halo' has been developed by the Mil bureau. It is a single-rotor helicopter with a conventional freight cabin and is considerably heavier than the Mi-6 'Hook' or Mi-10 'Harke'. It had not entered service in early 1980, but is believed to be very close to doing so. The 'Halo' represents a substitute for the monster Mi-12 'Homer' which was flown in 1968 but abandoned some years later. The 'Homer' was a transverse-twin-rotor helicopter basically comprising a massive fuselage with two Mi-6 powerplants and rotors on strutted wings. The mechanical and control problems of the helicopter seem to have defeated the Soviet engineers, although the 'Homer' did manage to lift more than 88,000 lb (40 000 kg) in record flights.

The design of the 'Halo' must have presented its own problems. According to *Jane's All the World's Aircraft,* the designers of the 'Halo' have spoken of eight-bladed rotors absorbing 25,000 shp (18 500 kW); this implies that the 'Halo' could be nearly as big as the Mi-12. Rotor diameter, however, is unlikely to be significantly greater than that of the Mi-6, because the latter's 114 ft 10 in (35 m) rotor is probably the largest achievable without excessive tip speeds. The 'Halo' would be far heavier than the elderly Mi-6, though, and a far greater proportion of its take-off weight would be lifted as payload. The

'Halo' could, for example, be used to airlift mobile tactical missiles complete with launchers as well as to carry heavy military equipment including medium armoured vehicles. Once the 'Halo' becomes fully operational it will bring a new dimension to the potential of helicopter-borne troops to overfly the battle line and establish themselves behind it.

The designation An-40 has been quoted for a heavy strategic freighter under development by the Antonov bureau. Little has been heard of this project since 1977, and it is possible that it has been delayed, like the long-haul version of the Il-86 wide-body, by the lack of a suitable engine in the 50,000-lb (22 200-kg) class. It is reported to be in the same class as the Lockheed C-5 Galaxy.

Only one other military aircraft programme has been reported under way in the Soviet Union, and that is the development of a new ASW helicopter to replace the Kamov Ka-25. The aircraft is not expected to be operation before the mid-1980s.

In the absence of any detailed information from the Soviet Union regarding the performance and characteristics of its contemporary military aircraft, the information in the following pages and in the discussion of new projects above has to be drawn from numerous sources. The primary sources for most information are the intelligence services of the NATO powers, through a number of channels which vary in sensitivity. Satellite reconnaissance, for example, is accepted as a fact of life. US reconnaissance satellites presumably make regular sweeps over the main Soviet aerospace manufacturing and research centres, and the Russians know it; the information drawn from satellite coverage is sensitive only so far as it reveals to the Soviet Union the power and efficiency of US space reconnaissance systems. Aircraft at a research base such as Ramenskoye are probably kept under cover as much as possible, but some will inevitably be caught in the open and their dimensions and planforms can be assessed quite accurately. The aircraft known as the RAM-H, RAM-J and so on fall into this category.

Another relatively insensitive source of informations opens up when aircraft are exported to third countries, and this flow of information becomes particularly fruitful when the customer country either maintains links with both East and West or when its allegiances changes, as in the case of Egypt. Usually, the Soviet Union will refrain from trying to export its latest aircraft for this very reason, but this rule may have been broken with the new STOVL fighter.

Straightforward defection of Soviet personnel represents a great windfall for Western intelligence services, especially as such information can be disseminated quite freely; the source is already known to the Soviet counterintelligence organisations and can hardly be prejudiced further. Summaries of information obtained from the defecting Soviet 'Foxbat' pilot, Lieutenant Victor Belenko, were leaked to the Western press within a few months of his arrival in Japan.

However, there is a considerable amount of data which reaches the Western intelligence agencies from sources which have to be protected, and this information has to be used with extreme care. In general, it will only be disseminated over a small area and in a form which reveals no clues as to the source. Receipt of this information may be confined to within the armed forces and to some persons employed by manufacturers who have to assess or counter any newly developed Soviet system.

Most of the information actually published about new Soviet efforts is provided to the media, officially or unofficially by Western manufacturers or by defence agencies. It has been pointed out that this leaves considerable room for distortion by the source, intended to exaggerate the Soviet threat and stimulate public sympathy for higher defence spending. The best example from recent years was the insistence of Western intelligence sources that the 'Backfire' was an intercontinental bomber fully com-

Soviet design bureaux could never be accused of conformism. One of the most distinctive of modern combat aircraft is the Yakovlev Yak-28P 'Firebar', interceptor member of a family of designs.

Typifying the Soviet Union's resurgent interest in sea-based air power, Yakovlev's Yak-36 'Forger' is nevertheless not as effective as the West's Harrier. However, there is no doubt that a more potent aircraft will follow.

parable with the B-1. Once the Rockwell bomber had been abandoned, and the campaign to support its development died away, the 'Backfire' was 'scaled down' to its present capability level. The actual performance attainable by any aircraft can broadly estimated without too much difficulty once its shape and size are known, by rule-of-thumb calculation and by analogy with Western aircraft in similar categories.

As far as possible the actual Soviet designations have been used in the following pages, but in many cases these are not known. Even long-established designations can be proved false, and in some cases, such as the designation Tu-22M for 'Backfire', the designation officially quoted by the Soviet Union may be inconsistent or incomprehensible. In that event one has to fall back on the NATO reporting system, supervised by the Air Standards Co-ordination Committee (ASCC). The system is memorable but has its quirks; it has to be remembered that the ASCC designation is a 'reporting name' in that it has to reflect externally visible differences. The 'Flogger-B' and 'Flogger-G' are

distinguished by the shape of the dorsal fin, but do not necessarily correspond to the distinction between early- and late-production MiG-23s. The ASCC system occasionally suffers breakdowns; the reporting name 'Brassard' for the Yak-28 was dropped when it was realised that it could be confused with the French Broussard utility aircraft. One wonders how long the new Mil heavy-lift helicopter will continue to be called 'Halo': the risk of confusion with the common and fashionable abbreviation 'helo' seems high.

There is one final note of caution which applies to any assement of Soviet aerospace technology at the present time. The last major air display in the Soviet union was in 1967, earlier displays having taken place in 1961 and 1955. Neither has Western intelligence recently received any recent windfall comparable to that brought to Europe by returning German internee designers at the end of the 1950s. However, the following is as comprehensive a summary of the Soviet Union's contemporary military aircraft as a nonclassified organisation can reasonably expect to publish.

Among the first recipients of the Soviet Union's first Mach 2 tactical fighter, the original MiG-21F, was Finland. This deal resulted in the first clear pictures of the MiG-21 reaching the West, laying to rest a great many misconceptions about the design.

Section 2
Soviet Military
Aircraft Exports

Soviet military aircraft are not only significant in the way they are used by the Soviet Union itself, but also in the way that they are exported to other countries. The Soviet Union is a massive exporter of arms of all kinds, and advanced military aircraft are no exception.

The terms on which Soviet aircraft are offered for export are often apparently generous, but are based on a shrewd assessment of what the potential customer can afford and the degree to which the buyer can draw on assistance to acquire combat aircraft from alternative sources. The interests of the supplier are taken into account: Angola and Mozambique were readily supplied with brand-new MiG-21s shortly after their independence from Portugal, because it suited the Soviet Union to maintain a military threat to South Africa and what was then Rhodesia.

This strategic use of arms exports is most in evidence in the Middle East, where any of the Soviet Union's regular customers may find itself involved in a high-intensity war which will make rapid drains on its armed forces. In this case, it is not enough simply to have a large force of Soviet aircraft; any country contemplating hostilities must know that it can count on swift resupply, replacement and reinforcement of its forces. Any Soviet-backed nation must ensure that the An-22s and Il-76s are waiting to start resupply before the attack is launched, giving the Soviet Union a high degree of control over its client's military plans. Libya, Syria and Iraq are in this class.

The straightforward exchange of military hardware for diplomatic goodwill is perhaps less in evidence than formerly. One reason for this could be the limited success which this policy has enjoyed. As is shown by the following country-by-country guide to aircraft exports, only about half the African nations wooed by the Soviet Union with giveaway fighter squadrons shortly after they gained independence have remained in the Soviet orbit. Others have decided that they simply do not need advanced combat aircraft, or have switched to Western or Chinese suppliers.

There is also a strong thread of straightforward commercialism in Soviet exports. Soviet military aircraft such as the MiG-21 have acquired a reputation for being cheap to buy, simple to operate and comparatively well-armed. Although their equipment standards are minimal, they represent a realistic choice for the budget-limited air force. In the unique case of India, the simplicity of the MiG-21 has allow-

Polish Air Force groundcrew work on an Su-7. Soviet aircraft have acquired the reputation of being amenable to simple maintenance by unskilled labour.

ed India's industry to build the aircraft, while the constant development to which the type has been subjected has meant that HAL is still able to build a competitive contemporary fighter in the shape of the MiG-21bis, without any drastic and expensive changes to the aircraft.

One apparent advantage of acquiring combat aircraft from the East rather than the West is that some very advanced and potent types are occasionally made available. A good example of this is the supply to some Arab nations of Tupolev Tu-22 'Blinder' supersonic medium bombers and Mach 3 MiG-25 'Foxbat-A' interceptors. The drawbacks of this policy are, firstly, that the more advanced types are kept under close control by Soviet 'advisors', and secondly that advanced technology in the most important — rather than glamorous or spectacular — areas of military aerospace is seldom released for export by the Soviet Union. This attitude on the part of the exporter has, if anything, hardened over the past few years. While all-weather versions of the MiG-21 were released for export within three or four years of their widespread introduction by Soviet forces in the mid-1960s, no non-Soviet force (apart from East Germany's entirely Soviet-controlled air force) has taken delivery of versions of the MiG-23 family comparable to the 'Flogger-B' and 'Flogger-G' interceptor and 'Flogger-D' strike aircraft used by Soviet forces. In the case of 'Flogger-G' it appears that the Soviet VVS has introduced a further improved fighter variant of the basic MiG-23, while export customers have to be satisfied with an aircraft consciously downgraded from the initial Soviet version nearly 10 years after the type entered service.

The differences are not unimportant. The MiG-23 offered for export is inferior in critical respects to the MiG-23 used by the Soviet forces. The export fighter lacks the beyond-visual-range combat capability of the 'domestic' model, which has a larger radar dish and medium-range AA-7 'Apex' missiles. Similarly, the MiG-23BM used in the strike role by Warsaw Pact and other export customers lacks many of the plethora of sensors and antennae featured by the Soviet Frontal Aviation MiG-27, and

appears to be armed mainly with 'iron bombs' rather than precision-guided weapons.

On the other hand, the policy of offering aircraft of limited capability for export has now been adopted by the United States. The development of the F-16D export version of the Fighting Falcon air superiority fighter, with an older and less powerful engine, has been conditioned by the desire to produce an aircraft which will not provoke an arms race should it confront a MiG-23. The country which turns to the West for combat aircraft may thus be thwarted if its aim is qualitative superiority.

One area where the Soviet Union has come in for criticism is its training of pilots for newly exported aircraft. Accounts of the short courses for new pilots in Southern Russia suggest that the techniques used are overwhelmingly didactic, that the pupils are expected to develop an instinctive allegiance to the flight manual and that the piloting techniques recommended are invariably cautious, exploiting neither the skill of the pilot nor the ultimate to-the-limits performance of the aircraft. In most cases, air

forces which have made successful use of Soviet aircraft are those where pilots have had some exposure to Western piloting techniques and Western instruction, or where the air force has had sufficiently long experience of the Soviet types to exploit them fully. The best example of this is the use of the MiG-21's low-speed manoeuvrability by the Egyptian Air Force in the 1973 Arab-Israeli war, a technique that was in none of the maker's manuals.

What follows is, necessarily, only a brief guide to Soviet exports of military aircraft rather than a comprehensive list. It does, however, reveal the extent to which the Soviet Union uses 'MiG diplomacy' as a tool to secure its objectives worldwide.

Soviet commercial aircraft are among the least efficient in the world. They are seldom operated except by airlines which, for political reasons, have no choice in the matter. This Tu-154B is operated by the Civil Aviation Administration of North Korea.

Europe

Albania

A few of the aircraft supplied to Albania by the Soviet Union before the country's break with the Warsaw Pact remain operational, but although Albania's front-line combat aircraft are of Soviet design they are manufactured and supplied by China. Chinese-built MiG-21s and MiG-19s are operated.

Bulgaria

One of the less advanced Warsaw Pact air forces, Bulgaria's air arm is only now in the process of retiring its obsolete MiG-17s in favour of MiG-21s. The air force may also have taken delivery of a small number of MiG-23BM 'Flogger-F' strike fighters.

Czechoslovakia

One of the most powerful members of the Warsaw Pact, Czechoslovakia possesses a capable aircraft industry and is thus not entirely dependent on the Soviet Union; in fact, the Czech industry produces the Aero L-39 Albatros advanced trainer for Soviet and other Eastern Bloc units and has also exported the L-39D armed version to the Middle East. On the other hand, there has been no production of modern Soviet military types under licence, as there was in the 1950s and early 1960s when Czechoslovakia produced the Ilyushin Il-28 and all the Mikoyan-Gurevich fighters up to and including the MiG-21F. Undoubtedly the trends towards independence

shown by major Warsaw Pact nations in the 1960s, culminating in the invasion of Czechoslovakia in 1968 and the Polish riots of 1970, influenced the Soviet Union's decision to terminate this 'dispersal' of production.

This much said, however, Czechoslovakia has been a favoured recipient of Soviet equipment since the events of 1968, operating some 340 MiG-21s including a large proportion of late models and at least one regiment (about 40 aircraft) of MiG-21RF 'Fishbed-H' electronic/photographic reconnaissance aircraft. In early 1978, too, the Czechoslovakian air arm became the first non-Soviet Warsaw Pact (NSWP) air force to take delivery of MiG-23BM 'Flogger-F' strike fighters.

East Germany

Dominated by the presence in East Germany of the Soviet Union's 16th Air Army, the East German *Luftstreitkräfte* (LSK) appears to enjoy rather less independence than other NSWP forces, being the only NSWP air force to fall under the command of the local Soviet forces in peacetime; Warsaw Pact agreements with other countries provide only for wartime Soviet takeover. On the other hand, its status as a German-manned extension of the Soviet Union's most important tactical air force endows it with priority over other NSWP forces in re-equipment. Its MiG-23s, for example, are fully fledged air-defence fighters rather than the compromise MiG-23BM 'Flogger-Fs' supplied to the other NSWP forces. The proportion of obsolescent types in the LSK is the lowest outside the Soviet Union itself.

Finland

Walking a delicate line between the West and the Soviet Union, Finland makes a point of meeting its needs equally from East and West. Its primary combat aircraft are limited-all-weather fighter-bombers: one wing operates Saab-Scania 35 Drakens, some new and some secondhand, while the other unit operates new Mikoyan-Gurevich MiG-21bis 'Fishbed-N' fighters. The Soviet aircraft were supplied to replace the country's ageing MiG-21F-13s, delivered in April 1962. They operate within an air-defence control system set up by the British industry in 1968.

Finland has chosen to buy advanced trainers from the West (British Aerospace Hawks, to be assembled in Finland) and to build its own basic trainer, the Valmet Leko-70. Some Soviet types are used for other support duties, however, including Mi-8 'Hip' transport helicopters. Finland is also expected to acquire Antonov An-32 'Cline' freighters to replace ageing Dakotas.

Hungary

Smallest of the Warsaw Pact air forces, the Hungarian Air Force is now beginning to take delivery of the MiG-23BM 'Flogger-F' export-standard strike fighter. These aircraft are replacing Su-7s and MiG-21s.

Poland

Largest of the NSWP force, the Polish air arm (Polish initials PWL) is associated with the Warsaw Pact's most capable and productive aircraft-manufacturing industry. How the events of 1980 will affect the status of the Polish industry and air force remains to be seen.

MiG-21s and Su-7s form the bulk of the PWL forces, but they have been supplemented by Su-20s, the first Soviet variable-sweep aircraft to be exported, since 1974. However, as yet Poland has not been confirmed to have taken delivery of MiG-23BMs.

Poland's aircraft industry manufactured MiG-15 and MiG-17 fighters in the 1950s, and developed the TS-11 Iskra jet trainer and LiM-6 ground-attack version of the MiG-17, but since the mid 1960s Poland has abandoned military aircraft development, possibly following a change in Soviet policy. Now,

the industry concentrates on commercial aircraft, with the exception of PZL Mi-2 helicopters supplied to the Soviet Union for military pilot/weapons operator training. Other programmes included development and production of the new Sokol helicopter and manufacture of Westernised versions of the Mi-2, development and manufacture of the M-15 jet crop-sprayer, and manufacture of the complete wing for the Ilyushin Il-86 wide-body transport. Powerplants manufactured in Poland include a wide range of piston engines and the turbine powerplants for the M-15 and Sokol.

Romania

Like Yugoslavia, Romania's air force finds itself in need of new Soviet combat aircraft unexpectedly as a result of disappointing progress with the Jugoslav-Romanian Orao attack fighter. A few Oraos are in service, but Romania will probably need MiG-21bis or MiG-23BM fighters to replace its rather elderly force of MiG-21F day fighters and limited-all-weather MiG-21PFs.

Romania's aircraft industry, however, is rapidly advanced in technology through collaborative programmes with Britain. Manufacture of Britten-Norman Islanders is being followed by licence manufacture of the British Aerospace One-Eleven and its Rolls-Royce Spey engine. The Spey, although not in the same category as the most modern military engines, has been chosen by Aeritalia to power the new Brazilian-Italian AMX strike fighter, and its application to a version of the Orao would radically improve the performance of the fighter.

Yugoslavia

A policy of independence from both East and West has affected aircraft procurement for the Yugoslav Air Force. It is, however, part of the Eastern Bloc in economic terms, and accordingly suffers from a shortage of foreign exchange to purchase Western combat aircraft. First-line, supersonic aircraft are thus exclusively supplied by the Soviet Union, the backbone of the air force being composed of various MiG-21 subtypes.

Yugoslavia's drive towards independence in military equipment has been frustrated by technical problems. Despite the success of the Galeb and Jastreb light trainer and attack aircraft, the country's attempt to build a more capable aircraft in co-operation with Romania has been unsuccessful. The Yugoslav-Romanian Orao fighter — originally known as the Jurom — is underpowered with its present Rolls-Royce Viper engines, and more powerful engines have not been available from the West.

The Yugoslav Air Force will now have to seek a more modern strike aircraft, but the price for supply of Su-20s or MiG-23BMs could be closer political links with the Soviet Union.

Middle East

Egypt

A serious embarrassment to the Soviet Union in security terms, the Egyptian Air Force has continued to operate its Soviet aircraft despite the rapid deterioration in its relations with the original supplier. Concurrently improving relations with the USA have reached the point where the air forces of the two countries have exercised together, giving the US Air Force invaluable information of the combat characteristics of the MiG-23 family.

Egypt operates both strike and air-to-air MiG-23s, in the shape of the MiG-23BM 'Flogger-F' strike aircraft, also supplied to the Soviet Union's allies in the Warsaw Pact, and the export MiG-23 'Flogger-E' with similar radar and missile armament to the MiG-21bis. According to one report, China has assisted Egypt by providing support for the MiG-23 and its R-27 engine, and Egypt has supplied a MiG-23 airframe in return for this help. Egypt has thus given both the Soviet Union's main potential adversaries technical details of the MiG-23.

Egypt's MiG-21s are apparently being supported and upgraded by a number of British companies under a little-publicised programme which involves the installation of head-up displays to replace the inadequate gunsights of the standard aircraft (later Soviet aircraft also have HUDs) and Ferranti inertial navigation systems, as well as engine and airframe maintenance. It is not known whether the Su-20 'Fitter-C' swing-wing strike aircraft will get similar treatment.

Iraq

In an active war situation by virtue of its proximity to the unstable and unpredictable regime in Iran, Iraq imports military aircraft from both East and West. However, the preponderance of Soviet equipment was secured under an agreement signed in 1977, which increased the number of Soviet personnel in the country in exchange for increased supplies of military equipment.

Iraq's Soviet aircraft include a high proportion of MiG-23s and Su-20s; which by now must almost outnumber the MiG-21s in service. A squadron of Tu-22s is also operated, together with MiG-25s. Iraq is also the only Middle East operator of the Czech Aero L-39D Albatros light strike fighter/trainer, and the only export customer anywhere for the Ilyushin Il-76 civil/military freighter. Antonov turboprop transports have also been supplied.

Libya

Since the deterioration of Soviet relations with Egypt, the Libyan Republic has been heavily armed by the Soviet Union to augment Mirages acquired from France. Mach 3 MiG-25R reconnaissance aircraft have been based in Libya, which also fields a squadron of 12 Tupolev Tu-22 'Blinder' supersonic medium bombers. It is not known to what extent these aircraft are under Libyan control: almost certainly their crews are either Russian or Soviet-trained foreigners, and the Soviet Union certainly has a considerable say in their use.

The most important combat aircraft supplied to Libya, however, are probably the MiG-23 'Flogger-E' fighter-bombers delivered in 1976. These will almost certainly be followed by more aircraft of the type. However, there must be some concern in Libya and Syria, arming as they are for an offensive war against Israel, at the increasing deployment by their potential adversary of advanced fighters such as the Kfir-C2 and US F-15 and F-16, with plans to introduce the F-18 or F-18L and IAI Lavy. It is hard to tell at what point the Soviet Union will be ready and willing to supply an aircraft in that class.

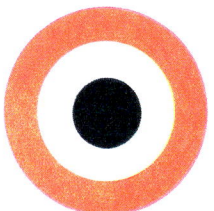

Syria

The September 1980 declaration of 'joint statehood' by Libya and Syria will, if put into effect, combine two of the strongest Soviet-armed forces in the Middle East in an alliance against Israel.

Syria has been a recipient of Soviet combat aircraft for longer than Libya, and despite heavy losses in the 1967 and 1973 wars with Israel it fields a formidable force of combat aircraft. Although this is still composed largely of MiG-21s, there is an increasing element of newer aircraft such as the MiG-23 'Flogger-E' and 'Flogger-F' and the Su-20 'Fitter-C'. Unlike its ally, Syria is armed almost exclusively with Soviet aircraft.

Like Libya, Syria will be anxiously awaiting the arrival of a Soviet fighter (such as the RAM-L discussed in the introduction to this volume) which can effectively challenge the strong force of modern fighters fielded or planned by Israel.

Yemen

Since 1972 Russian and Cuban instructors and technical personnel have assisted the People's Democratic Republic of Yemen (PDRY) to operate a small group of not very advanced Soviet combat aircraft, of which the most sophisticated are a single squadron of MiG-21 fighters.

Africa

Algeria

Since 1966 the main combat strength of the Algerian Air Force has been supplied by the Soviet Union,

and the country is now taking delivery of MiG-23 'Flogger-E' and 'Flogger-F' fighters and Su-20 'Fitter-C' ground-attack aircraft. Common dependence on Russia for supplies has been a factor in aligning Algeria with Libya and Syria in recent years, although in 1975 Algerian Su-7s could still be seen training at Egyptian bases. According to some reports, the country has now taken delivery of the latest Third World status symbol: a squadron of Mach 3 MiG-25 'Foxbat-A' interceptors. More significantly, in view of Algerian support for the Polisario guerillas in Morocco and Mauritania in the Spanish Sahara, the air force has received the first of a planned two squadrons of Mi-24 'Hind' helicopters, in gunship and transport versions.

Angola

Formed after the civil war which followed Portuguese withdrawal from the country in December 1975, Angola's air force rests heavily on Cuban technical aid. MiG-21MFs form the backbone of the air force, and An-26 transports have also been supplied.

Congo

The Congo Air Force operates mainly in liaison and transport roles, and its strength includes about five An-24RV transports delivered in the 1960s.

Ethiopia

Heavily supported by the Soviet Union against a former Soviet client, Somalia, in 1977-78, the Ethiopian Air Force relies on Soviet supplies and Soviet and Cuban skilled manpower. Apart from a few remaining F-5As and Canberras, the EAF's front-line combat aircraft are all Soviet-supplied. They include new-generation MiG-21s and some MiG-23s, probably MiG-23BM 'Flogger-F' strike fighters. Almost certainly Cuban-operated and Cuban-maintained are Mi-6 helicopters, which played an important role in the war against Somalia by lifting heavy equipment behind Somali lines.

Guinea

Although this small country was thought at one time to be on the point of becoming an important ally of the Soviet Union, by virtue of its port and airfield facilities at Conakry, relations have cooled in recent years and the last major use of the airfield was during the Angolan war. The small combat force of MiG-17s, supported by a number of transport aircraft, is not likely to be increased.

Madagascar

The small air force of this island republic has been strengthened over the past two years by another of the Soviet Union's 'aircraft dealers'. North Korean personnel have assisted in the introduction of a small number of MiG-21FL fighters, presumably supplied secondhand by India.

Mali

One of many newly independent states to be wooed with gifts of arms by the Soviet Union in the mid 1960s, Mali may still operate its single squadron of MiG-17s.

Morocco

Another less-than-successful exercise in "MiG diplomacy" was the supply of MiG-17s and MiG-15UTIs to Morocco in 1961. Since then, however, the air arm has acquired Western supersonic fighters and the elderly MiGs have almost certainly been put out to grass.

Mozambique

Armed by the Soviet Union and its agents as a base for operations against white-ruled South Africa, Mozambique is believed to possess a force of nearly 40 MiG-21MF 'Fishbed-J' fighter-bombers. Operation and support of the aircraft are almost certainly Cuban-manned, as in the case of Angola.

Nigeria

Dividing military procurement between East and West, Nigeria has chosen the cheap and simple MiG-21MF, which with its four pylons and internal gun is at least comparable to contemporary Western fighters in multi-role capability. Some of the country's mid-1960s acquisition of MiG-17s may still be in service.

Somalia

Following the war with Ethiopia, also Soviet-armed, in 1977-78, Somalia's air force no longer has any support from the Soviet Union or Cuba. Western replacements have been sought for the Soviet aircraft in the inventory, the most modern of which are a single squadron's ten MiG-21s.

Sudan

Like Somalia, Sudan has severed links with the Soviet Union and has expelled Soviet and Cuban advisors. A few MiG-21PF interceptors and Chinese-built MiG-17s may remain in service, but they are being steadily replaced with Western equipment.

Tanzania

Uniquely among African air forces, Tanzania operates military equipment of Soviet design and Chinese manufacture, under an assistance programme put into effect in 1972. TF-2 (MiG-15UTI), F-4 (MiG-17), F-6 (MiG-19) and a few F-7 (MiG-21) fighters remain in service, supported mainly by Tanzanian personnel.

Uganda

Soviet support for the Ugandan air force is now in doubt following the overthrow of the Amin regime in 1979. Previously, a small force of MiG-21s had been supported by the Soviet Union and brought up to strength after the destruction of half the aircraft in an Israeli raid on Entebbe.

Indian Subcontinent

Afghanistan

The Soviet-equipped forces of Afghanistan have to a considerable extent been absorbed into the Soviet forces occupying the country since the invasion at the end of 1979. Previously, the equipment of the Afghan air arm with the latest Soviet combat aircraft, including late-model MiG-21s and Mil Mi-24 'Hind' armed helicopters, provided the Soviet Union with an opportunity to place its 'advisors' throughout the Afghan forces; this proved instrumental in extending Soviet control over the armed forces.

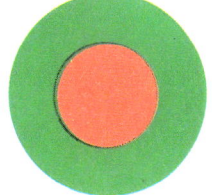

Bangladesh

Formed by secession from Pakistan in 1971, Bangladesh, like many other new states, received MiG-21s and other aircraft from the Soviet Union within a couple of years of its formation. However, once again the role of Soviet advisors and influence was questioned and Bangladesh has now turned to China for military equipment, operating the Shenyang F-6 (MiG-19S) as its main combat aircraft.

India

Possessing one of the ten largest air forces in the world, India retains a unique relationship with the Soviet Union's aircraft industry. Following licence production of the British Gnat fighter by Hindustan Aeronautics Limited (HAL) in the late 1950s, India

decided to seek rights to build a supersonic interceptor alongside the home-grown Marut strike fighter, and this role was filled by the Mikoyan-Gurevich MiG-21FL, roughly equivalent to the Soviet-built MiG-21PF but with provision for a ventral gunpack. A few MiG-21F day fighters were delivered in the early days of the programme, but HAL took on a steadily increasing share of the manufacture and assembly of the Soviet fighter. It has been followed on the production line by the MiG-21MF (known as the MiG-21M in India) and the MiG-21bis.

Recently, however, India has resumed purchase of combat aircraft from the West, with Sea Harriers for the Navy and Jaguars forming a major part of the Air Force in the 1980s. The Anglo-French Jaguar is to be built by HAL as the main penetration strike fighter for the IAF, but MiG-23s are on order to supplement the MiG-21s in the air-defence role.

India is also the only export customer for the Ilyushin Il-38 'May' anti-submarine aircraft, although it is not likely that the equipment on these aircraft is up to the same standard as that of the standard AVMF model. HAL is also expected to build An-32 freighters for the IAF.

Pakistan

The only Soviet-built aircraft in Pakistan military service are Mi-8 helicopters, acquired in 1969 and probably being replaced by Aérospatiale Pumas. However, Soviet-designed Chinese-built Shenyang F-6 (MiG-19) fighters are the most numerous type in PAF service.

Sri Lanka

The main combat element of this small force comprises ageing British Jet Provosts and a few MiG-17Fs, which are still partly operational.

Central and East Asia

China

All China's combat aircraft appear to be derived from aircraft supplied by the Soviet Union, including the 'flagship' A-5 'Fantan' strike fighter. Chinese copying of Soviet aircraft has become a major factor in undermining Soviet 'MiG diplomacy' because support for Soviet types is available from China.

Mongolia

The Mongolian Air Force is little more than an extension of the Soviet forces based in the region, and its equipment appears to be largely obsolescent.

North Korea

Mainly reliant on the MiG-21, the North Korean air force will almost certainly take delivery of MiG-23s and Su-20s in the near future, if it has not already done so. North Korea has also played a part in training Third World countries to operate Soviet aircraft.

South-east Asia

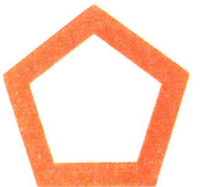 

Indonesia

A classic example of the political implications of Eastern Bloc military aid, Indonesia built up the most powerful air force in the South-East Asian region between 1958 and 1966; by the end of that period the Indonesian air force included MiG-21s and missile-armed Tu-16 'Badger-B' bombers. Following a *coup d'état* against the pro-Soviet government in 1966, support for the aircraft ceased totally and by 1970 the air force was grounded in its entirety.

Laos

A small number of MiG-21s have been supplied to Laos since the 1975 Communist takeover, together with a few support types such as An-26 transports and Mi-8 helicopters. More equipment will presumably be supplied as US-built aircraft inherited from the previous regime become unserviceable.

Vietnam

The use of apparently obsolescent MiG-17s as air-combat fighters by the North Vietnamese forces during the Vietnam war was a prime example of the way enterprising export customers have found new ways of using Soviet equipment, far transcending the conservative flying techniques taught by Soviet instructors.

Since the end of hostilities, however, Vietnam does not appear to have enjoyed the priority in new equipment which marks deliveries to, for instance, Libya and Syria. The present slow pace of re-equipment can probably be explained by the weakness in air power of Vietnam's closest adversary, China; the present Vietnamese air defences are adequate to inflict crippling losses on such a primitive force.

The Americas

Cuba

Playing an important role as an 'agent and distributor' for Soviet military aircraft, Cuba's small Revolutionary Air Force (FAR) is equipped with modern equipment — including a squadron of MiG-23BM 'Floggers' — well in advance of anything operated by neighbouring countries. The deployment of MiG-23s to Cuba caused a political storm in the United States, when it was realised that the strike fighters had adequate range to attack the mainland USA; however, it is likely that the MiG-23s are in Cuba so that the FAR can gain experience with the type and pass it on to other export recipients. Peru, Angola and Mozambique are examples of air forces built up with the aid of Cuban specialists trained in the Soviet Union.

Peru

The only operator of Soviet military aircraft on the American mainland, Peru decided to acquire Soviet equipment as a result of an evaluation of Western and Soviet strike aircraft. Deliveries of 36 Sukhoi Su-22s started in 1976, and more of the aircraft may be ordered despite some dissatisfaction with the spartan equipment standard. Peru also operates some Soviet-built transport and support aircraft, including Mil Mi-6 'Hook' helicopters — the largest rotary-wing aircraft on the American continent.

Cruising with wings spread over the Baltic, an
AVMF 'Backfire' makes no effort to avoid the
shadowing RSAF Drakens. 'Backfires' rarely
practise supersonic dash. Apparent in this view
are the twin tail cannon and the boost and cruise
nozzles of the AS-4 missile. The strake under the
body of the AS-4 appears to house elements of its
guidance system.

Section 3
Soviet
Military Aircraft

Antonov An-2 Colt

History and notes

Believed to have been built in larger numbers than any other aircraft designed since World War II, the Antonov An-2 'Colt' was reported to be continuing in production in 1980 in the absence of any complete replacement. The Antonov bureau was reported in that year to be working on a new general-purpose and agricultural aircraft, a single-turboprop cabin monoplane designated SE-100,but until this appears there is likely to be a continuing market for this inelegant but supremely practical aircraft.

The An-2 has several claims to uniqueness. It was the only large biplane to be put into production on any scale after World War II, and as well as being the first aircraft specifically designed for agricultural duties, it is the only aircraft of that type ever to succeed in many other roles. As well as excelling as a light transport, with its outstanding STOL performance, it is also widely used as a parachute trainer by organisations such as DOSAAF, the Soviet Union's paramilitary training organisation.

The Antonov design bureau was formed in May 1946 with the specific task of producing a utility aircraft for the Soviet Union's Ministry of Agriculture and Forestry. The new type was to replace the Polikarpov Po-2, which had itself been built in greater numbers than almost any other aircraft. To begin with, the aircraft was designated Skh-1 (Agricultural-1), but later the designation An-2 was adopted.

The first aircraft of the type flew in August 1947, and after flight-testing and some modification the aircraft went into production in late 1948. The biplane layout was chosen for its combination of good field performance with viceless low-speed handling, both of paramount importance for the agricultural role. The layout was unique for an air-

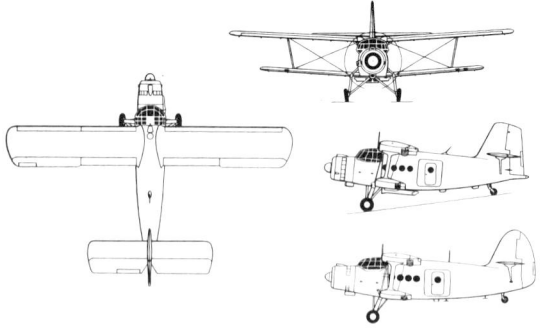

Antonov An-2M 'Colt' with (lower side-view) early An-2.

craft of its time in that the fuselage filled the entire gap between the wings, which were braced by a single I-strut on each side. The structure was all-metal apart from the fabric-skinned wings and tailplane. The wings carry slotted trailing-edge flaps, and the ailerons droop at low speeds.

More than 5,000 An-2s were built in the Soviet Union between 1948 and 1960, and production in that country ceased temporarily in 1962. In 1957, however, production of the An-2 had started in China, as the Fong Shou No 2, and several thousand of these are reported to have been built. Many remain in service under the designation C-5. The Soviet bloc's main source of aircraft has, however, been WSK-Mielec in Poland. Production of the An-2 by WSK started in 1960, and still continues. Soviet production was resumed in 1964, with several hundred of the An-2M type, with larger tail surface, a new

Improvements to later Polish-built An-2s included a more conventional variable-pitch propeller as well as a new fin.

Antonov An-2 Colt

Although the PWL (Polish Air Force) now relies on more modern types for transport, the An-2 soldiers on throughout the world.

variable-pitch propeller and a hermetically sealed cabin to exclude chemicals from the cockpit during spraying operations. Polish production switched to this improved version.

Special versions of the An-2 include the An-2TD parachute trainer and the An-2V floatplane (designated An-2W in Poland), which has a reversible-pitch propeller for deceleration on water. The An-2 can also be fitted with skis. A military observation version with an almost entirely glazed rear fuselage was tested in 1948, but did not go into production. Another special version was the WSK-Mielec Lala-1, converted from an An-2 as a testbed for the M-15 agricultural aircraft, designed as a replacement for the Antonov type. However, the An-2 continues in service in transport and paratrooping roles, and is likely to continue to do so for some time to come.

Specification

Type: 14-seat transport and general-purpose aircraft

Powerplant: one 1,000-hp (746-kW) Shvetsov ASh-62R nine-cylinder radial engine

Performance: maximum speed at 5,750 ft (1750 m) 160 mph (256 km/h); cruising speed 105 – 120 mph (170 – 190 km/h); ceiling 14,750 ft (4500 m); range 525 miles (845 km); take-off run 490 – 590 ft (150 – 180 m); landing run 560 – 590 ft (170 – 180 m)

Weights: empty 7,500 lb (3400 kg); fuel load 2,000 lb (900 kg); payload 2,850 lb (1300 kg); maximum take-off 12,125 lb (5500 kg)

Dimensions: span (upper) 59 ft 8 in (18.18 m), (lower) 46 ft 9 in (14.24 m); length 40 ft 8 in (12.4 m); height (tail up) 20 ft 0 in (6.10 m); wing area 769.8 sq ft (71.52 m²)

Operators: military operators include Afghanistan, Albania, Bulgaria, China, Cuba, Egypt, Ethiopia, East Germany, Hungary, Iraq, Mali, Mongolia, North Korea, Poland, Romania, Somalia, Sudan, Syria, Tanzania, Tunisia, USSR, Vietnam

Antonov An-12 Cub

History and notes

The Soviet equivalent of the Lockheed C-130 Hercules, the Antonov An-12 'Cub' was the result of a chain of development which started in the mid-1950s. By that time it was recognised that the turboprop engine, offering far higher power/weight ratios than the piston engines, as well as power outputs considerably greater than most piston engines, would revolutionize the design of military transport aircraft. Such aircraft generally operate over short distances; the fact that the fuel consumption of the turboprop was at the time higher than that of the piston engine was thus of secondary importance compared with the prospect of a military freighter with sufficient power to lift a large payload from a short and unprepared field.

The first Antonov aircraft designed around this formula was the twin-engined An-8, which was designed in 1953 – 54 and made its first flight in the autumn of 1955. Like the contemporary C-130, it adopted what has become the classic layout for a military freighter, with high wing, landing gear in side fairings on a fuselage with a flat, low-level floor, and a rear loading door with integral ramp under the unswept rear fuselage.

The An-8 was tested with turboprops from the Kuznetsov and Ivchenko bureaux, both these Soviet design teams including many German engineers captured in 1945. Invchenko's AI-20 was chosen as the powerplant for the An-8, about 100 of which were built for the VTA (the Soviet military air transport force). Some remain in service.

An Aeroflot requirement for an airliner designed for rough-field operations led to the development of the four-engined An-10 airliner from the An-8, and it was this type which formed the basis for the An-12. The wing and tail were initially largely unchanged, despite the 40% greater weight of the airliner, but the An-10 had a much larger, pressurized fuselage and four AI-20s. Lateral and longitudinal stability problems resulted in anhedral being applied to the outer wing panels, an Antonov trademark which

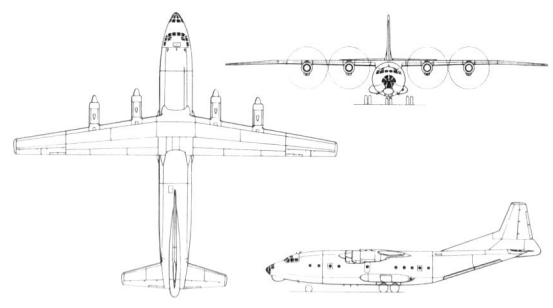

Antonov An-12 'Cub-A' with tail turret removed.

was to persist until the appearance of the An-72 in 1977. The An-10 entered service in 1959, but following an accident at Kharkov in May 1972 the entire fleet was withdrawn, apparently because of structural problems.

The military An-12PB, differing from the airliner in having a more upswept rear fuselage and an integral rear loading ramp, flew in 1958 and from the early 1960s became the standard Soviet military transport. A peculiarly Soviet feature of the military versions is the rear gun turret, although this lacks radar guidance and can be only a token defence. (Indian An-12s were, however, used as bombers in the 1965 Indo-Pakistan war, escaping without loss.) Later in their service life, Russian air force An-12s were fitted with improved radar equipment. A serious drawback of the An-12PB is that its cabin is not pressurised; if used as an airlifter for troops, therefore, its range is heavily reduced due to the fact that is has to fly at low altitudes.

Although the type does not seem to have been pressed into service in as many roles as the C-130, the An-12 has since 1970 been seen in the electronic counter measures (ECM) and electronic intelligence

Aeroflot's reserve military role is well illustrated here; a civil freighter does not normally need tail guns.

Antonov An-12 Cub

(Elint) role, joining the increasing number of Russian aircraft loitering in the vicinity of war zones and NATO exercises. The Elint version, known to Nato as 'Cub-B', features a number of ventral bulges covering variously-tuned receiver aerials, and the cabin is presumably equipped with operators' consoles. The fact that the 'Cub-B' has been seen in the vicinity of naval exercises may suggest that it forms part of the growing AV-MF (Soviet Naval Aviation) fleet of long-range land-based aircraft. The ECM Cub-C features prominent radomes, including a rear installation which replaces the tail turret. Like the Ilyushin Il-38, 'Cub-C' was seen in Egyptian markings before the rift between the two states widened, but this is probably no more than a cover for overseas basing of Soviet-manned aircraft, feeding their gleanings of monitored data back to the Soviet Union for interpretation.

One of half-a-dozen Iraqi Air Force An-12 'Cub-A' transports, now supplemented by Ilyushin Il-76s.

Specification

Type: heavy tactical freighter, (Cub-C) ECM aircraft and (Cub-B) electronic intelligence (Elint) platform

Powerplant: four 4,000-shp (2984-kW) Ivchenko AI-20K turboprops

Performance: maximum cruising speed 400 mph (640 km/h); economic crusing speed 360 mph (580 km/h); service ceiling 33,500 ft (10200 m); range with 22,000-lb (10000-kg) payload 2,100 miles (3400 km)

Weights: empty (estimated) 75,000 lb (35000 kg); maximum payload 44,000 lb (20000 kg); maximum take-off 134,500 lb (61000 kg)

Dimension: span 124 ft 7 in (38.0 m); length 108 ft 6 in (33.1 m); height 32 ft 3 in (9.83 m); wing area 1,309 sq ft (121.73 m^2)

Armament: two 23-mm NR-23 cannon in tail turret

Operators: Algeria, Bangladesh, Egypt, India, Indonesia, Iraq, Poland, Sudan, USSR, Yugoslavia

Antonov An-14 Clod/An-28 Cash

History and notes

The Antonov An-14 'Clod' was designed in 1957 as a STOL (short take-off and landing) freighter and feederliner, with handling characteristics which would enable it to be flown by inexperienced pilots. With its high-aspect-ratio braced wing and twin fins, it shows signs of inspiration from the French Hurel-Dubois transports of the early 1950s, the experimental designs which also led to the British Short Skyvan and 330.

The development of the An-14 was protracted, and it was not until 1965 that the type entered service. Production versions feature a very different tail design from the prototype, and the planform of the wing and the arrangement of the high-lift devices are also modified. The nose was slightly lengthened, and clamshell doors were fitted to the rear fuselage.

If the evolution of the An-14 had been slow, that of its turboprop development, the An-28, has been even less hurried. It was announced in 1967 that a turboprop version was under development, and the first prototype, designated An-14M, flew at Kiev in September 1969. Powered by two 810-shp (604-kW) TVD-850 turboprops, the new version was stretched to accommodate up to 15 passengers, and weighed 12,500 lb (5600 kg) fully loaded. It was selected for production in competition with the Beriev Be-30. The production An-28 seats up to 20 passengers and is powered by more powerful engines derived from those of the Ka-25 helicopter.

The aircraft is to follow the An-2 into production in Poland by PZL. Deliveries are due to start in 1980-81.

All variants of the An-14 and An-28 share the same pod-and-boom fuselage layout, permitting easy loading of cargo in the freight role. The high wing carries full-span double-slotted flaps and slats, ailerons being built into the outer flap sections.

Specification

An-14
Type: light STOL transport
Powerplant: two 300-hp (224-kW) Ivchenko AI-14RF radial piston engines
Performance: cruising speed 105 – 120 mph (170 – 180 km/h) at 6,560 ft (2000 m); maximum

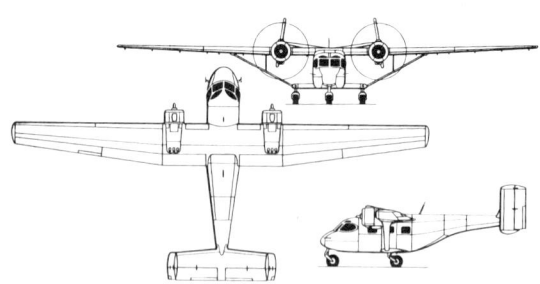

Antonov An-14 'Clod'

range with six passengers or 1,200 lb (570 kg) payload 400 miles (650 km); service ceiling 16,400 ft (5000 m); take-off run 330 – 360 ft (100 – 110 m); landing run 360 ft (110 m)
Weights: empty 5,700 lb (2600 kg); normal take-off 7,600 lb (3450 kg); maximum take-off 8,000 lb (3630 kg)
Dimensions: span 72 ft 3 in (22.0 m); length 37 ft 3½ in (11.36 m); height 15 ft 2½ in (4.63 m); wing area 422.8 sq ft (39.72 m²)
Operators: Bulgaria, East Germany, Yugoslavia, USSR (air forces and Aeroflot)

An-28
Type: light Stol transport
Powerplant: two 960 shp (715-kW) PZL-built Glushenkov TVD-10B turboprops
Performance: max cruise speed 217 mph (350 km/h); economical cruise speed 185 mph (300 km/h); take-off run to 50 ft (15 m) 1,180 ft (360 m); range with 20 passengers 317 miles (510 km)
Weights: empty 7,700 lb (3500 kg); max payload 3,750 lb (1700 kg); max take-off 13,450 lb (6100 kg)
Performance: span 72 ft 4½ in (22.06 m); length 42 ft 7 in (12.98 m); height 15 ft 1 in (4.6 m); wing area 433.5 sq ft (40.28 m²)

After 14 years of development, the Soviet-built prototypes of the Antonov An-28 have led to a production version, to be built in Poland.

Antonov An-22 Cock

History and notes

One of the most technically impressive of Soviet aircraft designs, the mighty Antonov An-22 'Cock' strategic freighter took the world by surprise when it arrived at the Paris air show in June 1965. It has since become a symbol of Soviet imperialism, spearheading the shipment of arms to client states in Africa and elsewhere, using its vast range and payload to fly long diversions and so avoid hostile territory. Its combination of range with field performance is outstanding, and in many respects it outshines the later Ilyushin Il-76 'Candid' by a large margin.

Following the development of the twin-engined An-8 into the An-10 and An-12, and the design and testing of the An-24, the Antonov bureau turned its attention to a very large strategic freighter closely based on the successful An-12. The An-22 is very unusual, in fact, in being a successful example of a direct scaling-up process. The wing of the An-22 is an almost exact 1.7:1 linear scale of the An-12 wing, and is typically Antonov with its anhedralled outer panels. The major difference in shape between the two aircraft is in the rear fuselage and tail. Rear fuselage aerodynamics and structure are probably the most demanding area in the design of a large military transport, with the linked problems of drag around a rear ramp and aerodynamic tail loads on an

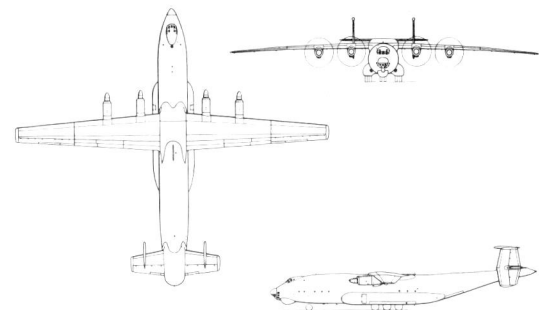

Antonov An-22 'Cock'.

open-ended fuselage. The An-22's twin-fin layout was chosen to overcome predicted problems with flexing of the rear fuselage, the original design having included a single fin.

The key to the An-22's efficiency is its high wing-loading, comparable with that of the Boeing 747. This is an almost inevitable effect of the square/cube law when the design of a smaller aircraft is scaled up so dramatically. Despite the high loading, however, the An-22 has an excellent field performance as a

Even on military supply flights, Antonov An-22 transports generally carry civilian markings.

Antonov An-22 Cock

The anhedralled outer wings which were found to cure instability problems on the An-8 and subsequent aircraft were found effective on the much bigger An-22. Unlike that of the similarly sized Lockheed C-5A, the cross-section of the An-22 fuselage is a circle.

Specification
Type: heavy strategic freighter
Powerplant: four 15,000-shp (11190-kW) Kuznetsov NK-12MV turboprops
Performance: maximum speed 460 mph (740 km/h); cruising speed 320 mph (520 km/h); service ceiling 25,000 ft (7500 m); range with 100,000-lb (45000-kg) payload 6,800 miles (11000 km); ground roll at maximum weight 5,000 ft (1500 m)
Weights: empty 250,250 lb (113500 kg); maximum payload about 175,000 lb (80000 kg); maximum take-off 550,000 lb (250000 kg); wing loading 148 lb/sq ft (725 kg/m^2)
Dimensions: span 211 ft 4 in (64.42 m); length (prototype) 189 ft 7 in (57.8 m); height 41 ft 2 in (12.55 m); wing area 3,713 sq ft (345 m^2)
Operator: USSR

Antonov's solution to the thorny problems of rear-fuselage design on a large rear-loading freighter was to abandon the single fin, incidentally reducing hangarage problems. The anti-flutter masses on the fins are noteworthy.

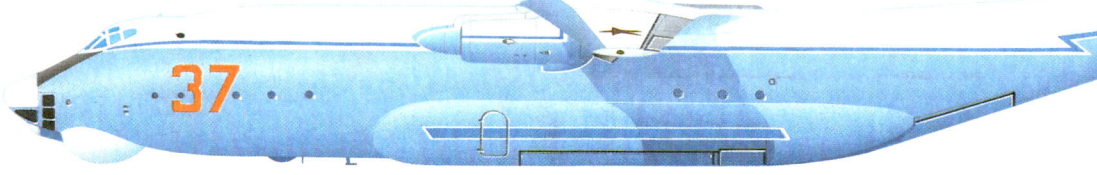

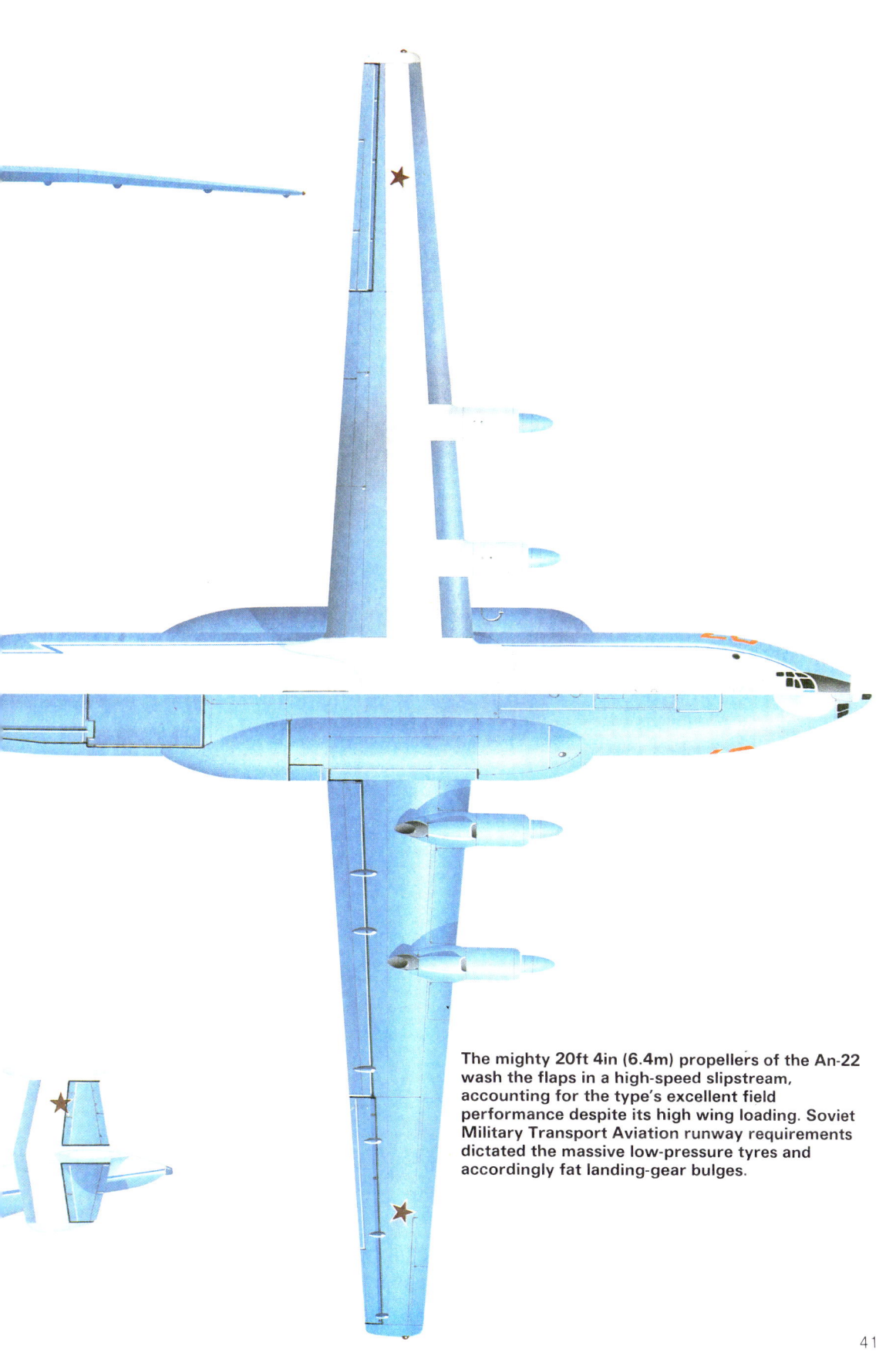

The mighty 20ft 4in (6.4m) propellers of the An-22 wash the flaps in a high-speed slipstream, accounting for the type's excellent field performance despite its high wing loading. Soviet Military Transport Aviation runway requirements dictated the massive low-pressure tyres and accordingly fat landing-gear bulges.

Antonov An-22 Cock

The An-22 stopped the Paris Air Show of 1965, and was still impressive at later shows (as seen here). Aircraft exhibited lack the nose radar equipment of production aircraft.

result of the fact that much of the wing is 'blown' by the slipstream of the four contra-rotating propeller units. Like those of the An-12, the flaps are double-slotted. Early An-22s had propellers with a diameter of 18 ft 6 in (5.6 m), similar to those of the Tu-95; production aircraft have propellers of 20 ft 4 in (6.4 m), presumably because the An-22 cruises at a lower speed than the swept-wing Tupolev, and propeller tip speeds are less critical.

Another operationally significant feature is the landing gear, designed to permit operations from unprepared strips. Each main gear is installed in a side blister, and comprises three twin-wheel units with large low-pressure tyres. An APU (auxiliary power unit) is fitted in the front of the right blister. The APU also seems to be used to pressurize the cabin (most large modern aircraft use engine bleed air for pressurization).

The An-22 carries a crew of five or six, and there is a cabin in the forward fuselage for about 28 passengers, possibly including a relief crew on long flights. The main hold can accommodate a twin SA-4 'Ganef' missile launcher on its tracked carrier, as well as any of the Soviet Union's armoured fighting vehicles, including main battle tanks. The hold is fitted with mechanical handling, including electric roof cranes and winches. The rear doors can be opened for air-dropping; like most Soviet freighters, the An-22 has a glazed nose and is extensively fitted with radar; later aircraft have a forward-looking weather radar in the tip of the nose, a large navigation/mapping set aft of the nose glazing, and an unidentified avionic housing ahead of the second radar.

Design of the An-22 started in early 1962 to meet civil and military requirements, following the Soviet government's decision to support the exploitation of natural resources in Siberia by air. The civil and military requirements were compatible, because the new aircraft was intended to carry heavy construc-

tion equipment and machinery as well as armoured vehicles. The first aircraft flew on 27 February, 1965, and was demonstrated at a day's notice at the Paris air show in June of that year. It was the world's largest and heaviest aircraft until the first flight of the Lockheed C-5 in June 1968. The first production An-22 entered service with Aeroflot in 1967 — a short gestation period, particularly by Soviet standards, for so large an aircraft.

Only about 100 of these giant freighters have been built, and production is generally thought to have been ended in 1974. Deliveries are believed to have been shared about equally between the Soviet VTA (air transport force) and Aeroflot, but the civil aircraft are equipped to the same standard as military variants and are always available for military use. Aeroflot aircraft have been used for military airlifts where the presence of a red-starred VTA aircraft might have been provocative.

Despite its spectacular weight-lifting capability and field performance, the An-22 is probably of only limited use to the Soviet Union. Perhaps its most im-

portant role in the future will be to sustain an internal airlift capability linking the European and Chinese fronts. It is also useful in its role of supporting client states, but so large a freighter is probably out of place at a short frontal airstrip. As the US Air Force has found with the Lockheed C-5A, it is hard to justify a large force of super-heavy freighters when most items of military equipment can be carried in smaller aircraft such as the Il-76 or Lockheed C-141; the only item which really demands C-5 or An-22 capacity is the main battle tank, and tanks cannot be airlifted in significant numbers except by a force of freighters that even the Soviet Union could scarcely contemplate acquiring.

In 1977 the Antonov bureau was reported to be working on the design of a more advanced replacement of the An-22, an aircraft in the C-5A class and designated An-40. The Soviet Union has, however, clearly encountered difficulties in developing an efficient high-output turbofan engine for such an aircraft. Efforts to import Western engines have been blocked.

Antonov An-24 Coke

History and notes

Originally a civil airliner, the Antonov An-24 'Coke' VIP and government transport became the progenitor of the An-26 'Curl' military freighter. The design was undertaken in 1957 to meet a requirement for a turboprop replacement for the Lisunov Li-2 'Cab' and Ilyushin Il-14 'Crate'. Flown in December 1959, the An-24 resembles earlier Antonov designs in the wing planform and the anhedralled outer wing panels, but the mainwheels retract into the engine nacelles rather than fuselage fairings, and the structure makes extensive use of welding and bonding rather than riveting. The type went into service with Aeroflot in October 1962. Most of the production aircraft were An-24Vs, with 28-40 seats and, in some cases, a side freight door and convertible cabin. The An-24V Series II was introduced in 1967 with the more powerful AI-24T engine to improve hot-and-high performance, and this was delivered in 46-seat and 50-seat layouts.

All An-24Vs were delivered with a TG-16 gas-turbine auxiliary power unit in the right nacelle, an unusual piece of equipment for an aircraft in this class. In the An-24RV, also introduced in 1967, this was replaced by a small Tumansky turbojet to boost take-off performance in hot-and-high conditions. The intake for the small auxiliary engine is located on the inboard side of the nacelle. Take-off weight of the An-24RV is increased to 48,060 lb (21800 kg) and this can be maintained up to ISA + 30° conditions. More than 1,000 An-24s are believed to have been built, and the type appears to be continuing in production alongside the later An-26 and An-32. Service experience is said to have proved the theoretical advantages of bonded structures in reducing maintenance costs and improving corrosion resistance.

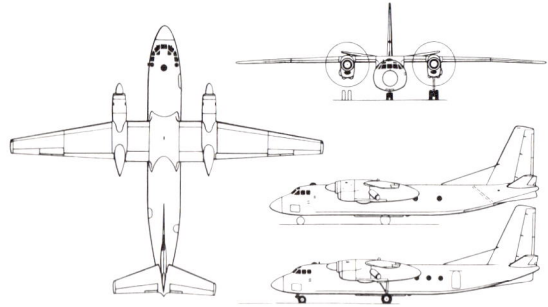

Antonov An-24V and (upper side-view) An-24TV 'Coke'.

Specification

Type: short-range transport or VIP aircraft
Powerplant: two 2,550-shp (2148-kW) Ivchencko AI-24 turboprops plus (An-24RV) one 1,980-lb (900-kg) Tumansky RU-19-300 turbojet
Performance: cruising speed 315 mph (500 km/h) at 20,000 ft (6100 m); maximum range with 30 passengers 1,490 miles (2400 km); range with 12,125-lb (5520-kg) payload 340 miles (550 km); take-off run to 35 ft (11 m) 2,900 ft (885 m); landing run from 50 ft (15 m) 3,700 ft (1130 m)
Weights: empty 29,320 lb (13600 kg); maximum take-off landing 46,300 lb (21000 kg)
Dimensions: span 95 ft 10 in (29.2 m); length 77 ft 3 in (23.5 m); height 27 ft 4 in (8.3 m); wing area 780 sq ft (72.5 m²)
Operators: Czechoslovakia, East Germany, Hungary, Poland.

Antonov's An-24 is the equivalent of the Western F.27 and BAe 748.

Antonov An-26 Curl/An-30 Clank/An-32 Cline

History and notes

Development of a military freighter from the Antonov An-24 'Coke' airliner was logical, especially in view of the increased performance available with the addition of an auxiliary engine in the An-24RV. (A similar development had been undertaken in the UK, where the Andover C.1 was modified from the Hawker Siddeley HS.748.)

The first rear-loading variant of the An-24 was the An-24TV, demonstrated in 1967. The aerodynamic shape of the rear fuselage was largely unchanged, but a loading hatch suitable for air-dropping was added beneath the rear fuselage, together with an internal winch and conveyor system. The original An-24TV had only two engines, but the first aircraft was modified in 1967-69 as the An-24RT with a booster engine as fitted to the An-24RV. The An-24RT could not accept large loads through the rear door, and does not appear to have gone into large-scale production. However, it forms the basis for the An-30 'Clank' photographic survey transport air-

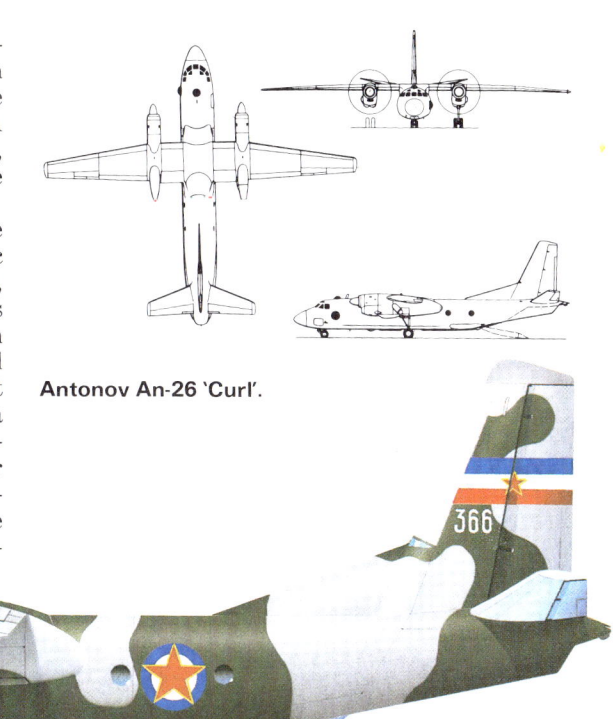

Antonov An-26 'Curl'.

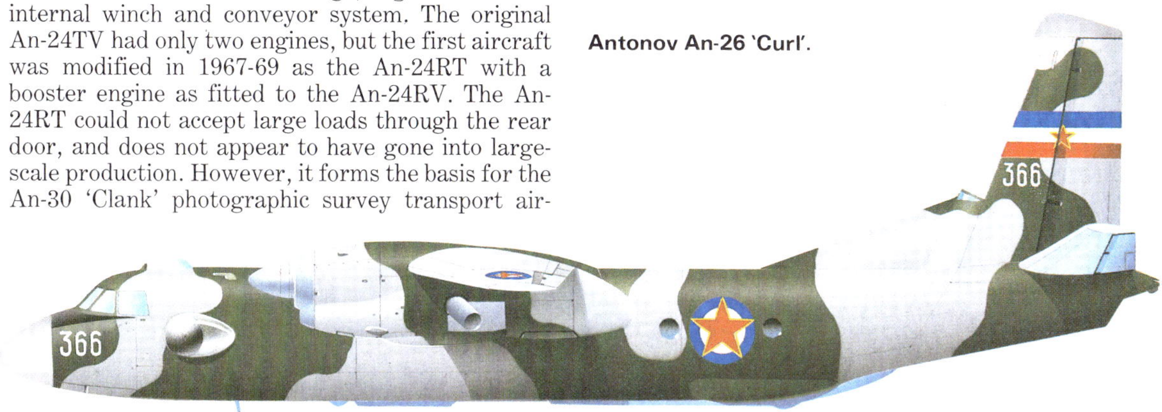

The An-26 is one of the 'standard-issue' Soviet types, being in service with allies as far apart as Yugoslavia (above) and the Pathet Lao Air Force (below).

Antonov An-26 Curl/An-30 Clank/An-32 Cline

craft, first displayed in 1974. This aircraft features an extensively glazed nose and ventral ports for cameras or other survey equipment. As far as can be seen it has no directly military role (although it could form the basis of a maritime-patrol aircraft), but is more likely to be used in the search for mineral resources within the Soviet Union.

Before the development of the An-30, however, a new version of the basic aircraft appeared. Displayed in 1969, the An-26 'Curl' introduced a redesigned rear fuselage, including a door large enough to admit any load which can be accommodated in the cabin and a rear-loading ramp. Small vehicles can be driven into the hold, while other cargoes can be handled by built-in powered conveyors and winches. A large bulged observation window is fitted to the left side of the fuselage, just aft of the flight-deck, presumably for increased accuracy in paradropping operations. The An-26 appears to be the standard light tactical transport of the Warsaw Pact air forces, and considerable efforts

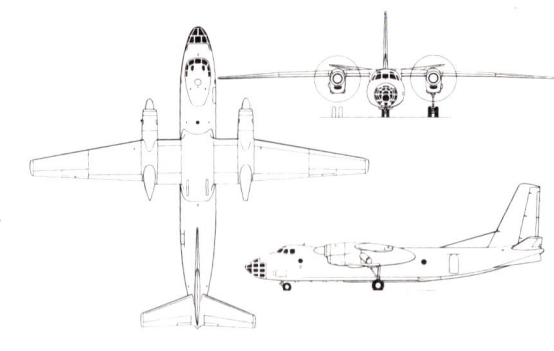

Antonov An-30 'Clank'

Antonov An-30 'Clank' combined photographic and transport aircraft flown by the Romanian air arm.

The An-30 is an unusually specialised aircraft, used by military operators as well as by Aeroflot.

Antonov An-26 Curl/An-30 Clank/An-32 Cline

Yugoslavia operates the An-26 (above), but some operators are likely to choose the Stol, hot-and-high An-32 'Cline' (below).

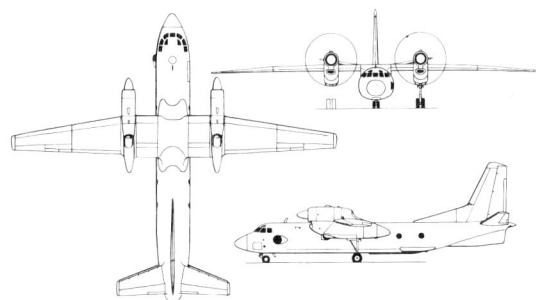

Antonov An-32 'Cline'.

to export the type have been made. It is likely to replace the remaining examples of the Ilyushin Il-14 'Crate' and Lisonov Li-2 'Cab' still in transport service.

The latest development of the An-26 appears to be intended to overcome the hot-and-high performance problems which afflict the earlier aircraft, even with the auxiliary engine in operation. First revealed in 1977, the An-32 is powered by completely different engines from those fitted to the earlier aircraft: 5,180-shp (3864-kW) Ivchenko AI-20Ms, yielding almost twice as much power as the AI-24s of the An-26. The AI-20M is an uprated version of the An-12 powerplant. The greater power demands propellers of greater diameter than those fitted to the An-26; in order to avoid total redesign of the wing, the engines have had to be mounted well above the wing, so that the propeller axes are above the widest point of the fuselage. Another advantage of this arrangement is that the engine-out control problems are less severe than they would be if the engines were moved outboard. Even so, the An-32 has more ventral fin area than the An-26, to compensate for the greater installed power and the destabilizing effect of the bigger cowlings and propellers. The

high thrust line has presumably caused some problems in pitch control; production versions of the An-32 feature extended chord on the outboard leading-edge of the wing, resulting in a dog-tooth, and fixed inverted slots on the tailplane leading edge. The wing may also be provided with spoilers. The An-32 dispenses with the booster engine and weighs 57,300 lb (24000 kg) for take-off, resulting in a great improvement in power/weight ratio. According to the Soviet exporters, the greater power of the An-26 permits operations at airfields as high as 15,000 ft (4600 m). The An-32 was reported to be in production in 1978.

The An-32 was ordered by India in 1979; 95 of the aircraft are to be acquired, with a steady move from direct purchase to licence manufacture.

Specification

Type: (An-26 and An-32) light tactical transport; (An-30) photographic survey aircraft (specifications for An-26)

Powerplant: two 2,820-shp (2104-kW) Ivchenko AI-24T turboprops and one 1,980-lb (900 kg) Tumansky RU-19-300 turbojets

Performance: maximum cruising speed 270 mph (435 km/h) at 20,000 ft (6100 m); range with 12,130-lb (5500-kg) payload 560 miles (900 km); range with 6,800-lb (3100-kg) payload 1,370 miles (2200 km); take-off field length 4,200 ft (1240 m); landing field length 5,700 ft (1740 m)

Weights: empty 33,120 lb (15020 kg); maximum take-off and landing 53,000 lb (24000 kg)

Dimensions: span 95 ft 9 in (29.2 m); length 78 ft 1 in (23.8 m); height 28 ft 6 in (8.575 m); wing area 807 sq ft (75 m²)

Operators: Angola, Bangladesh, Cuba, Hungary, Laos, Peru, Poland, Romania (An-30), Somalia, USSR, Yugoslavia.

Antonov An-72 Coaler

History and notes

The prototype of the Antonov An-72 twin-turbofan STOL military freighter, the first jet aircraft produced by the Antonov bureau, is reported to have flown in December 1977 and was revealed to the West shortly afterwards. Its service status is uncertain; the second prototype was shown at the 1979 Paris air show in Aeroflot markings, but the type has obvious military applications.

The aircraft is being evaluated as a replacement for the An-26, in civil and military service. The An-72 bears a close resemblance to the Boeing YC-14 military transport. The Antonov bureau has elected to adopt the Boeing-developed concept of 'upper-surface-blowing', in which the exhaust from high-bypass-ratio turbofans is directed across specially designed trailing-edge flaps, which divert the jet thrust downwards by the so-called Coanda effect. This principle demands the location of the engines above and ahead of the wing, close inboard to minimize the engine-out asymmetric problems. Movable ramps divert the engine exhaust outwards for greater effectiveness. A T-tail is in consequence necessary, to lift the tailplane out of the wash from the engines.

The wing of the An-72 is fitted with full-span slats and triple-slotted trailing edge flaps on its outer sections, with the special double-slotted USB flaps inboard. The main landing gear comprises four independent single-wheel units, carrying low-pressure tyres and retracting into bulges on the fuselage side. The fuselage is pressurized and is fitted with a rear loading door and integral ramp for the accommodation of small vehicles. Two ventral fins are fitted to the rear fuselage on either side of the ramp; they may be designed to reduce turbulence around the tail for parachute dropping. Folding seats installed along the sides of the starboard freight cabin can accommodate 24 passengers, or the aircraft can be configured to carry 20 stretchers in a casevac role.

It has been suggested that the An-72 may be a fly-

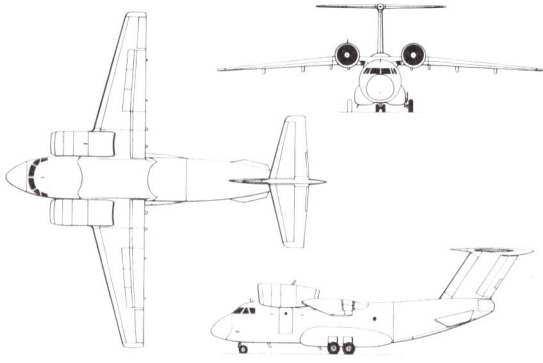

Antonov An-72 'Coaler'.

ing scale model of a larger military freighter, intended to prove the upper-surface-blowing concept, and that the aircraft may have flown before its 'official' first flight in 1977. The main problem in the design of an upper-surface-blowing STOL aircraft is ensuring stability and control in the event of an engine failure in partially jet-borne flight, and this demands high-authority sophisticated autopilots.

Specification

Type: experimental light tactical transport
Powerplant: two 14,300-lb (6500 kg) Lotarev D-36 three-shaft high-bypass turbofans
Performance: Max cruising speed 450 mph (720 km/h) between 26,250 ft and 33,000 ft (8000 m and 10000 m); range with max fuel and reserves 2,000 miles (3200 km); range with max payload 620 miles (1000 km)
Weights: Max payload 16,500 lb (7500 kg); max take-off weight from 4,000-ft (1200 m) runway 67,250 lb (30500 kg)
Dimensions: span 84 ft 9 in (25.83 m); length overall 87 ft 2¼ in (26.576 m); height overall 27 ft 0¼ in (8.325 m)

The intended operational use of the An-72 is not yet certain, but it may well be used to replace the An-26.

Beriev Be-6 Madge

History and notes
Designed by G.M. Beriev, who had been responsible for a long line of seaplane and flying-boat designs since 1928, the Beriev Be-6 'Madge' flew in prototype form in 1947 under the project designation LL-143, powered by two 2,000-hp (1492-kW) Shvetsov ASh-72 engines. After successful trials the type was ordered into production as the Be-6 with the more powerful Shvetsov ASh-73 radials of 2,300 hp (1716-kW). It replaced several antiquated single- and twin-engined flying-boats built in small numbers after World War II. In the production aircraft, the single 23-mm cannon in the nose and twin 20-mm cannon in a tail turret were deleted, retaining only a dorsal barbette with twin 20-mm cannon. The tail gun position was replaced by magnetic anomaly detection (MAD) gear, and after the type entered service a retractable radome was fitted in the hull behind the second 'step'. Offensive weapons (mines, depth charges and torpedoes) are carried on underwing pylons outboard of the engine nacelles.

The Be-6 normally carried a crew of eight and was in a similar class to the US Martin Mariner. It served with the Soviet Navy (AV-MF) in the long-range maritime reconnaissance role from about 1949 to 1967, when it was replaced by the turboprop-powered Be-12 'Mail' amphibian.

A few Be-6s are still in service, mainly on fishery patrol and protection duties, and the type is still used in its original role by China.

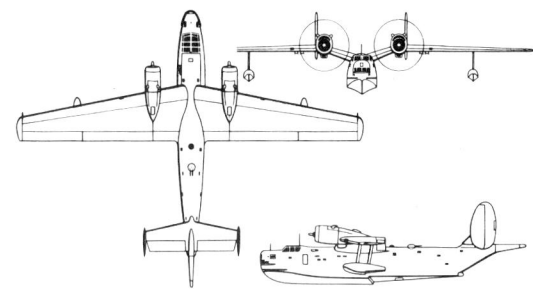

Beriev Be-6 'Madge'.

Specification
Type: twin-engine maritime reconnaissance flying-boat
Powerplant: two 2,300-hp (1716-kW) Shvetsov ASh-73TK radial piston engines
Performance: maximum speed 258 mph (415 km/h) at 7,875 ft (2400 m); maximum range 3,045 miles (4900 km); maximum endurance 16 hours
Weight: loaded 51,588 lb (23400 kg)
Dimensions: span 108 ft 3 in (32.91 m); length 73 ft 10 in (22.50 m); height 24 ft 7 in (7.45 m)
Armament: twin 20-mm cannon in a remotely-controlled dorsal barbette; mines, torpedoes and depth charges carried beneath wings
Operators: USSR

One of the oldest aircraft types still in service, the Be-6 is still used by China.

Beriev Be-12 Tchaika

History and notes

Together with the Japanese Maritime Self-Defence Force, the AVMF (Soviet Naval Aviation) is the last major service to operate fleets of combat flying-boats and amphibians. Elsewhere, the role of the patrol flying-boat was taken over by long-range landplanes in the 1950s. This process may continue, as no amphibious replacement for the Beriev Be-12 *Tchaika* (seagull), codenamed 'Mail' by NATO, has been reported, and the AVMF has now introduced its first specialized landplane for the maritime reconnaissance role, the Ilyushin Il-38 'May'.

The Beriev design bureau, based at Taganrog on the Sea of Azov, has been the main supplier of marine aircraft to the Soviet navy since 1945, most of its aircraft going to the Northern and Black Sea Fleets. The origins of the Be-12 go back to the LL-143 prototype of 1945, which led in 1949 to the Be-6 'Madge'. This latter twin-engined flying-boat served with success until 1967.

Following the Be-6, the Beriev team carried out a considerable amount of research into jet-powered flying boats, producing the straight-winged Be-R-1 of 1952 and the swept-wing Be-10 of 1960-61. The latter, powered by two Lyulka AL-7RVs (unreheated versions of the Su-7 powerplant), established a number of seaplane records in 1961, but only three or four are believed to have been built.

The lessons learned in the design of the Be-R-1 and Be-10, however, were incorporated in the design of a much improved flying-boat based loosely on the Be-6 and originally identified by NATO as a re-engined version of the older type. In fact, the Be-12,

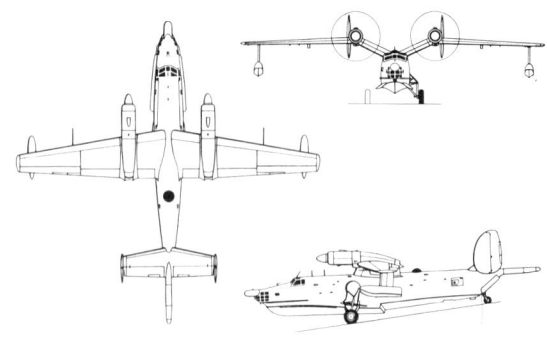

Beriev Be-12 'Mail'.

designated M-12 in AVMF service, bears little more than a general resemblance to the Be-6, sharing only the gull-wing layout and twin tail of its predecessor. The greater power and lighter weight of the turbo-prop engines have permitted the forward extension of the hull, with a new planing bottom similar to that of the Be-10. The prominent spray suppressor around the bows of the Be-10 is also a feature of the turboprop aircraft. The most significant change, however, was the addition of a massive and sturdy retractable landing gear, making the Be-12 amphibious and thus considerably more versatile than the earlier Beriev designs. The turreted gun armament of the Be-6 has been deleted, being replaced by a MAD (magnetic anomaly detector) 'sting' in the tail, above the tailwheel well, while the search radar

Far more than a turboprop-powered version of the Be-6, the 'Mail' was the Soviet Union's primary anti-submarine warfare aircraft until the appearance of the Ilyushin Il-38.

Beriev Be-12 Tchaika

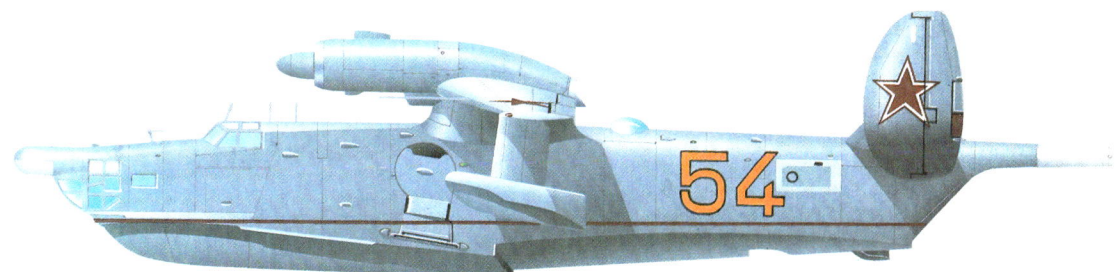

The Soviet Navy is the sole operator of the Be-12 amphibian, used for patrol and rescue.

is carried in a long nose housing instead of the ventral retractable 'dustbin' radome of the Be-6. One of the drawbacks of the high-wing layout, the excessive height of the engines above the ground, has been mitigated by the design of the engine cowling panels, which drop down to form strong working platforms.

The considerable weight-lifting capability of the Be-12 was demonstrated in a series of class records for amphibians set up in 1964, 1968 and 1970, suggesting a normal weapons load as high as 11,000 lb (5000 kg). The Be-12 can load on the water through large side hatches in the rear fuselage, and stores can be dropped through a watertight hatch in the hull aft of the step. Unlike land-based ASW platforms, a marine aircraft can, in reasonably calm conditions, settle on the water and search with its own sonar equipment, rather than relying exclusively on sonobuoys. It is assumed that the Be-12 has this capability.

With the increasing use of the Mil Mi-14 'Haze' ASW helicopter and the Ilyushin Il 38 'May', there would seem to be a diminishing ASW role for the Be-12, although the type will certainly remain in service as a high-speed search-and-rescue (SAR) vehicle. It is also believed to have been used for mapping, geophysical survey and utility transport. By Soviet standards the type was not built in large numbers, only 75 being reported in service in the late 1970s.

Specification

Type: maritime patrol and reserve amphibian
Powerplant: two 4,190-shp (3126-kW) Ivchenko AI-20D turboprops
Performance: maximum speed 380 mph (610 km/h); economical patrol speed 200 mph (320 km/h); maximum range 2,500 miles (4000 km)
Weights: estimated empty 47,840 lb (21700 kg); maximum take-off about 66,140 lb (30000 kg)
Dimensions: span 97 ft 6 in (29.7 m); length 99 ft (30.2 m); height on land 23 ft (7.0 m)
Armament: bombs, rockets or guided ASMs on underwing pylons; depth charges and sonobuoys in fuselage bays
Operators: USSR

The gull wings and twin tail of the Be-6 were echoed in its turbine-powered successor.

Ilyushin Il-14 Crate

History and notes

Although obsolescent in its original roles as airliner and military freighter, the Ilyushin Il-14 'Crate' remains in service for secondary duties, and in 1976 it was reported that the type was entering service with Russian Frontal Aviation electronic intelligence (Elint) units in East Germany. The type is also used as a navigation trainer by a number of air forces.

The Il-14 was developed as an improved version of the Il-12, which had been designed in 1944 and flown in 1946 as a replacement for the Lisunov Li-2 (Soviet-built Douglas C-47). Compared with its predecessor, the Il-14 featured more powerful engines and a redesigned wing of slightly thicker section, intended to improve handling character-istics. The fin and rudder were enlarged to improve engine-out behaviour. The type made its maiden flight in 1950 and entered service with Aeroflot in 1954.

About 1,200 Il-14s are believed to have been built in the Soviet Union in 1950-58, when the type was superseded on Soviet production lines by turbine-powered transports. However, about 80 of the type were built by VEB in the German Democratic Republic, and some 120 produced in Czechoslovakia as the Avia-14. The Avia-14 corresponded to the Il-14M, a stretched version of the original aircraft, while the Avia-14T was a freighter version with op-tional wing-tip tanks. Some Czech-built aircraft were supplied to the Soviet Union.

The Russian air force Elint version of the Il-14 preceded the Il-18 'Coot-C' into service, and has largely been replaced in this role by the more ad-vanced aircraft. The older type may, however, be re-tained in second-line units and as an Elint trainer.

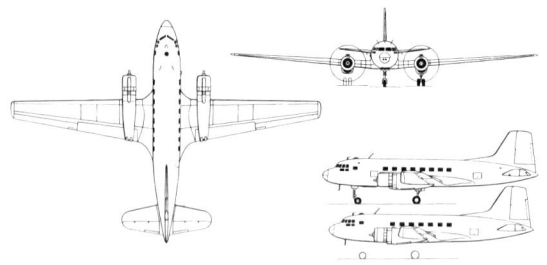

Ilyushin Il-14M 'Crate' and (lower side-view) Il-14.

Specification

Type: medium transport, electronic intelligence (Elint) aircraft, and navigation trainer

Powerplant: two 1,900-hp (1417-kW) Shvetsov ASh-82T radial piston engines

Performance: maximum speed 268 mph (430 km/h) at 7,800 ft (2400 m); cruising speed 200-215 mph (320-350 km/h) at 8,200-9,800 ft (2500-3000 m); range with 7,300-lb (3300-kg) payload 250 miles (400 km); range with 3,500-lb (1600-kg) payload 1,000 miles (1750 km)

Weights: (Il-14M) empty 28,000 lb (12700 kg); maximum payload 7,300 lb (3300 kg); maximum fuel with tip-tanks 7,000 lb (3175 kg); maximum take-off 38,500 lb (17500 kg)

Dimensions: span 104 ft (31.7 m); length 69 ft 11 in (21.31 m); wing area 1,080 sq ft (100 m²)

Operators: Czechoslovakia, Poland, India, Iraq, Egypt, USSR, Yugoslavia

An Il-14 flown by Iraq.

Ilyushin Il-18 Coot

History and notes

The first Soviet airliner designed from the outset as a turbine-powered commercial transport, the Ilyushin Il-18 'Coot' made its initial flight in July 1957. Although a close contemporary of the US Lockheed Electra, it was rather larger, being closer in size to the Vickers Vanguard and Bristol Britannia. Despite this, it relies on manual controls, commonly found on Soviet commercial aircraft.

Early Il-18s were flown with both Kuznetsov NK-4 and Ivchenko AI-20 turboprops. The latter was standardized, but severe problems with this engine caused accidents in the early years of operations from 1958. The capacity of the Il-18 was increased from 80 passengers in early versions to 120 in later aircraft. The Il-18D featured increased power, weight and fuel capacity and became the main production version in airliner form. Its economics, although not outstanding, were better than those of contemporary Soviet jet transports and the type was extensively used by Aeroflot and other airlines in Warsaw Pact countries. Other examples have been used as government and VIP transports, but no convertible passenger/freight version has been produced, and its value as a military transport is therefore limited.

About 600 Il-18s are reported to have been built by the late 1960s, but by 1975 the type was being phased out of service with Aeroflot in favour of the Tupolev Tu-154 'Careless' tri-jet. About this time, with the closely related Il-38 'May' maritime reconnaissance aircraft in production, it was decided to use the basic Il-18 for the electronic intelligence (Elint) role, backing up Antonov An-12 'Cub-Bs'. It seems likely that both the 'Cub-B' and the Elint Il-18, codenamed 'Coot-A', are based on old airframes retired from the VTA (Military Transport Aviation) or Aeroflot, and remanufactured for their new roles.

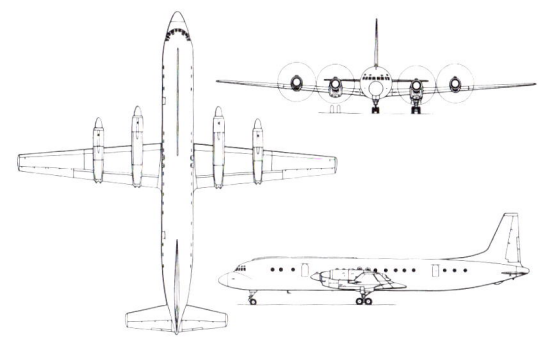

Ilyushin Il-18 'Coot'.

The 'Coot-A' was observed in early 1978, and has been seen in overland and over-water service. Given the wide-ranging nature of Elint activities, it is probable that both the 'Coot-A' and 'Cub-B' are operated by the AVMF (Soviet Naval Aviation). Their missions involve monitoring transmissions on the periphery of NATO-controlled areas, and patrolling in the vicinity of NATO exercises, suggesting that they may be involved in communications between widely-spaced Soviet units (the US forces use the similar Lockheed Hercules for the same role.)

Seen here in Aeroflot insignia, the Il-18 was also used by several governments before being adapted for the electronic jamming role.

Ilyushin Il-18 Coot

Another activity is the so-called 'provocative' mission, colloquially known to the Royal Air Force as 'ringing the fire alarm': a 'Coot-A' was intercepted and photographed by an RAF fighter in 1978, suggesting that it was involved in an investigation of the UK Air Defence Region. The value of such missions is that they provoke a flurry of communications among the defending forces and provide a mass of data for later analysis.

The 'Coot-A' is fitted with a very large canoe fairing below the fuselage, possibly containing a highly sensitive directional receiver antenna. Other aerials are mounted in pods on the fuselage side, and in dorsal and ventral radomes. The prominent dorsal radomes may indicate the use of satellite communication for real-time transmission of intercepted signals to a processing station. (The radar installations are strongly reminiscent of those on the US Navy's Lockheed EP-3E Orion, which also has an Elint role). The crew presumably includes a complement of systems operators, and working conditions are presumably far superior to those aboard the converted bombers which previously bore the brunt of Russian Elint work.

Specification
Type: medium transport and ('Coot-A') electronic intelligence/communications aircraft
Powerplant: four 4,250-ehp (3170-kW) Ivchenko AI-20M turboprops
Performance: cruising speed 380-390 mph (610-625 km/h) at 26,250 ft (8000 m); range with 30,000-lb (13500-kg) payload 2,500 miles (4000 km); range with maximum fuel 4,000 miles (6500 km)
Weights: empty 77,000 lb (35000 kg); maximum fuel load 51,920 lb (23550 kg); maximum take-off 141,000 lb (64000 kg)
Dimensions: span 122 ft 8½ in (37.4 m); length 117 ft 9½ in (35.9 m); wing area 1,507 sq ft (140 m²)
Operators: Afghanistan, Algeria, Bulgaria, Czechoslovakia, East Germany, North Korea, Poland, Romania, USSR, Vietnam, Yugoslavia

'Coot-A' bristles with electronics, including a massive 'canoe' fairing beneath the fuselage. The type is very active around the European central region and UK air defence region.

Ilyushin Il-28 Beagle

History and notes

China is by far the most important user of the Il-yushin Il-28 'Beagle', a now elderly tactical bomber. Some hundreds of the type were manufactured in China under a licence taken out before the Sino-Soviet rift. Production of the bomber, designated B-5, and of a trainer version continues despite the age of the design. Other air forces continue to use the Il-28 for various second-line duties: the Finnish air force operated several as target-tug into the late 1970s. The last Soviet force to use the type for combat duties was the AVMF (Soviet Naval Aviation) which adopted the Il-28T torpedo-bomber fairly late in the type's career. The AVMF Il-28Ts were almost certainly adapted from surplus Frontal Aviation Il-28s when the AVMF Tupolev Tu-14 'Bosuns' were retired in the mid-1960s.

The Il-28 was, like many first-generation Soviet jets, powered by derivatives of the Rolls-Royce Nene turbojets which had been supplied to the Soviet

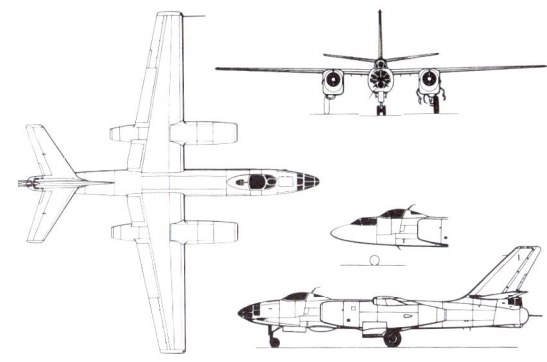

Ilyushin Il-28 'Beagle' with scrap view of Il-28U 'Mascot'.

Main user of the Il-28 is China, which refers to its indigenously-built aircraft as the B-5.

The forward-slung engines and large swept tail of the Il-28 are very apparent in this shot of an unmarked Soviet-operated aircraft.

Ilyushin Il-28 Beagle

The first generation of effective Soviet jet combat aircraft were powered by derivatives of British Rolls-Royce engines. Among the last to see service outside China were the Il-28R target tugs of the Finnish air arm.

Ilyushin Il-28 Beagle

The Il-28 was the last bomber type to be delivered to Warsaw Pact allies of the Soviet Union until the mid 1970s, when Su-20s and MiG-23BMs entered service.

Union by the British government immediately after World War II. These offered greater power and better reliability than the engines then being developed by Russian and German engineers in the country's own establishments. The first prototype flew in August 1948 on the power of two British-built Nenes: the later aircraft were fitted with Soviet-built RD-45s or VK-1s. The Il-28 was of rather unusual appearance; the leading-edge of the wing was completely unswept and the trailing-edge was swept forwards, giving the aircraft a long-nosed appearance. The tail was abbreviated, possibly because of the weight of a bulky tail gun turret similar to that on the Tupolev Tu-4 'Bull', a copy of the Boeing B-29. Unlike contemporary US bombers, the Il-28 had a manned tail turret rather than a radar-controlled installation. In contrast with the wings, the tail surfaces were sharply swept back. Swept tail surfaces were standard on all straight-wing Soviet bombers of the day, for reasons which are not altogether clear; the intention may have been to avert compressibility problems around the rear turret or to ensure stability at high diving speeds.

Pre-production aircraft with RD-45s began to appear in late 1949, and deliveries of production aircraft, powered by the VK-1, started in 1951. Deliveries to Frontal Aviation greatly increased the striking power of the force, which hitherto had relied on the piston-engined Tu-2 'Bat'. The Il-28 retained the visual bombardier nose of the older piston-engined bombers, but at a fairly early stage in production the type was also fitted with all-weather bombing radar in a ventral fairing. Later aircraft were fitted with a tail-warning radar beneath the rear turret, but the guns remained manually aimed.

The Il-28 formed the main striking strength of the initial Warsaw Pact air forces, particularly those of Poland, Czechoslovakia and, later, East Germany. Other versions included the Il-28U 'Mascot' conversion trainer, with a second pilot's station and canopy

in place of the bombardier nose. Like many Soviet conversion trainers, the Il-28U has no combat capability. Some Il-28R photographic and electronic reconnaissance aircraft were also put into service.

At least 1,000 Il-28s were built in the Soviet Union and the type has been built in China as the B-5. The type was replaced in Soviet air force service by the Yakovlev Yak-28 'Brewer'. In general, however, non-Soviet Warsaw Pact forces have not been re-equipped with comparable offensive aircraft. The Il-yushin bomber also possesses the distinction of being the first jet aircraft operated by Aeroflot; a few examples of the type, designated Il-20, were put into service by the airline in 1955 carrying high-priority freight and mail, as a means to gain jet experience before the arrival of the Tu-104 'Camel'.

Specification
Type: three-seat light bomber
Powerplant: two 6,040-lb (2740-kg) Klimov VK-1 centrifugal-flow turbojets
Performance: maximum speed at 14,765 ft (4500 m) 560 mph (900 km/h); maximum speed at sea level 500 mph (800 km/h); cruising speed 480 mph (770 km/h) at 33,000 ft (10000 m); range with a 2,200-lb (1000-kg) bombload 1,350 miles (2180 km) at 33,000 (10000 m)
Weights: empty 26,455 lb (13000 kg); maximum 46,300 lb (21000 kg)
Dimensions: span 70 ft 4½ in (21.45 m); length 57 ft 11 in (17.65 m); wing area 654.4 sq ft (60.8 m²)
Armament: internal bay for up to 6,500 lb (3000 kg) of bombs or two air-launched torpedoes; two fixed NR-23 23-mm cannon in nose and two NR-23 in tail turret
Operators: Afghanistan, Algeria, Bulgaria, China, Czechoslovakia, Iraq, North Korea, Nigeria, Poland, Romania, Somalia, South Yemen, Syria, USSR, Vietnam.

Ilyushin Il-38 May

History and notes

The Soviet Union was a latecomer in the field of specialized maritime reconnaissance and anti-submarine-warfare (ASW) aircraft, as it came late to the manufacture of airborne early warning systems. For this reason it is usually assumed that Soviet systems such as the Ilyushin Il-38 'May' and the Tu-126 'Moss' are not up to the same standards as Western counterparts; but their operational effectiveness depends on hard-to-assess details of their sensors and internal equipment.

The closest Western equivalent of the Il-38 is the Lockheed P-3 Orion. Both were developed from medium-range airliners of about the same vintage, although the Il-18 which forms the basis of the Il-38 is a rather larger aircraft than the Lockheed Electra. However, the histories of the two types are different. The first Orion entered service some 10 years before the Il-38 appeared, and by the time the Soviet aircraft had entered service the P-3's systems had been modernized twice to keep abreast with the growing threat from Russian ballistic-missile-firing submarines (SSBNs). More recently, the P-3C has undergone various Update programmes, acquiring new types of sensor and improved versions of systems already fitted. None of this development effort has been paralleled visibly on the Il-38, no

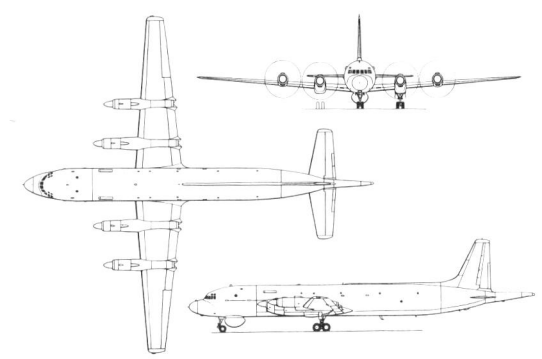

Ilyushin Il-38 'May'.

changes in equipment having been observed since the type entered service.

Neither has the Soviet Union the benefit of the West's long experience of ASW, dating back to the Battle of the Atlantic in World War II. The Lockheed Neptune, for example, had no known equivalent in the Soviet Union. Jet aircraft such as the Tu-16 were too inefficient at low speeds and altitudes to be used effectively in the ASW role, which was mainly the province of flying-boats such as the Beriev Be-6 and M-12, with relatively short range.

Weapon doors open, an Il-38 drops a sonobuoy during a naval exercise.

Ilyushin Il-38 May

Specification

Type: maritime reconnaissance and ASW aircraft
Powerplant: four 5,200-shp (3879-kW) Ivchenko AI-20M turboprops
Performance: maximum speed 400 mph (640 km/h); patrol speed 290 mph (460 km/h); endurance 16 hours; range 5,200 miles (8300 km)
Weights: empty 90,000 lb (40000 kg); maximum take-off 150,000 lb (68000 kg)
Dimensions: span 122 ft 9 in (37.4 m); length (including MAD boom) 129 ft 10 in (39.6 m); height 33 ft 4 in (10.3 m); wing area 1,500 sq ft (140 m²)
Armament: internal weapons bay for homing torpedoes, nuclear and conventional depth charges and sonobuoys
Operators: India, USSR

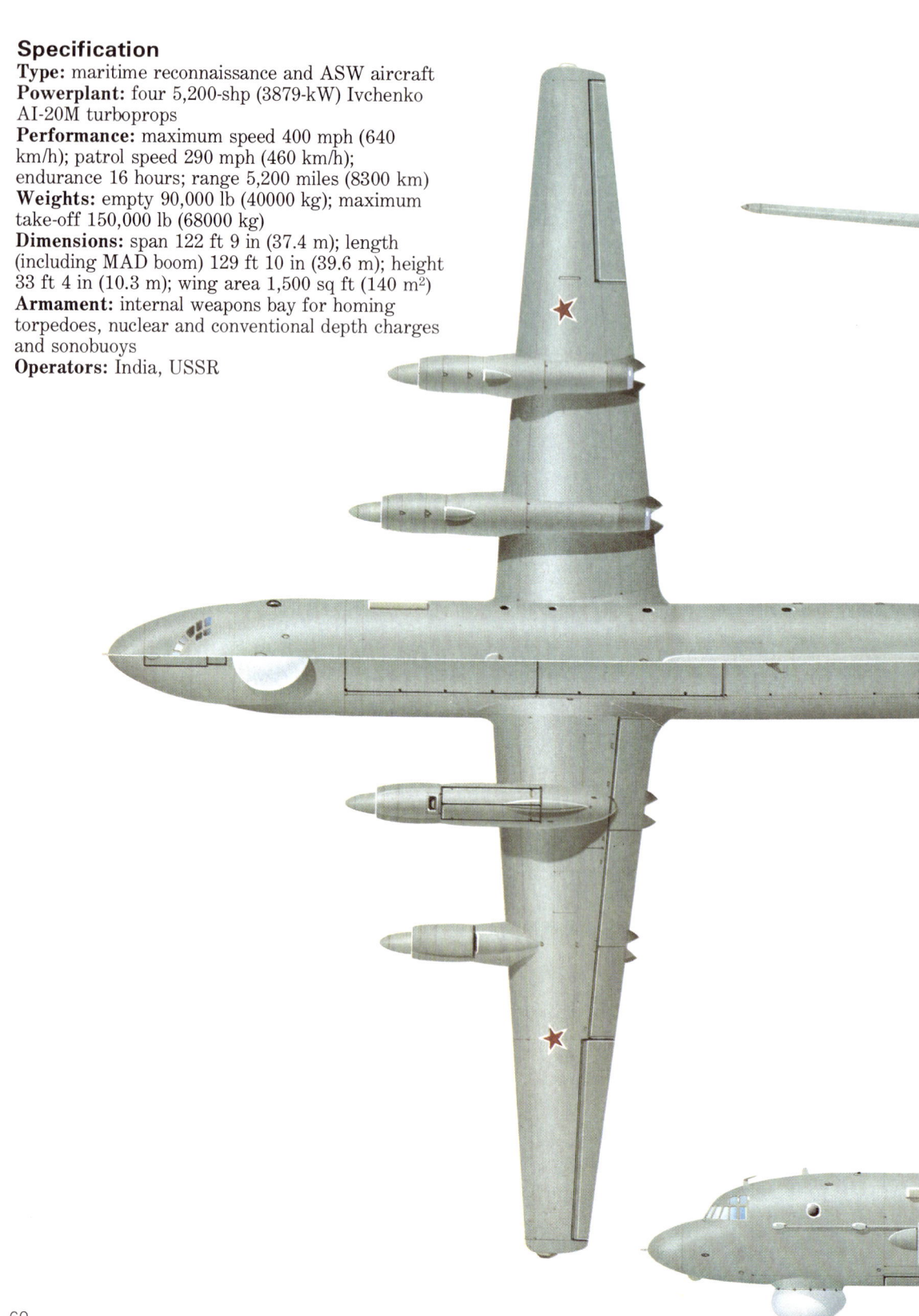

The cross-section of the Il-38 is narrower than that of the Lockheed P-3 Orion and considerably smaller than that of the British BAe Nimrod, limiting its weapon load.

The Il-38 probably differs extensively from its parent, the Il-18, in structural detail. The wing is further forward, and this would mean restressing the fuselage even without the completely different window arrangement.

Fuselage detail such as the location of observation blisters suggests that the Il-38 tactical and sensor-operating crew are located aft, with electronics in the forward fuselage.

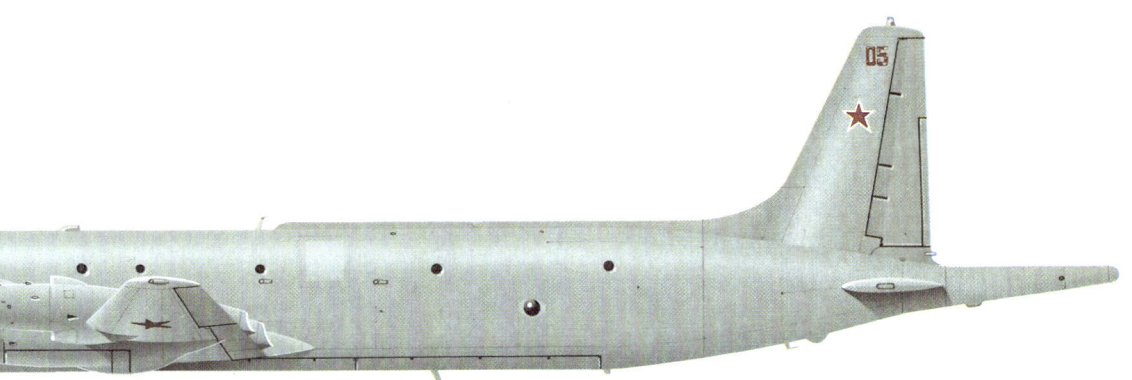

Ilyushin Il-38 May

In the early 1960s, when the United States Navy's force of Polaris-armed SSBNs was being built up, there was no aircraft in the Soviet naval air force (AVMF) which could counter the increasing threat. With the development of the Poseidon missile, the area from which US SSBNs could threaten large sectors of the Soviet Union increased well beyond the area which could be covered, even partially, by Be-6s and M-12s. The need for a specialized ASW aircraft grew with the deployment of the longer-ranged missile to replace the Polaris, and Il-38 development appears to have coincided with the introduction of Poseidon. The aircraft was first observed in 1974, but by that time it appears to have been in service for some years, and so design probably began in about 1965. About 100 Il-38s have been delivered to the AVMF, and some have been supplied to India; it is possible that the latter aircraft have a reduced standard of equipment, like the Lockheed P-3F supplied to Iran.

The airframe of the Il-38 is certainly stronger than that of the Il-18 airliner, in order to withstand the stresses of manoeuvring at low altitude in gusty weather. It is also likely that the ASW aircraft can take off at a higher gross weight than the airliner (the P-3C for instance, is very much heavier than the Electra) and it would be logical to expect the engines to be similar to the uprated AI-20s fitted to the Antonov An-32 STOL freighter.

A highly significant feature of the Il-38 design is the fact that the wing is set much farther forward than on the airliner. This indicates that the forward fuselage contains a concentration of heavy equipment. On either side of the fuselage, ahead of the wing, there is fitted what appears to be an air intake and outlet. One explanation for this feature, and for the short front fuselage, is that a large processor is installed forward, with the main tactical control compartment above the wing and extending towards the rear. The aft fuselage presumably includes sleeping accommodation for relief crews and galley facilities, which account for little weight.

Unlike that of the Orion, the main radar of the

No significant changes have been observed to the Il-38 since this early photo was taken in 1970.

Il-38 is mounted under the forward fuselage immediately aft of the nosewheel bay. Radar is a major search aid for an ASW aircraft, but in these days of nuclear-powered submarines it has to be of high performance if it is to be effective. It is not known whether the Il-38 radar can match Western sets in its ability to distinguish small solid echoes such as periscopes from 'glint' off the water surface.

The weapon bay of the Il-38 is installed well forward; this feature does not in itself account for the forward shift of the wing, as it is shared by the P-3, where the wing is in the same relative position as on the original Electra. The weapon bay houses sonobuoys as well as offensive weapons, whereas the P-3 has separate sonobuoy stowage in the rear fuselage. Underfloor capacity immediately ahead of the wing is probably used for fuel tankage. The Il-38 carries the symbol of the ASW aircraft's trade: a magnetic anomaly detector (MAD) installed in a long tailboom.

Radar, MAD and acoustic sensors appear to be the main sources of raw data for the Il-38, but its effectiveness will also depend on the processing equipment fitted and its ability to select and pass information to the crew. Electronic surveillance measures (ESM) are not conspicuous, although there is a fin-top antenna. Also apparently absent are infra-red and low-light level visual sensors, both standard on the latest Western types. Going purely on external signs, the Il-38 as so far observed appears to be a first-generation type in terms of its operational equipment; however, it can be expected that more effective versions are under development and will appear in AVMF service in due course.

Development of a large, long-range subsonic military aircraft was reported in 1979, with both the strategic missile-launching and ASW roles apparently in mind. However, the new type may be intended more for the high-altitude surveillance role formerly undertaken by the Tu-142 than for ASW of the sort carried out by the Il-38 and its Western equivalents.

Ilyushin Il-76 Candid

History and notes

Superficially similar to the Lockheed C-141 StarLifter, the Ilyushin Il-76 'Candid' is in fact a heavier and more powerful aircraft, more capable of operations from short, unpaved runways. It is replacing the Antonov An-12 'Cub' as the main tactical transport of the Soviet VTA (air transport force); it is also in service with Aeroflot, and Il-76s of both operators have been used to supply arms to Soviet client states.

The design of the Il-76 started in the late 1960s, to meet a joint civil/military requirement. Aeroflot needed an aircraft smaller and more flexible than the An-22 'Cock', while the VTA could presumably see a requirement for a faster aircraft than the big Antonov turboprop for use in forward areas. The requirement which emerged was for an aircraft which could carry twice the maximum payload of the An-12 over sectors longer than the older aircraft's maximum range. The new transport had to be able to use the same short and semi-prepared strips as the An-12, setting problems in undercarriage and wing design.

There is little room for flexibility in the design of a heavy military freighter. Loading and unloading requires a rear ramp and a floor at truck-bed height, so that a low wing is ruled out; wing wake then makes a

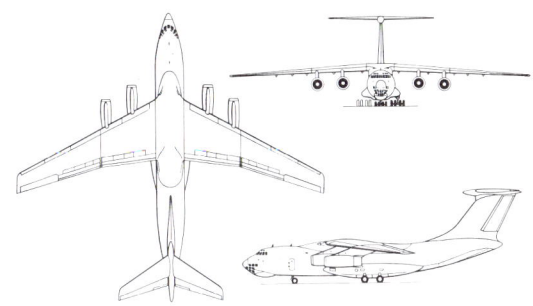

Ilyushin Il-76 'Candid'.

low-set tailplane risky, so that aircraft of this type tend to have T-tails. The Ilyushin design bureau, headed from the mid-1960s by General Designer Novozhilov, adopted this generally conventional layout for the Il-76. It was the first Soviet transport to have podded engines, hung on low-drag pylons reminiscent of those of the Douglas DC-8-62. The engines are set well inboard compared with those of Western airliners, and are probably set too low to have any blowing effect on the flaps. The wing is fitted with extensive high-lift devices, including slats,

Iraqi Airways has taken delivery of Il-76s, but as these aircraft are fully equipped with radar-aimed tail cannon they clearly have a military reserve role.

Ilyushin Il-76 Candid

Iraqi Airways is the ostensible operator of a few Il-76s, but these are fully equipped for military operations, including paradropping of troops and supplies.

triple-slotted trailing-edge flaps, and spoilers for low-speed roll control.

A unique feature of the Il-76 is its rough-field landing gear, more complex than that of the C-141. The main gear comprises four units, each a single axle with four wheels abreast, while the nose gear also has four wheels abreast. The original Il-76 was designed to have a 'footprint pressure' no higher than that of the An-12.

Internally, the Il-76 is equipped with a cargo roller floor, two 6,500-lb (3000-kg) winches and two roof cranes with a total capacity of 22,000 lb (10000 kg).

In addition to the normal crew of two pilots, a flight engineer and a navigator, there is accommodation for a loadmaster and a radio operator. The navigator occupies a cabin below the flight deck, with a glazed nose. Production Il-76s have two radomes similar to those of late-production An-22s, one housing a weather radar and the other containing mapping equipment. The final member of the crew, on military Il-76s, is the tail gunner: the apparently archaic armament of twin 23-mm cannon fitted to the An-12 is retained on its jet replacement. Unlike the An-12, however, the jet aircraft carries a tail-warning radar.

The first Il-76 was flown in March 1971, and was demonstrated at the Paris air show two months later. Prototype and early production aircraft were designed closely to the original specification, which demanded 3,100-mile (5000-km) range with 88,000-lb (40000-kg) payload, and had a maximum take-off weight of 346,000 lb (157000 kg). This is believed to have been matched by limited fuel capacity. From 1977 production appears to have concentrated on the Il-76T, with some 20 per cent more fuel. It is likely that more of the Il-76T wing is wet, allowing payload to be traded for extra range.

Take-off and landing runs for the lighter early Il-76 are quoted at 2,800 ft (850 m) for the 1,500 ft (450 m) respectively; these are almost certainly ground rolls, but still suggest that the Il-76 could comfortably use a 5,000 ft (1500 m) strip. This performance is impressive, if not in the class of the US Advanced Medium STOL Transport (AMST) prototypes, and makes the Il-76 a tactical transport to be reckoned with. It has also been used extensively in the airlift role, and air-dropping trials have been carried out.

About 100 Il-76s are now in service; production is continuing at about 30 aircraft/year, and the VTA is probably replacing all its 600 An-12s with the new type. Reports of a tanker version under development may have been premature: the Il-86 wide-body airliner would seem to be a more suitable basis for such a development and would now be available in the same timescale. Deliveries to Aeroflot appeared to be gaining momentum in 1978, suggesting that the VTA was relaxing some of its demands for

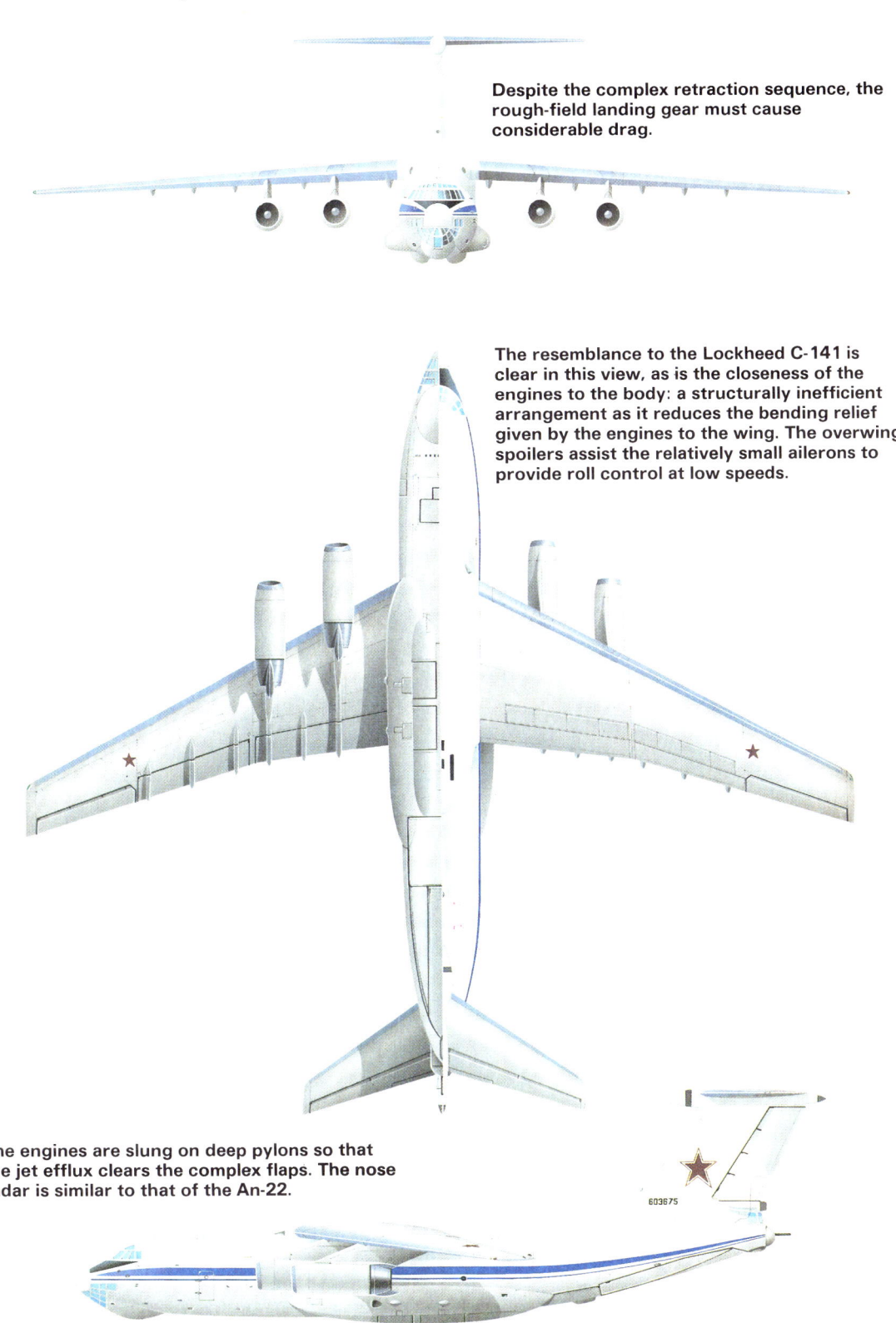

Despite the complex retraction sequence, the rough-field landing gear must cause considerable drag.

The resemblance to the Lockheed C-141 is clear in this view, as is the closeness of the engines to the body: a structurally inefficient arrangement as it reduces the bending relief given by the engines to the wing. The overwing spoilers assist the relatively small ailerons to provide roll control at low speeds.

The engines are slung on deep pylons so that the jet efflux clears the complex flaps. The nose radar is similar to that of the An-22.

priority in deliveries.

The Il-76T is probably the definitive version of the type for the time being, in the absence of any more advanced Soviet powerplant. An Il-76 was used as the flying test-bed for the Kuznetsov NK-86 engine, and the type was mentioned as a possible application for the engine, but there seems to be no sign that such a version is being built.

Specification

Type: strategic or tactical freighter
Powerplant: four 26,500 lb (12000 kg) Soloviev D-30KP turbofans
Performance: maximum speed 530 mph (850 km/h) or Mach 0.8; economical cruising speed 500 mph (800 km/h) or Mach 0.75; range with 77,000-lb (35000-kg) payload 4,000 miles (6500 km); ceiling 42,000 ft (13000 m)
Weights: empty 135,000 lb (62000 kg); maximum payload about 88,000 lb (40000 kg); maximum take-off 375,000 lb (170000 kg)
Dimensions: span 165 ft 8 in (50.5 m); length 152 ft 10½ in (46.59 m); height 48 ft 5 in (14.76 m); wing area 3,230 sq ft (300 m²)
Armament: (when fitted) two 23-mm cannon in radar-directed manned tail turret
Operators: Iraq, USSR

Design for short-runway, rough-field operation is evident in this front view of an Il-76 on approach, with flaps and slats fully deployed.

Kamov Ka-25 Hormone

History and notes

The Soviet naval air arm (AVMF) has for many years been a loyal customer of the design bureau named after Nikolai Kamov. Like the similarly named Kaman concern in the United States, the Kamov bureau has been associated with compact helicopters of close-coupled twin-rotor layout, but whereas Kaman developed the Flettner intermeshing rotor concept, the Soviet team chose the co-axial layout, originally applied to the experimental pre-World War II Breguet-Dorand. With no need for a long tail boom to counter torque, the fuselage of the co-axial helicopter can be made small and compact. This renders it particularly suitable for shipboard use, and all the helicopters operated by the AVMF from ships have been Kamov co-axial types.

The Ka-8 and Ka-10 'flying motorcycle' designs of 1945-55 aroused naval interest in the potential of shipboard helicopters for over-the-horizon target spotting; this 'airborne crow's nest' concept had been explored by the German navy in World War II. The Ka-15 cabin helicopter and the improved Ka-18

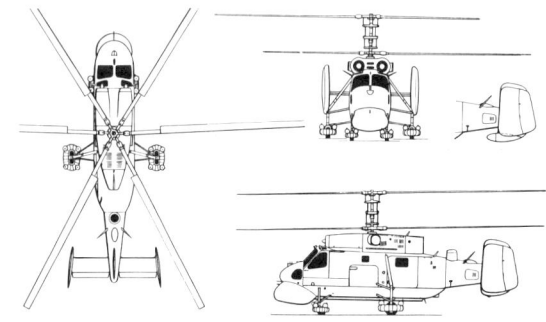

Kamov Ka-25 'Hormone-A'.

were ordered for AVMF service, but appear to have been used only on a small scale for experimental shipboard operations.

The Soviet Union's definitive shipboard helicopter, however, made its public debut in 1961, at the Tushino air display. More than four times as

Kamov Ka-25 Hormone

Ka-25s operating from the antisubmarine cruiser Moskva. The nets on the deck presumably form part of a restraint system.

heavy as the Ka-15, the new helicopter was powered by twin turbines, six times as powerful as the piston engine of the older type, with scarcely any increase in weight and volume. As with land-based helicopters, the availability of the turboshaft engine vastly increased what could be achieved. Together with the natural compactness of the co-axial layout, the powerplant makes the Ka-25 look deceptively small; in fact it is almost as heavy as the Mil Mi-4, and rather bigger than the Westland Wessex. At the time of writing it is probably the largest and most capable helicopter operated from normal warships, and in effectiveness it comes into the same class as the much later Kaman SH-2F and Westland Lynx. The prototype Ka-25 was demonstrated with air-to-surface missiles on outriggers, but these appear to have been dummies.

Details of the Ka-25 design probably reflect lessons learned in trials with smaller helicopters. The twin-engine layout presumably confers a degree of security in the event of an engine failure, although the type does not seem over-endowed with power unless the engines can be run at a contingency rating higher than the figure quoted for the Ka-25K civil derivative. Both engines, however, have their own independent fuel supplies, a feature not always found on Soviet land-based helicopters; the type is fitted with autostabilization, powered controls, comprehensive communications and full all-weather navigation equipment. Most Ka-25s are fitted with emergency flotation 'boots' on each of the four landing gear legs, which inflate automatically in the event of a ditching.

The 'missile-armed' prototype seen in 1961 was codenamed 'Harp' by NATO, but for some reason best known to NATO the very similar production version was christened 'Hormone'. The first version of the Ka-25 to see service appears to have been the 'Hormone-B' fitted with a large chin radome broader than that of the 'Harp' prototype. The 'Hormone-B' is deployed on 'Kresta I' class cruisers and 'Kiev' class aircraft-carriers, and appears to be associated with long-range surface-to-surface cruise missiles such as the SS-N-3 'Shaddock' (on the cruisers) and the SS-N-12 fitted to the 'Kiev' class. (The lead ship of the latter class, *Kiev*, made her maiden voyage in 1976, followed by *Minsk* in 1979.) The 'Hormone-B' seems to be a modern extension of the 'flying crow's nest' principle, using its radar to provide guidance and targeting information for the long-range missiles. The 'Kresta I' class appeared in 1967, marking the first shipboard deployment of the Ka-25. It would be logical for the 'Hormone-B' to lack some of the ASW equipment of the 'Hormone-A', in order to

Kamov Ka-25 Hormone

Economical use of space accounts for the Ka-25's success in Soviet Navy service, despite its relatively poor performance. Equipment standards vary even among aircraft of the Hormone-A subtype pictured here. However, nearly all carry the nose-mounted Yagi aerials on this aircraft. Long-range tanks are not always carried, leaving pylons free for stores.

Kamov Ka-25 Hormone

increase its range and ceiling and hence the area over which it can offer missile guidance.

The 'Hormone-A', the basic ASW variant, appeared shortly after the 'Hormone-B' on the helicopter-carriers *Moskva* and *Leningrad*, and on the new 'Kresta II' and 'Kara' cruiser classes. It also equips the 'Kanin' class destroyers. It forms the bulk of the helicopter complement of the 'Kuril' class carriers, which also carry a number of 'Hormone-B' radar pickets.

Little is known about the operational equipment of the 'Hormone-A', and equipment standards appear to vary; some aircraft are fitted with a box-like container on the fuselage side, while others have been seen with nose aerials possibly connected with ESM (electronic surveillance measures). As well as radar, the 'Hormone-A' almost certainly carries dunking sonar equipment in the cabin, and is likely to be fitted with a magnetic anomaly detector (MAD) in a towed 'bird'. The radome is smaller than that of the 'Hormone-B' and the radar is presumably less powerful. There may be an internal weapons bay, but usually the 'Hormone-A' crew would leave the 'kill' to the SS-N-14 ASW missiles of the mother ship.

A new naval helicopter is expected to appear shortly, but there would seem to be no need in the immediate future for a Ka-25 replacement. The type appears well suited to the shipboard role, in which its compactness — without the complication of tail folding — counts for a great deal and the need for high performance or low silhouette is not urgent. The Ka-25 may fill other roles in addition to ASW and radar-picket duties, but as yet no details of these have been revealed. The existence of the Ka-34, a 20-passenger helicopter probably derived from the Ka-25, was reported in 1979.

This 'Hormone-A' differs from the aircraft pictured on the previous pages in having a box-like container on the starboard side of the fuselage, and a beacon-like assembly above the boom.

Specification

Type: multi-role shipboard helicopter
Powerplant: two 900-shp (671-kW) Glushenkov GTD-3 turboshafts
Performance: maximum speed 135 mph (220 km/h); cruising speed 120 mph (200 km/h); hovering ceiling 2,000 ft (600 m); service ceiling 16,500 ft (5000 m); maximum endurance 4 to 5 hours; range with external fuel 400 miles (650 km)
Weights: empty about 10,500 lb (4750 kg); normal maximum 15,500 lb (7100 kg); overload 16,500 lb (7500 kg)
Dimensions: rotor diameter 51 ft 8 in (15.75 m); fuselage length about 34 ft (10.35 m); height 17 ft 8 in (5.4 m); rotor disc area 4,193 sq ft (389.7 m²)
Armament: two homing torpedoes or depth charges in internal weapons bay
Operator: India, Jugoslavia, Syria, USSR

As well as equipping many conventional warships, the Ka-25 is carried by the much larger Kiev-class carriers. Compactness of the co-axial configuration is shown here.

Mikoyan-Gurevich MiG-15 Fagot/15UTI Midget

History and notes

Although obsolete in its basic fighter version, the Mikoyan-Gurevich MiG-15 'Fagot' survives in considerable numbers in its two-seat trainer version and will remain in use, in some countries, until it is replaced by the Aero L-39 Albatros.

German and Russian research gave rise to the design of the MiG-15 in 1945-46, and the first prototype was not unlike the Focke-Wulf Ta 183 study of the late war years. Early difficulties occasioned by the lack of a suitable powerplant for the proposed fighter were solved when the British government decided to supply the Soviet Union with a batch of Rolls-Royce Nene turbojets. A copy was produced by the Klimov bureau under the designation RD-45; later uprated versions were designated in the VK-1 series.

The first prototype was lost soon after its first flight in July 1947, but a second and extensively revised prototype flew towards the end of the same year, and the aircraft was ordered into production in March 1948. Deliveries started in 1949, by which time the improved MiG-15SD, better known as the MiG-15bis, was flying in prototype form. The MiG-15UTI conversion trainer flew shortly afterwards.

The combat debut of the MiG-15 in Korea in November 1950 proved an unpleasant shock to the West. There was only one Allied fighter in the same class, the North American F-86 Sabre. Its better

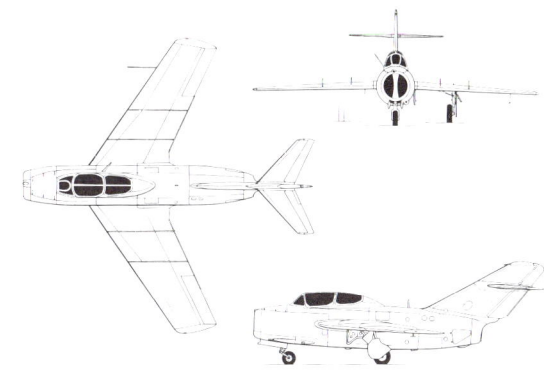

Mikoyan-Gurevich MiG-15UTI 'Midget'.

equipment, and the better training of the US pilots, allowed the US Air Force to achieve superiority over the MiG-15, but the Soviet fighter had a better climb rate, ceiling and acceleration even than this outstanding US type.

China, Poland and Czechoslovakia built MiG-15s, (the first-named under the designation F-2) and the latter two countries converted many single-seaters into two-seaters after the MiG-15 was phased out of first line service. In the absence of any production trainer version of the MiG-17 or MiG-19, the MiG-

The MiG-15UTI remains in use in a great many air forces; Finland is acquiring British Aerospace Hawks to replace its aircraft.

Mikoyan-Gurevich MiG-15 Fagot/15UTI Midget

Key to MiG-15bis cutaway
drawing

1 Bifurcated engine air intake
2 Landing light (moved to port
   wing root on later production
   aircraft)
3 Combat camera fairing
4 Accumulator
5 Radio transmitter
6 Radio receiver
7 Armour-glass windscreen
8 Gyro gunsight
9 Starboard electrics control
   panel
10 Ejector seat
11 Aft-sliding canopy (open
   position)
12 VHF blade antenna
13 Wing fence
14 Slipper-type drop tank (247,5
   1/54·4 Imp gal capacity)
15 Pitot pressure head
16 Compass unit
17 Starboard navigation light
18 Starboard aileron
19 Main fuel tank

20 Rear fuselage attachment joint
21 Engine bearers
22 Klimov VK-1 turbojet
23 Control rods
24 Rear fuselage frames
25 Fin mainspar
26 Rudder balance weight
27 Rudder (upper section)
28 Tail navigation light
29 Elevator trim tab
30 Port elevator
31 Single-spar tailplane
32 Jetpipe fairing
33 Air brake (partly extended)
34 Walkway (rubber coated)
35 Split landing flap
36 Trim operating mechanism
37 Aileron operating rods
38 Trim tab
39 Port aileron
40 Port rear spar

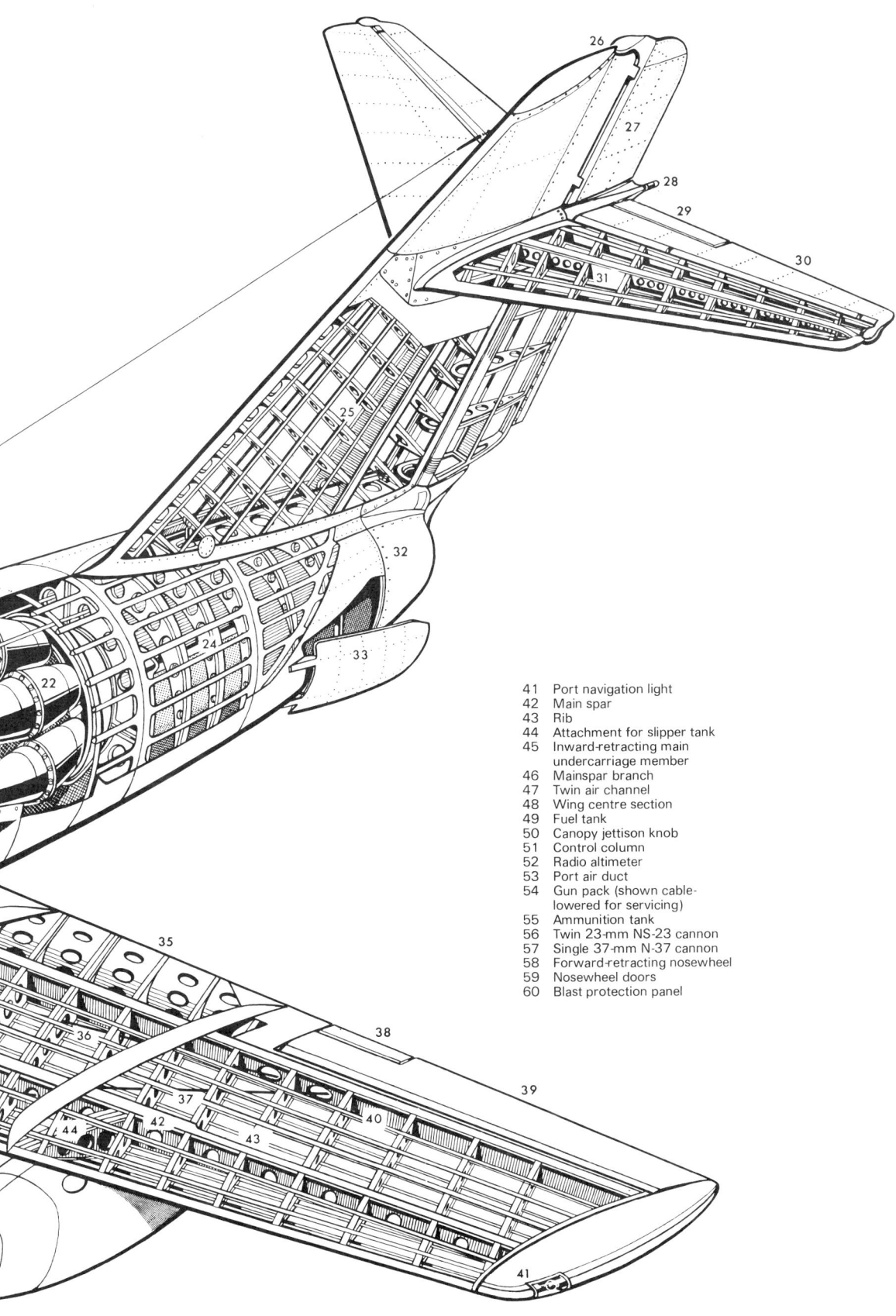

41 Port navigation light
42 Main spar
43 Rib
44 Attachment for slipper tank
45 Inward-retracting main
    undercarriage member
46 Mainspar branch
47 Twin air channel
48 Wing centre section
49 Fuel tank
50 Canopy jettison knob
51 Control column
52 Radio altimeter
53 Port air duct
54 Gun pack (shown cable-
    lowered for servicing)
55 Ammunition tank
56 Twin 23-mm NS-23 cannon
57 Single 37-mm N-37 cannon
58 Forward-retracting nosewheel
59 Nosewheel doors
60 Blast protection panel

Mikoyan-Gurevich MiG-15 Fagot/15UTI Midget

15UTI moved out of its original role as conversion trainer and became the Eastern bloc's standard advanced trainer. Even today it is found in service all over the world.

Specification

Type: single-seat fighter and (MiG-15UTI) two-seat advanced trainer

Powerplant: one 5,950-lb (2700-kg) Klimov VK-1 centrifugal-flow turbojet

Performance: maximum speed 668 mph (1076 km/h) at 39,500 ft (12000 m); ferry range 1,250 miles (2000 m); initial climb rate 9,050 ft (2760 m) per minute; ceiling 51,000 ft (15500 m)

Weights: empty 7,500 lb (3400 kg); normal loaded 11,000 lb (4960 kg); maximum take-off 12,750 lb (5786 kg)

Dimensions: span 33 ft 1 in (10.08 m); length 35 ft 7½ in (10.86 m); height 11 ft 1¾ in (3.4 m); wing area 221.7 sq ft (20.6 ²)

Armament: one 37-mm N-37 and two 23-mm NS-23 cannon (later aircraft had the NS-23s replaced by NR-23 revolver cannon); underwing hardpoints for slipper tanks or up to 1,100 lb (500 kg) of stores

Operators: Albania, Algeria, Angola, Bulgaria, China, Cuba, Czechoslovakia, East Germany, Egypt, Finland, Guinea, Hungary, Iraq, Mali, Mongolia, Nigeria, North Korea, Poland, Romania, Somalia, South Yemen, Sri Lanka, Syria, Tanzania, Uganda, USSR, Vietnam

(1) *Prototype MiG-15 (I-310 or Type S) after replacement of wing leading-edge slats by wing fences;* (2) *Initial production MiG-15 with rear fuselage-mounted air brakes, full-length tab on lower rudder component, enlarged fairing at rudder base, fairings over shell-case ejection ports, and provision for 250 l/55 Imp gal or 300 l/66 Imp gal slipper-type drop tanks, the latter (fitted with fins) being shown dotted;* (3) *Production MiG-15bis with undercarriage extended. External differences from preceding model include attachment of cable aerial directly to fuselage on the starboard side of cabin, the adjacent mast becoming VHF blade antenna, IFF post antenna on centre fuselage replacing flat loop aerial, and aerials for radio altimeter beneath port wingtip and starboard wing root. The redesigned air brakes were introduced on the late production MiG-15;* (4) *The MiG-15bisR fighter reconnaissance aircraft with camera pack mounted below cannon magazines and 400 l/88 Imp gal pylon-mounted tank (dotted);* (5) *MiG-15bis modified for ground attack rôle with tandem stores stations on projecting pylon;* (6) *MiG-15P all-weather interceptor with twin 23-mm cannon armament and early Izumrud AI radar. Note rearview mirror over canopy;* (7) *Mig-15UTI tandem two-seat conversion trainer. Note retention of early-style air brakes. Armament reduced to single 12,7-mm or 23-mm weapon to port, and 250 l/55 Imp gal slipper tank shown dotted;* (8) *Mig-15UTI (SP-5) two-seat radar trainer. Similar to standard conversion trainer apart from extended nose accommodating Izumrud AI.*

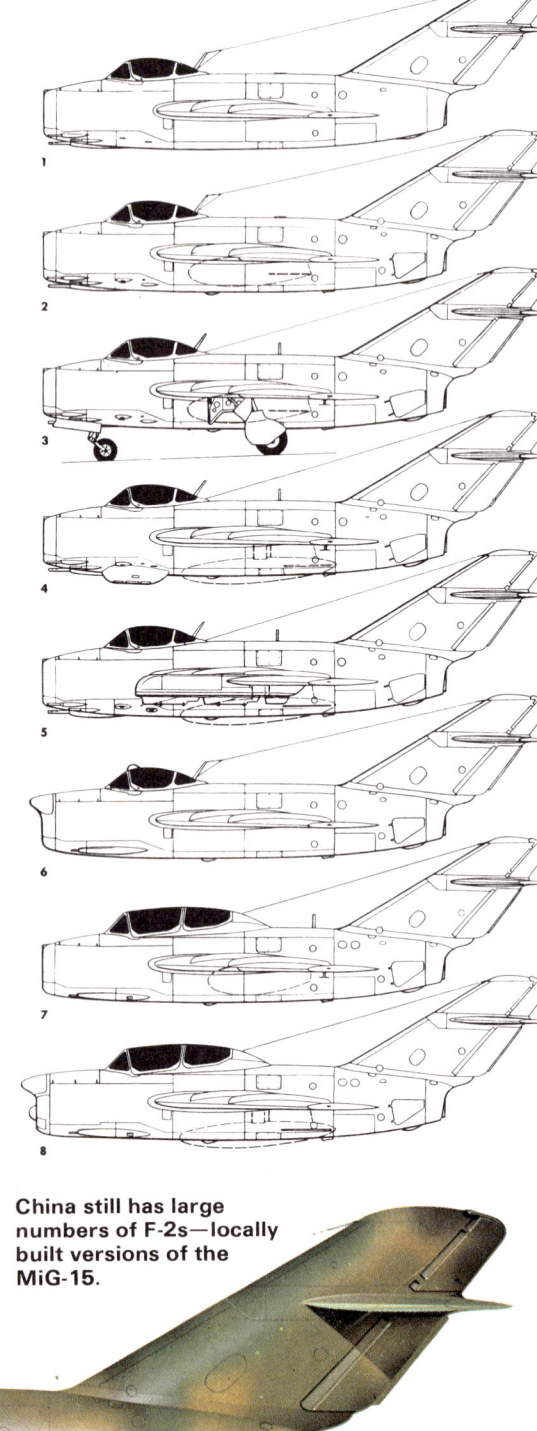

China still has large numbers of F-2s—locally built versions of the MiG-15.

Mikoyan-Gurevich MiG-17 Fresco

History and notes

The Mikoyan-Gurevich MiG-17 'Fresco' was a completely redesigned development of the MiG-15, intended to remove the maximum speed restriction of Mach 0.92 which affected the earlier type. During flight trials the MiG-17 is claimed to have exceeded Mach 1 in level flight, but this performance was not attained in service.

Early production MiG-17s were fitted with the same VK-1 engine as the MiG-15, but the main production model, the MiG-17F, introduced the VK-1F with a simple afterburner. The wing of the MiG-17 was thinner and more sharply swept than that of its forebear, and the rear fuselage was slightly extended to reduce drag. First seen in 1955 was the MiG-17PF, a limited all-weather interceptor with radar in a central inlet bullet and the inlet lip. A further development was the MiG-17PFU, armed with four AA-1 'Alkali' guided air-to-air missiles, the Soviet Union's first missile-armed interceptor.

Although the MiG-17 was in theory obsolete by the mid-1960s, the type gave a good account of itself over Vietnam, being flown by most of the leading North Vietnamese pilots. Its US adversaries were hampered by rules under which they had to close to within visual range before firing, and unlike the MiG-17 they were not designed for close-range dogfighting.

The MiG-17 has been built in Poland (as the LIM-5

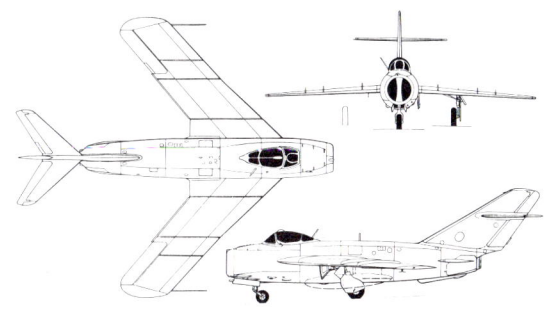

Mikoyan-Gurevich MiG-17 'Fresco'.

and -5P), Czechoslovakia (as the S-104) and China (as the Shenyang F-4 and all-weather F-5). China has also developed a two-seat trainer version of the aircraft. A special close-support version was developed in Poland as the LIM-6, with a deeper, longer-chord inner wing section, and dual mainwheels, rocket-assisted take-off gear and a braking parachute for operation from unprepared fields.

A derelict MiG-17 of the Egyptian Air Force, abandoned after suffering damage in an airstrike.

Mikoyan-Gurevich MiG-17 Fresco

Specification

Type: single-seat fighter

Powerplant: one 7,500-lb (3400-kg) Klimov VK-1 afterburning turbojet

Performance: maximum speed 710 mph (1145 km/h) at 10,000 ft (3000 m); range 1,400 miles (2250 m); rate of climb 12,795 (3900 m) per minute; ceiling 54,500 ft (16600 m)

Weights: empty 9,000 lb (4100 kg); maximum take-off 14,750 lb (6700 kg)

Dimensions: span 31 ft 7 in (9.63 m); length 36 ft 4½ in (11.09 m); height 11 ft (3.35 m) wing area 243.3 sq ft (22.6 m²)

Armament: (MiG-17P, PF) three 23-mm NR-23 cannon and/or four AA-1 'Alkali' AAMs; two underwing hardpoints for drop tanks or stores up to 1,100 lb (500 kg)

Operators: Afghanistan, Albania, Algeria, Angola, Bulgaria, China, Cuba, Czechoslovakia, East Germany, Egypt, Guinea, Hungary, Iraq, Mali, Nigeria, North Korea, Poland, Romania, Somalia, South Yemen, Sri Lanka, Sudan, Syria, Tanzania, Uganda, USSR, Vietnam, Yemen

(1) *Prototype MiG-17 with similar air brakes to those of Mig-15bis;* (2) *Initial production version of MiG-17 (Fresco-A) with enlarged air brakes featuring external actuating jack fairings, rudder tab, and pitot tube at each wingtip. Pylon-mounted 400 l / 88 Imp gal drop tank shown dotted;* (3) *MiG-17F (Fresco-C) with revised rear fuselage for afterburning VK-1F, and redesigned air brakes. Undercarriage illustrated extended;* (4) *LIM-6 modification of MiG-17F with deeper, extended inboard wing sections to house twin-wheel main undercarriage members and additional fuel;* (5) *LIM-5M fighter-bomber with forward-projecting inboard stores pylons, brake chute housing and RATOG lugs;* (6) *MiG-17PF (Fresco-D) with lengthened nose, increased windscreen rake, extended upper intake lip for ranging scanner of Izumrud AI and bullet fairing on intake splitter for scan dish. Note that size of bullet differed with version of Izumrud mounted;* (7) *MiG-17PFU (Fresco-E) with cannon armament removed and provision for four AAMs.*

39	Port control console (throttle quadrant)	63	Nosewheel doors
40	Pilot's headrest	64	Nosewheel fork
41	Canopy heating web	65	Forward-retracting nose-wheel
42	Rear-view mirror	66	Nosewheel strut
43	Rocket-sight	67	Forward fuselage members
44	Radar-scope shroud	68	Inboard-section wing leading edge
45	Enlarged cockpit quarter-light	69	Three wing/fuselage attach-ment points
46	Instrument panel	70	"Y"-section inner main spar
47	Control column	71	Inboard wing fence
48	Rudder pedals	72	Forward main spar
49	Windscreen	73	Undercarriage indicator spigot
50	RDF ranging unit	74	Inner wing skinning
51	VHF transmitter/receiver	75	Split landing flap (inner section)
52	Accumulator	76	Split landing flap structure outer section)
53	Radar ranging unit	77	Centre wing fence
54	Radar scanner	78	Outboard wing fence
55	Extended upper intake lip	79	Wing construction
56	AI scanner in central intake bullet	80	Rear spar
57	Combat camera housing	81	Aileron construction
58	Bifurcated intake	82	Starboard navigation light
59	Intake centre-body	83	Wingtip
60	Centre-section nosewheel well	84	Starboard pitot head
61	Intake trunking		
62	Nosewheel retraction radii		

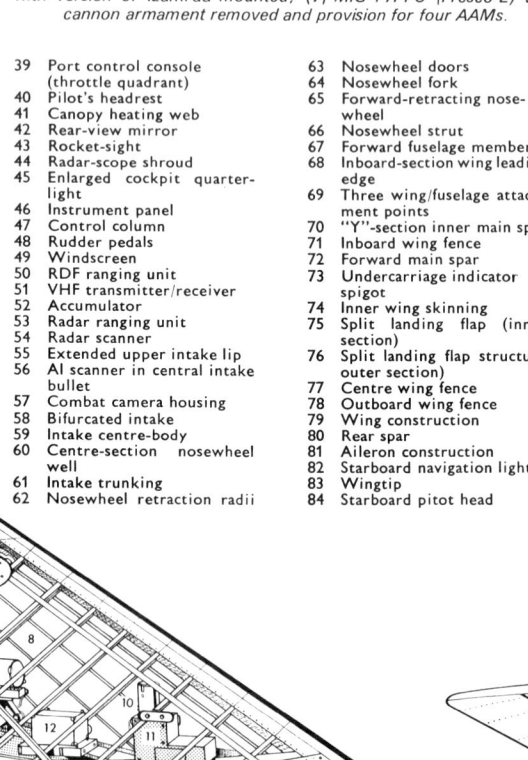

Key to MiG-17PFU (Fresco-E) cutaway drawing

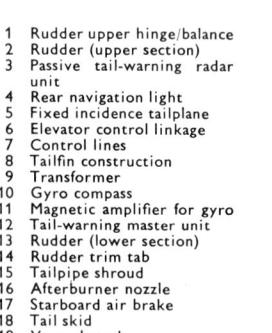

1 Rudder upper hinge/balance
2 Rudder (upper section)
3 Passive tail-warning radar unit
4 Rear navigation light
5 Fixed incidence tailplane
6 Elevator control linkage
7 Control lines
8 Tailfin construction
9 Transformer
10 Gyro compass
11 Magnetic amplifier for gyro
12 Tail-warning master unit
13 Rudder (lower section)
14 Rudder trim tab
15 Tailpipe shroud
16 Afterburner nozzle
17 Starboard air brake
18 Tail skid
19 Ventral strake
20 Air brake hydraulic activator
21 Control linkage assembly
22 Rear fuselage structure
23 Afterburner pipe
24 Aft fuselage fuel tank
25 Afterburner outer casing
26 Klimov VK-1F turbojet
27 Inspection panel
28 IFF antenna
29 Engine intake grille
30 Inspection panel
31 Engine auxiliaries
32 Aft/forward fuselage break-point
33 Main fuselage fuel tank
34 Intake trunking
35 VHF antenna
36 Canopy track
37 Bulkhead
38 Ejector seat

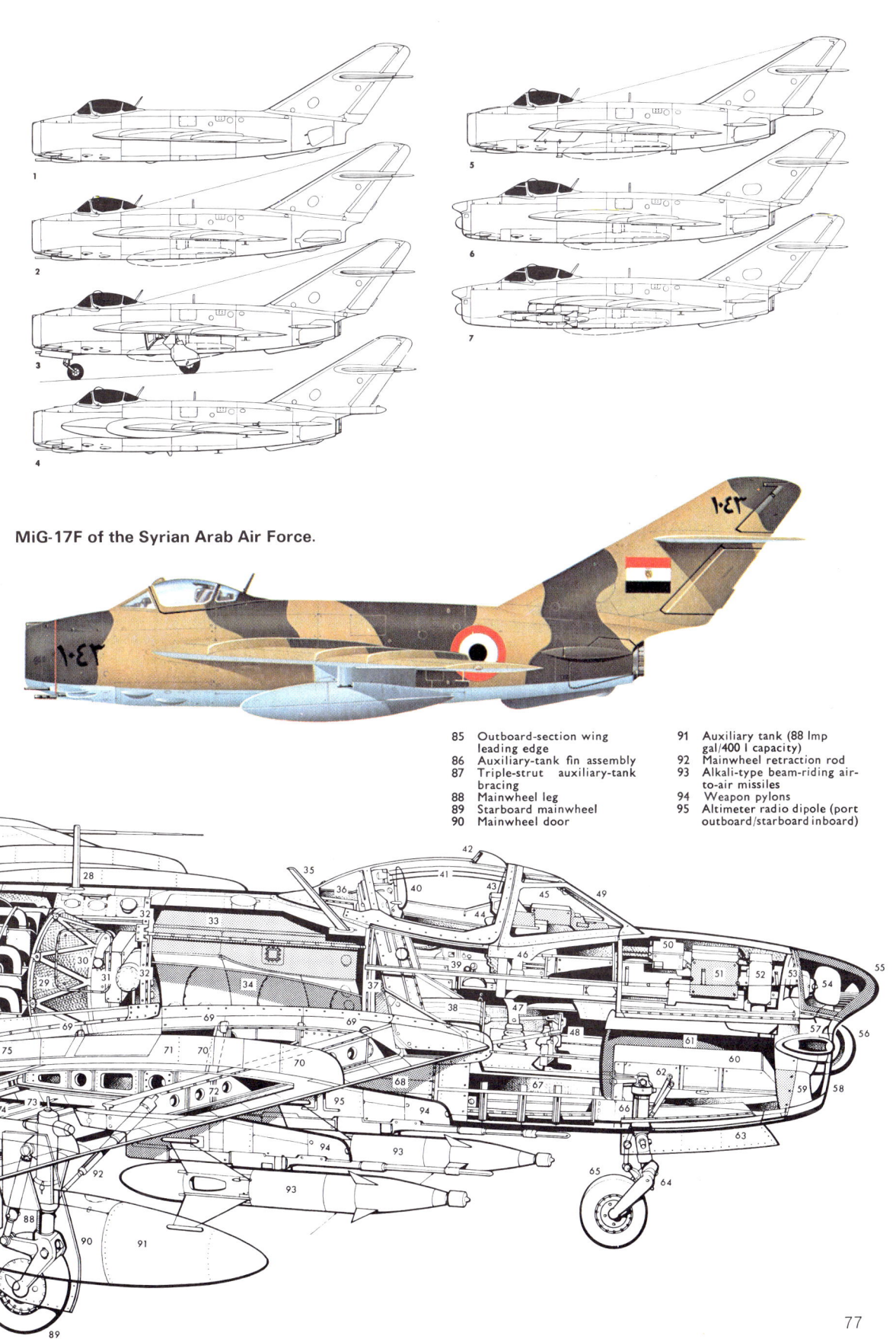

MiG-17F of the Syrian Arab Air Force.

85 Outboard-section wing leading edge
86 Auxiliary-tank fin assembly
87 Triple-strut auxiliary-tank bracing
88 Mainwheel leg
89 Starboard mainwheel
90 Mainwheel door
91 Auxiliary tank (88 Imp gal/400 l capacity)
92 Mainwheel retraction rod
93 Alkali-type beam-riding air-to-air missiles
94 Weapon pylons
95 Altimeter radio dipole (port outboard/starboard inboard)

Mikoyan-Gurevich MiG-17 Fresco

A Syrian MiG-17 hugs the desert in a low-level fighter-bomber mission. The elderly MiG-17 has a distinguished combat record, including service in the Middle East and Vietnam wars.

Mikoyan-Gurevich MiG-19 Farmer

History and notes

The Mikoyan-Gurevich MiG-19 'Farmer', the world's first production supersonic fighter, remained in production in 1980, and currently forms the backbone of the Chinese tactical air force in its Shenyang F-6 version. In the hands of Pakistan air force pilots it has proved its worth against considerably more modern and more costly opponents, with agility in combat which would do credit to a contemporary air-superiority fighter. Another good feature is the hard-hitting gun armament, with much greater projectile weight and muzzle velocity than most western 30-mm weapons.

Development of the MiG-19 started in the late 1940s, with a requirement for a new fighter designed around the newly developed Lyulka AL-5, the Soviet Union's first large axial-flow jet engine. Disappointing progess with this powerplant, however, led to the decision to redesign the Mikoyan prototype around two small-diameter Mikulin AM-5s. The first aircraft, the I-360, was distinguished by a T-tail, but was destroyed in flight-testing as a

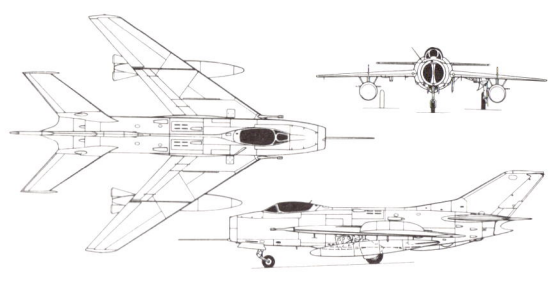

Mikoyan-Gurevich MiG-19S 'Farmer'.

result of tailplane flutter. The I-350(M) was completed with a low-set tailplane, and was flown in late 1952. It was soon followed by the production MiG-19F with afterburning AM-5Fs, the first version to go supersonic in level flight in early 1953.

The initial MiG-19F and limited-all-weather MiG-19PF were less than successful, and were eventually withdrawn from service as a result of high accident

Standard supersonic fighter of the Chinese Air Force of the People's Liberation Army is the Chinese-built copy of the MiG-19, the Shenyang F-6.

Mikoyan-Gurevich MiG-19 Farmer

rates. They were replaced by the MiG-19S, with an all-moving tailplane, refinements to flying controls and systems, and RD-9 engines. The latter was a largely redesigned development of the AM-5 produced by the Tumansky bureau, and was the first of many Tumansky engines believed to power all MiG fighters up to the MiG-27 'Flogger-D'. Deliveries of the definitive MiG-19S started in mid-1955 and the basic airframe thereafter continued almost completely unchanged to the end of the type's Russian production life. A measure of the basic good handling characteristics is the fact that the two-seat MiG-19UTI, although completed and flown, was never put into production in the Soviet Union; pilots found little difficulty in converting from the MiG-15UTI to the supersonic fighter. However, a trainer version of the F-6 is widely used in China.

The MiG-19S was rapidly followed by the MiG-19P, with Izumrud radar in an intake bullet fairing and the inlet lip, and from this version was developed the Soviet Union's first missile-armed fighter. The MiG-19PM suffered from engine problems resulting from rocket-plume ingestion, but formed the spearhead of the PVO air defence force for some years. However, more advanced versions of the MiG-19 were overtaken by the MiG-21 'Fishbed' and its developments.

Production of the MiG-19 was transferred from the Soviet Union to Czechoslovakia in 1958, the Aero works producing some 850 aircraft between 1958 and 1961. In that year, the Chinese Shenyang works produced the first examples of an unlicensed copy of the MiG-19S, designated F-6. By the mid-1970s at least 1,800 F-6s had been built in China. A substantial number of F-6s was supplied to Pakistan in 1965-66 and 1972; Vietnam, Albania and Tanzania have also taken delivery of similar aircraft. The MiG-19 has also formed the basis for the Chinese F-6bis or A-5 strike fighter, an enlarged MiG-19 with side air intakes.

The Pakistani aircraft have been modified with launch pylons for AIM-9 Sidewinder missiles, and Chinese aircraft probably carry a version of the equivalent K-13 'Atoll'. Points in favour of the MiG-19 include its excellent manoeuvrability and initial climb rate, products of its modest size, high power/weight ratio and (by modern standards) low wing-loading.

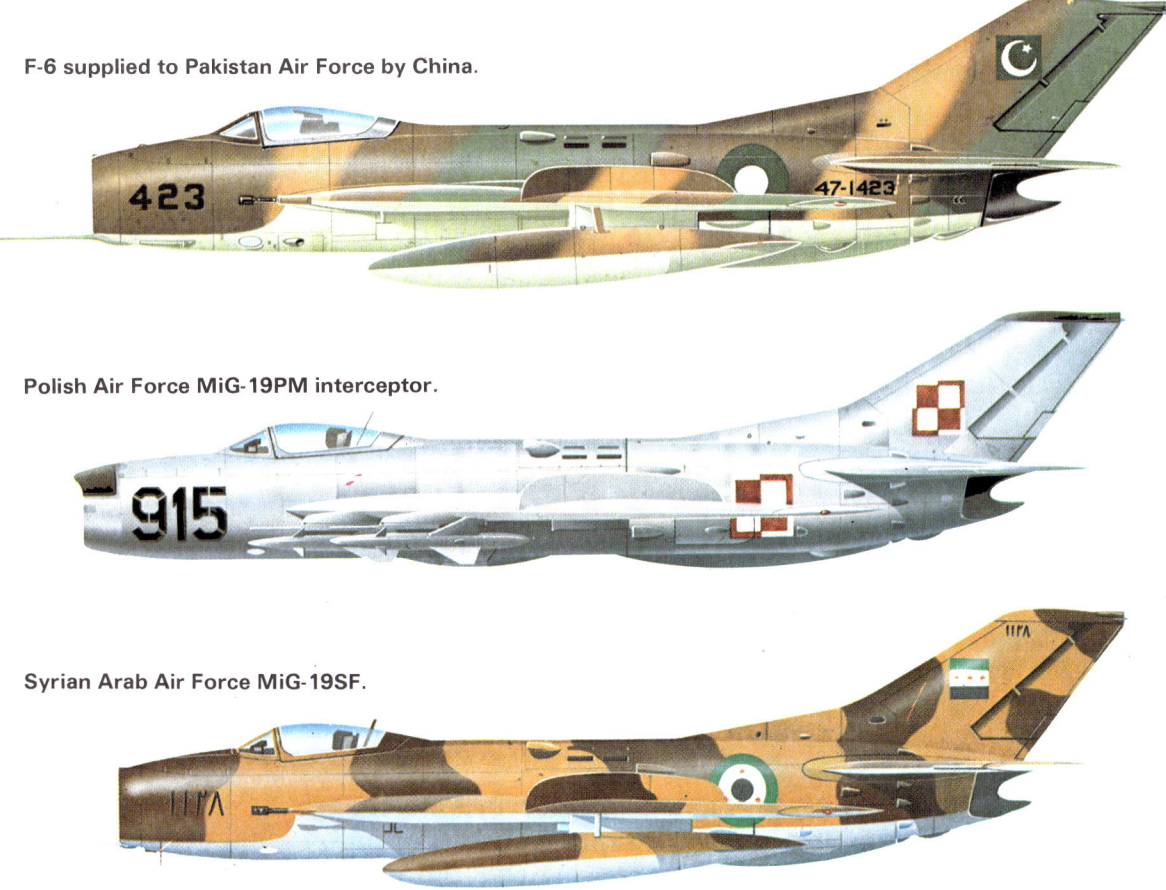

F-6 supplied to Pakistan Air Force by China.

Polish Air Force MiG-19PM interceptor.

Syrian Arab Air Force MiG-19SF.

The term 'Chinese copy' might have been coined for the F-6, which is virtually indistinguishable from the original MiG-19. Chinese production has brought a new lease of life to the Soviet bureau's versatile design, and has moreover proceeded to include two new versions of the type: a trainer, different from the Soviet Union's one-off MiG-19UTI, and the A-5 'Fantan' strike fighter, with side intakes, a small internal weapon bay and equipment relocated in a pointed nose.

Mikoyan-Gurevich MiG-19 Farmer

1 Pitot tube (hinged)
2 Bifurcated intake
3 Combat camera (offset to starboard
4 Nose intake ring
5 Access panel
6 Nosewheel retraction cylinder
7 Nudelmann-Rikhter NR-30 revolver-type cannon (starboard lower fuselage) of 30mm caliber
8 Nosewheel doors
9 Taxiing light
10 Nosewheel leg assembly
11 Axle fork
12 Forward-retracting nosewheel (500 × 180mm tyre)
13 Shock absorber
14 Ranging aerial
15 Oxygen bottles
16 Intake trunking (port)
17 RSIU-4 VHF receiver
18 RSIU-4 VHF transmitter
19 Accumulator
20 RV-2 altimeter transmitter/receiver
21 Windshield
22 ASP-5N automatic gyroscopic gunsight (coupled with SRD rangefinder)
23 Instrument panel shroud
24 Starboard console
25 Control column
26 Rudder pedal assembly
27 Intake duct section
28 NR-30 cannon muzzle
29 Landing light
30 NR-30 cannon barrel fairing
31 Ejector seat pan
31 Canopy external release/lock
33 Ejection seat
34 Headrest
35 Single-piece jettisonable canopy
36 ARK-5 radio compass antennae (in canopy)
37 Cabin pressurization compressed air system
38 RSIU-4 VHF antenna
39 4 spar wing structure (main and three auxiliary)
40 Mainspar (inboard section)
41 Mainspar midspan full-chord boundary layer fence

42 Wing skinning
43 Starboard navigation light
44 Starboard aileron
45 Fuel dump vents
46 Starboard auxiliary fuel tank of 200.4 gal (760 l) capacity
47 Starboard hydraulically-powered Fowler-type flap
48 Flap hinge fairing
49 Ram air intakes
50 Dorsal spine housing control rod tunnel
51 Fuel filler cap
52 Main (Nos. 1 and 2) fuel tanks of 387.6 gal (1,470 l) and 87.12 gal (330 l) capacity
53 Intake cut out frames
54 Hydraulics accumulator
55 Port Tumansky RD-9B turbojet
56 Slot intakes
57 Air conditioning system
58 Slab-type tailplane control rod linkage
59 Fuselage break point
60 Air intake
61 Hydraulics tank
62 Oil tanks
63 Rudder control linkage
64 Fuselage aft frames
65 Filler cap for aft tanks (Nos. 3 and 4) of 47.52 gal (180 l) and 46.08 gal (175 l) capacity
66 Air intake
67 Tailplane control hydraulic actuator
68 Tailfin front spar
69 Starboard hydraulically-actuated 1 piece tailplane
70 Antiflutter weight
71 Tailfin structure
72 ARK-5 radio compass mounting

73 Tail warning radar amplifier
74 Rudder balance
75 Tail warning antenna fairing
76 Rear navigation light
77 Rudder hinges
78 Tailfin rear spar
79 Rudder tab
80 Pen nib exhaust fairing
81 Antiflutter weight
82 1 piece tailplane structure
83 Exhaust nozzle (three position) hydraulic control
84 Afterburner
85 Afterburner cooling air intakes
86 Tail bumper
87 Slab tailplane spigot
88 Slab tailplane actuator fairing
89 Tailplane (fixed) fillet
90 PR-19 braking chute packing panel
91 Ventral strake
92 Aft (No. 4) fuel tank of 46.08 gal (175 l) capacity
93 Filler neck
94 Air brake hydraulic actuating ram
95 Air brake (port and starboard)

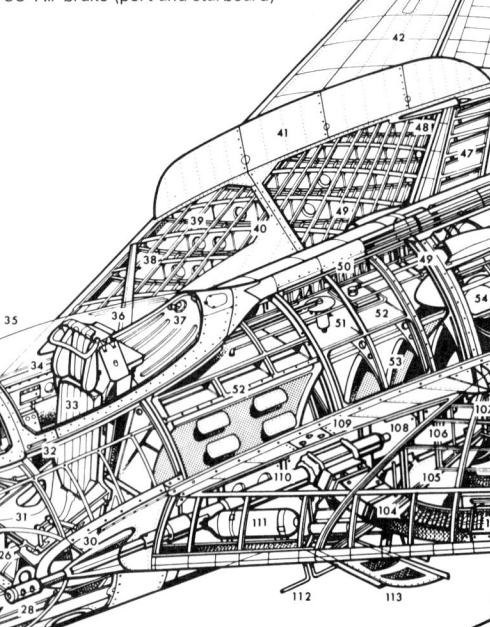

96 Wing root fillet
97 Flap hinge fairing
98 Port flap structure
99 Aileron control linkage
100 Mainspar (inboard section)
101 Port mainwheel retraction cylinder
102 Port mainwheel well
103 Ammunition track
104 Ammunition feed
105 Undercarriage door (inboard section)
106 Angled rib
107 Mainspar/fuselage attachment
108 Port wing root cannon bay

109 Cannon cooling louvres
110 Port 30-mm Nudelmann-Rikhter NR-30 revolver type cannon
111 Compressed air bottle
112 RV-2 radio altimeter dipole

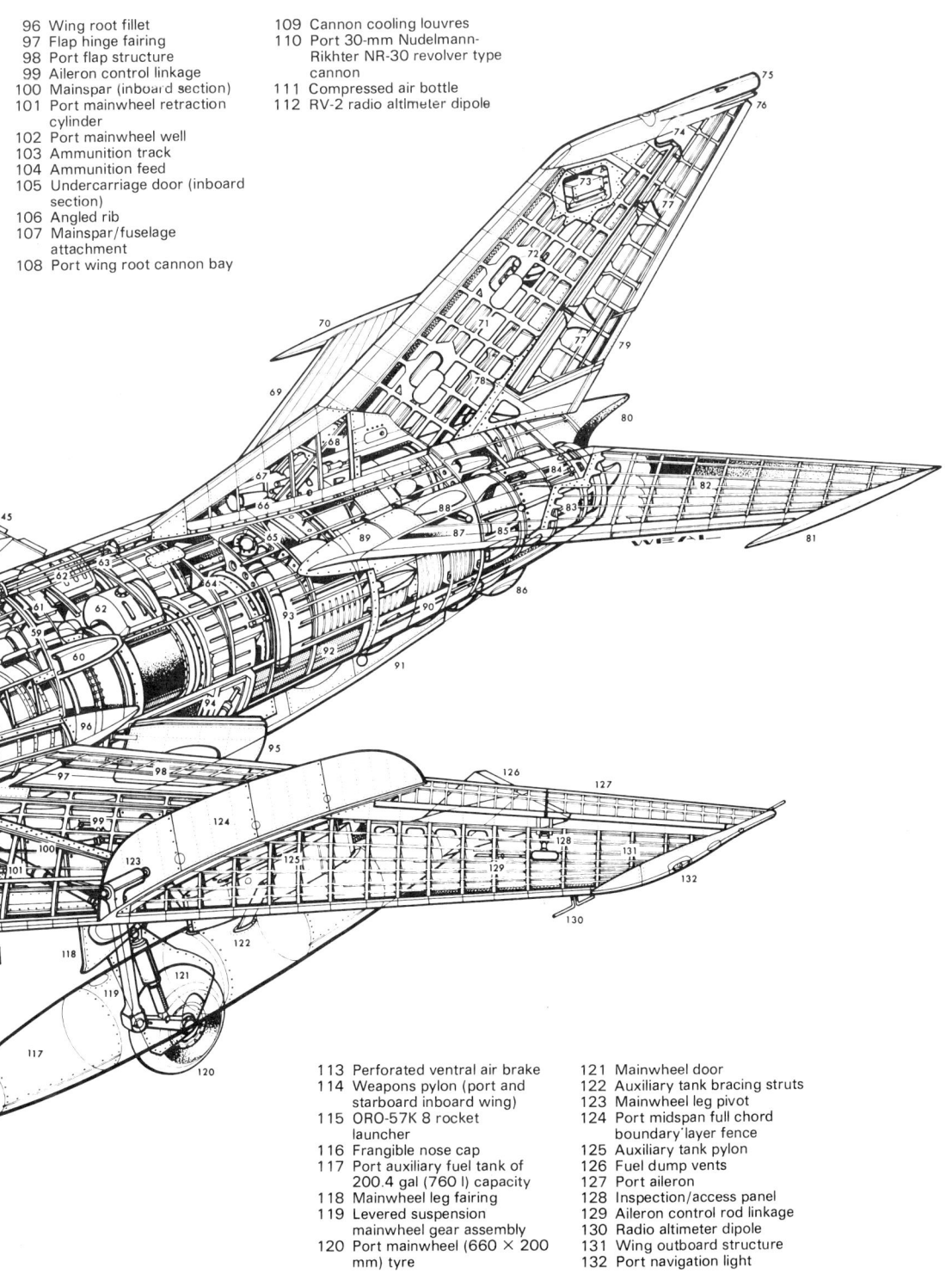

113 Perforated ventral air brake
114 Weapons pylon (port and starboard inboard wing)
115 ORO-57K 8 rocket launcher
116 Frangible nose cap
117 Port auxiliary fuel tank of 200.4 gal (760 l) capacity
118 Mainwheel leg fairing
119 Levered suspension mainwheel gear assembly
120 Port mainwheel (660 × 200 mm) tyre

121 Mainwheel door
122 Auxiliary tank bracing struts
123 Mainwheel leg pivot
124 Port midspan full chord boundary layer fence
125 Auxiliary tank pylon
126 Fuel dump vents
127 Port aileron
128 Inspection/access panel
129 Aileron control rod linkage
130 Radio altimeter dipole
131 Wing outboard structure
132 Port navigation light

Mikoyan-Gurevich MiG-19 Farmer

Specification

Type: single-seat fighter and limited all-weather interceptor

Powerplant: two 7,165-lb (3250-kg) after-burning Tumansky RD-9B turbojets

Performance: maximum speed (clean) 900 mph (1450 km/h) at 33,000 ft (10000 m) or Mach 1.4; maximum speed with external fuel tanks 715 mph (1150 km/h) at 33,000 ft (10000 m); initial climb rate 22,640 ft (6900 m) per minute; ceiling 57,400 ft (17500 m); ferry range with external fuel 1,350 miles (2200 km)

Weights: empty 11,400 lb (5172 kg); loaded (clean) 16,300 lb (7400 kg); maximum take-off 19,600 lb (8900 kg)

Dimensions: span 29 ft 6½ in (9.0 m); length (excluding pitot tube) 41 ft 4 in (12.6 m); height 12 ft 9½ in (3.9 m); wing area 269 sq ft (25 m²)

Armament: three 30-mm NR-30 cannon plus rocket pods on underwing pylons; Pakistani aircraft have AIM-9 Sidewinders; MiG-19PM has no cannon but four K-5M 'Alkali' AAMs

Operators: Afghanistan, Albania, Bangladesh, Bulgaria, China, Cuba, Iraq, North Korea, Pakistan, Somalia, Sudan, Tanzania, Uganda, USSR, Vietnam, Zambia

As the first Soviet fighter capable of breaking the then-redoubtable "sound barrier", the MiG-19 was a propaganda card to be played on all occasions. The fighter was even demonstrated publicly in its profoundly unsafe initial version, before the introduction of an all-moving tailplane. These MiG-19s, possibly of the early type, formed an aerobatic display team.

Mikoyan-Gurevich MiG-21 Fishbed/ MiG-21U Mongol

History and notes

The Mikoyan-Gurevich MiG-21 'Fishbed', still in production and apparently under development more than 25 years after it first flew, must be judged a classic combat aircraft. Although its combat record has been mixed, it has had a profound influence on Western fighter design. At the time of writing, it remains the principal low-level tactical air defence fighter of the Eastern bloc, working in conjunction with MiG-23s, and is unlikely to be fully replaced before the second half of the 1980s, even in Soviet service.

The origins of the MiG-21 lie in Korean War experience as do those of the Lockheed F-104. Both types stemmed from demands from pilots for an 'air-superiority' fighter from which all unneccessary equipment would be eliminated, and in which all aspects of the design would be subordinated to combat performance. Armament would be the minimum needed to knock down an enemy fighter.

The Mikoyan design bureau went even further in the direction of miniaturization than Lockheed, producing in 1955 the first of a series of prototypes

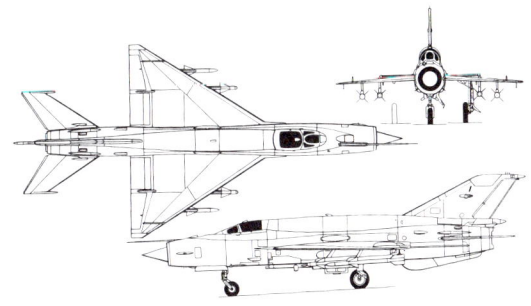

Mikoyan-Gurevich MiG-21SMT 'Fishbed-K'.

designed around an engine not much larger than the Tumansky RD-9; two of the latter powered the MiG-19, itself not a large aircraft. The new engine, also of Tumansky design, was not available by 1955, so the swept-wing E-50 of that year was powered by an uprated RD-9E and a booster rocket.

In the following year the design bureau flew the

Finland's MiG-21F 'Fishbed-C' day fighters were among the first to be exported and the last to be retired. In 1980 they were being replaced by MiG-21bis 'Fishbed-N' fighter/strike aircraft.

Mikoyan-Gurevich MiG-21 Fishbed/MiG-21U Mongol

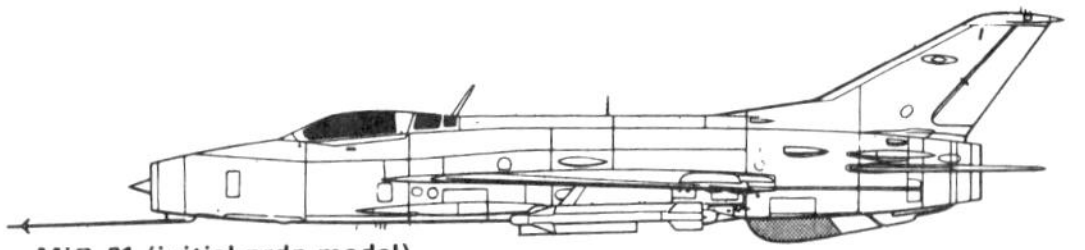

MiG-21 (initial prdn model)

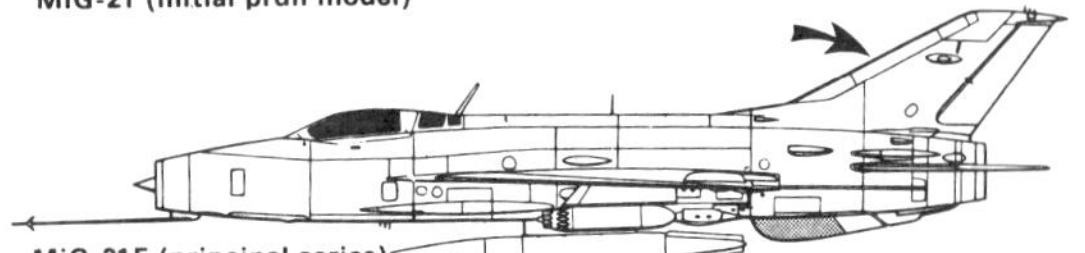

MiG-21F (principal series)

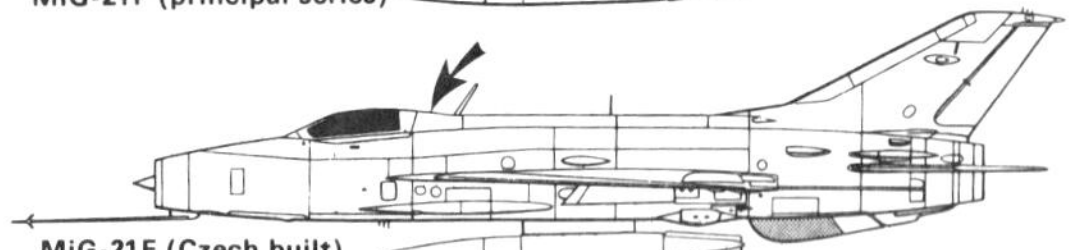

MiG-21F (Czech built)

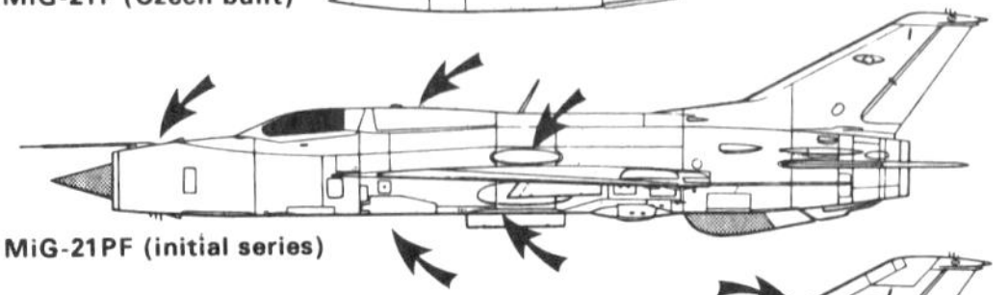

MiG-21PF (initial series)

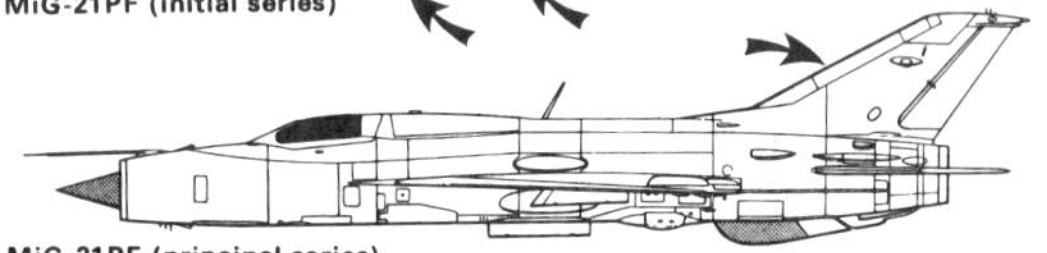

MiG-21PF (principal series)

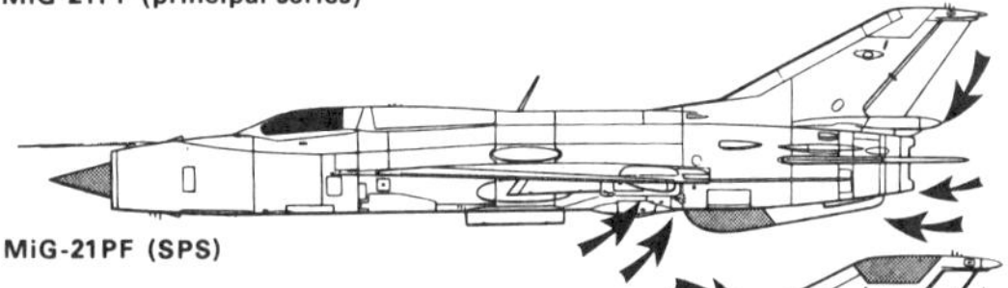

MiG-21PF (SPS)

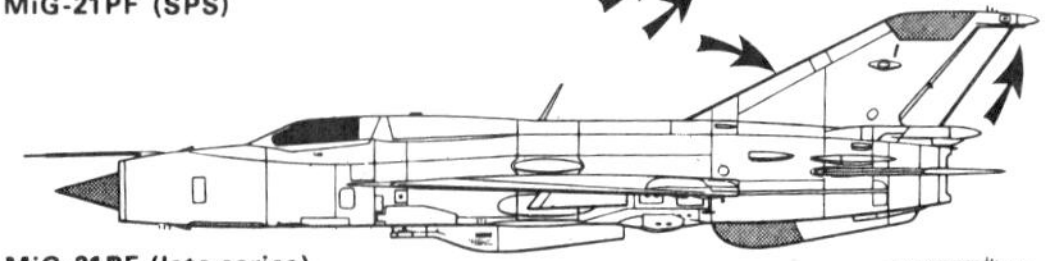

MiG-21PF (late series)

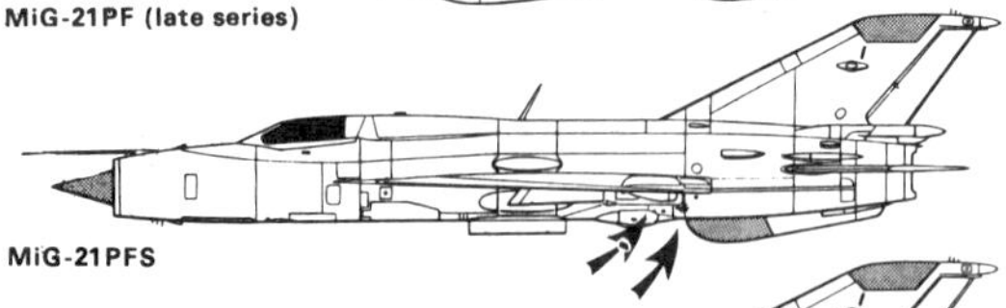

MiG-21PFS

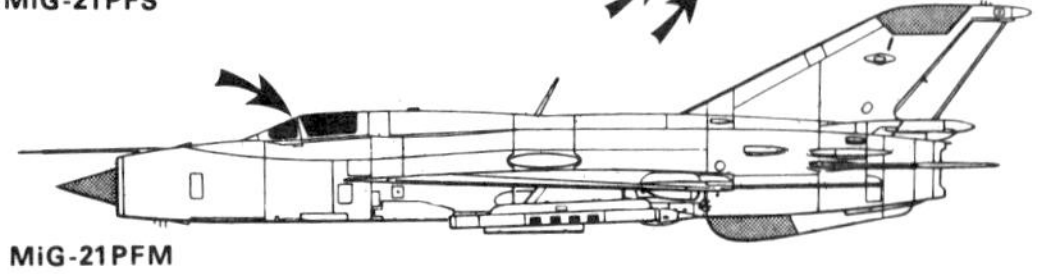

MiG-21PFM

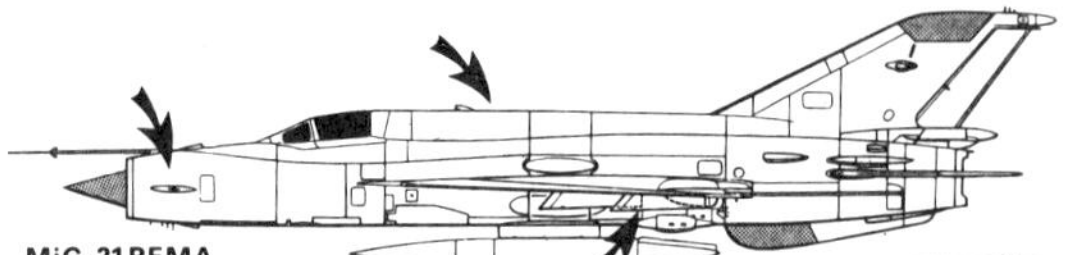

MiG-21PFMA

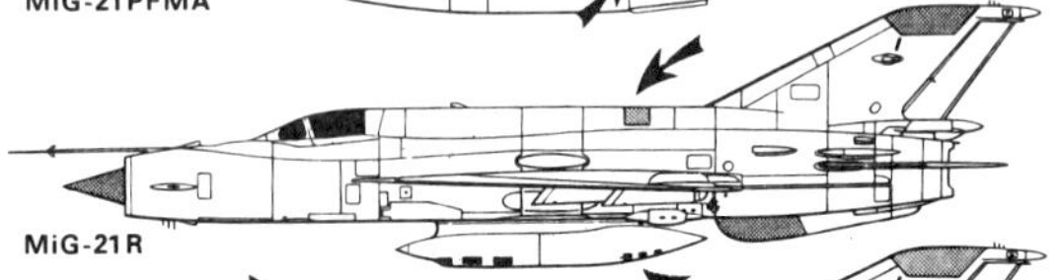

MiG-21R

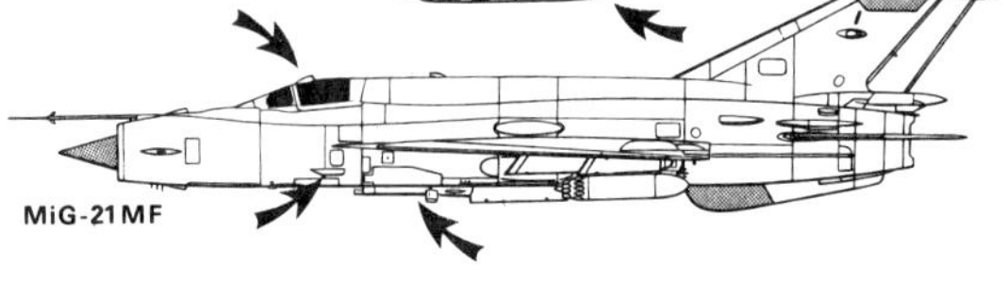

MiG-21MF

swept-wing E-2A and the tailed-delta E-5, both powered by the newly developed RD-11 and armed with three 30-mm cannon. The tailed-delta layout of the E-5 resembled that of the Douglas Skyhawk in plan view, but featured a mid-set wing in line with the tailplane. The advantages of the layout included low drag and, as it turned out, excellent handling; on the debit side, its low-speed performance was not good and it was structurally complicated. However, the E-5 offered generally better performance than the E-2, and the tailed-delta was selected for production.

The first series aircraft were developed from the E-6 production prototype and were themselves designated E-66 by the Mikoyan bureau. They carried a simple radar-ranging sight and two K-13 'Atoll' air-to-air missiles in addition to two 30-mm

Continuous development has kept the MiG-21 in production for more than 20 years. Sideview drawings illustrate the development of the basic fighter from the early day fighter to the MiG-21MF 'Fishbed-J', itself now supplanted by the MiG-21bis. Arrows indicate new features associated with each new version, such as successively deeper dorsal spines and broader-chord fins, and modified canopies. Tactical reconnaissance and trainer versions are also shown. In general, the MiG-21 has absorbed extra armament and operational equipment without too serious a detrimental effect on its basic handling qualities. However, the MiG-21SMT version, not shown here, seems to have been an exception to the rule. It will be interesting to see whether any more substantial developments of the MiG-21 will follow the latest aircraft, the MiG-21bis.

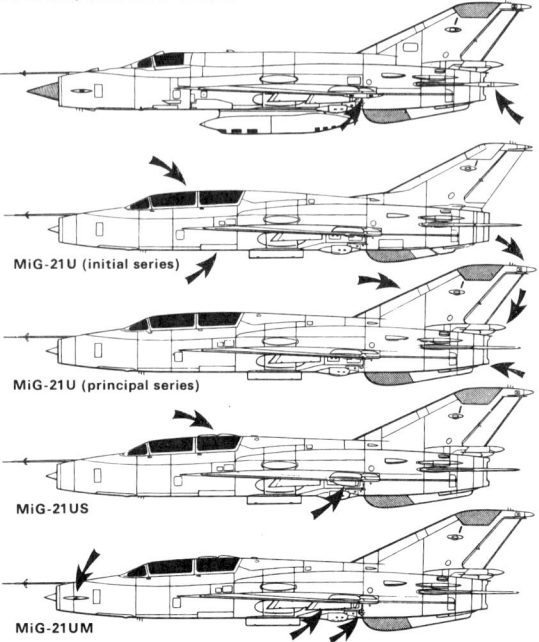

MiG-21U (initial series)

MiG-21U (principal series)

MiG-21US

MiG-21UM

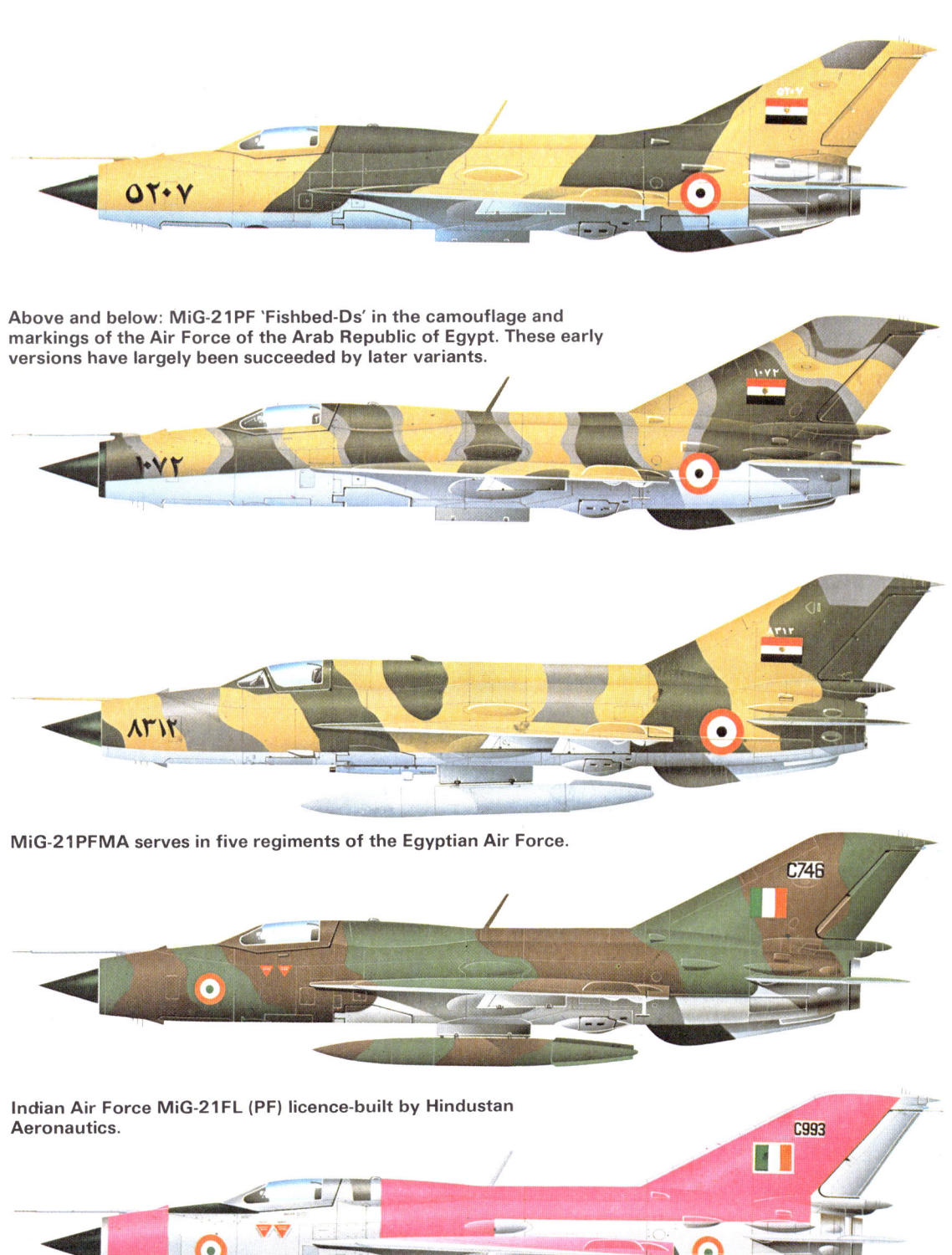

Above and below: MiG-21PF 'Fishbed-Ds' in the camouflage and markings of the Air Force of the Arab Republic of Egypt. These early versions have largely been succeeded by later variants.

MiG-21PFMA serves in five regiments of the Egyptian Air Force.

Indian Air Force MiG-21FL (PF) licence-built by Hindustan Aeronautics.

MiG-21(PF) of the Indian Air Force's 'Red Archer' aerobatics team.

Mikoyan-Gurevich MiG-21 Fishbed/MiG-21U Mongol

Still one of the most numerous variants of the MiG-21 is the 'third-generation' MiG-21MF 'Fishbed-J' developed from the initial limited-all-weather MiG-21s in the late 1960s and mainly distinguished from these by its new R-13 powerplant. It forms the basis for the current MiG-21bis 'Fishbed-N'.

cannon, but with only 11,250-lb (5100-kg) maximum thrust they were underpowered. A few aircraft of the type entered service with a trials unit in late 1957, with the designation MiG-21. The first large-scale production variant was the MiG-21F, powered by an uprated Tumansky R-11F-300 of 12,600-lb (5750-kg) thrust, which entered service in late 1959. Most of these had the left gun removed to save weight, and had a fin of longer chord than that of the early MiG-21.

After the appearance of the MiG-21F, the process of improving the MiG-21 began in earnest. The early MiG-21 was a clear-weather interceptor with little payload, range and armament. However, there were strict limits to what could be done to rectify the situation, because any extra equipment could have disastrous effects on the performance of what was basically a small aircraft.

The MiG-21F was delivered to India and Finland as well as to Warsaw Pact states, and was put into production in China (as the F-7) and Czechoslovakia.

By the time it was established in service, development of a limited-all-weather version was under way, a considerably more advanced aerodynamic prototype being demonstrated at Tushino in 1961. This was the MiG-21PF, with an R1L radar in the centrebody of a redesigned inlet. Guns were removed, and the cockpit was faired into the fuselage, sacrificing rear vision for low drag.

Between 1964 and 1970 the MiG-21PF formed the basis for numerous modified subvariants. In the course of production, a new brake-chute installation was added at the base of the fin. On the MiG-21SPS, plain flaps blown by engine-bleed air replaced the chord-extending Fowler flaps. Later the fin was again extended forwards, and some aircraft had provision for a GP-9 gun-pack containing the newly developed GSh-23 cannon. Also covered by the MiG-

MiG-21MF of the Luftsteitkräfte und Luftverteidigung of the GDR.

Late-model MiG-21 of the Egyptian air arm. Only two of the four pylons are loaded with weapons, and the usual ventral drop tank is absent for this aerobatic sortie.

Soviet Air Force MiG-21PF interceptor.

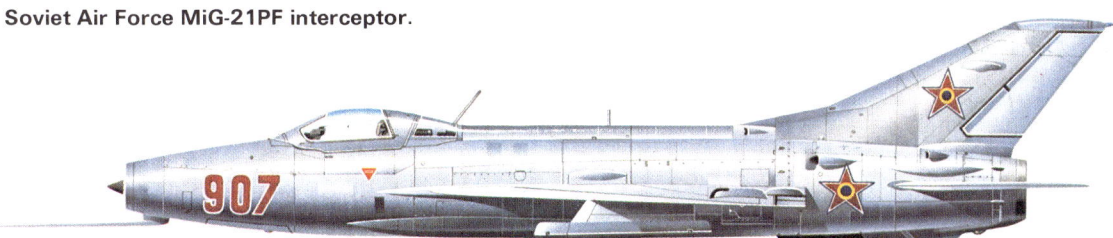

MiG-21F day interceptor of the Hungarian Air Force.

MiG-21F (F-7) of the Air Force of the People's Liberation Army of China.

MiG-21F of a Romanian Air Force interceptor regiment, 1967.

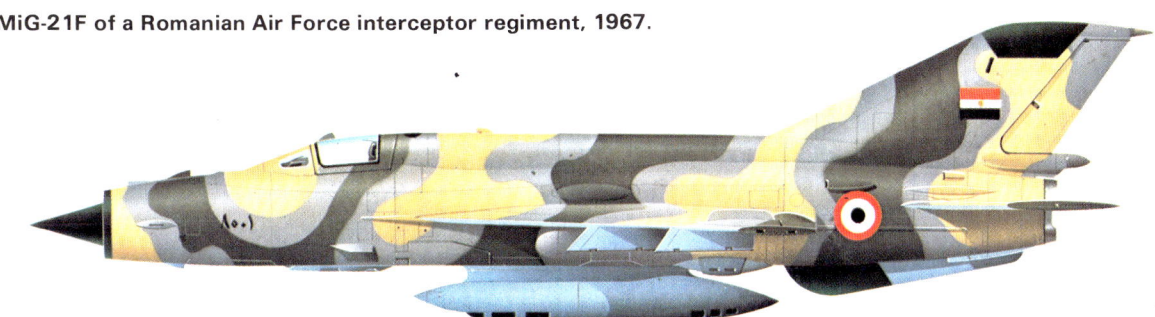

Sand-camouflaged MiG-21RF of the Arab Republic of Egypt Air Force.

Mikoyan-Gurevich MiG-21 Fishbed/MiG-21U Mongol

India has both built the MiG-21 under licence and used it in action. The aircraft seen here are of the version originally built in India, equivalent to the MiG-21PFM but known to India as the MiG-21FL.

21PF designation was the introduction of the 13,700-lb (6200-kg) R-11F2S-300 engine and improved R2L radar.

The next recognisable modification produced the MiG-21PFM, with a conventional sideways-hinged canopy and separate windscreen replacing the forward-hinged one-piece hood of the MiG-21F. It was followed by the MiG-21PFMA, with a deeper dorsal spine and four wing pylons, which formed the basis for the MiG-21R reconnaissance version with optical and electronic sensors in ventral and wing-tip pods. The next major modification came in 1970, with the service introduction of the MiG-21MF. This has an internal GSh-23 and the new Tumansky R-13 rated at 14,500 lb (6600 kg). The equivalent reconnaissance version is designated MiG-21RF. Egypt and India have both fitted MiG-21s with British avionics, and Egyptian MiG-21s may be modified to carry Sidewinder missiles.

In 1973 there appeared the first examples of a new MiG-21 development, the MiG-21SMT, with internal fuel and avionic equipment in a bulged dorsal spine. It has been followed by the structurally redesigned and simplified MiG-21bis, with the Tumansky R-25 and further improved avionics including a new gun-sight; the new type may also carry the AA-8 'Aphid' missile. Despite the development of the MiG-21 in the direction of multi-role capability, it is now mainly used for air defence of tactical air bases.

However, the MiG-21 is limited in range and payload by comparison with the MiG-27, while its dogfighting performance is not in the class of the latest Western fighters. The MiG-21bis may be an interim development, pending production of a new aircraft to fill the air-to-air slot in the Soviet air arm. Meanwhile, the MiG-21bis has become the standard export version. Another MiG-21 development is reported to be the Chinese fighter designated F-8.

Other versions of the MiG-21 have included the MiG-21M, generally similar to the MiG-21MF but powered by the older R-11, which was built under licence in India and has been superseded on the Indian production lines by the MiG-21bis. All trainer versions of the MiG-21 have similar forward fuselages and lack search radar: the MiG-21U is basically equivalent to an early MiG-21PF, the MiG-21US is equivalent to the MiG-21PFS and the MiG-21UM is derived from the MiG-21MF. It is likely that a MiG-21bis-derived trainer will emerge in due course.

MiG-21MF of the Czeskoslovenske Letectvo.

Indian Air Force Hindustan-built MiG-21PFM hastily camouflaged for service in the 1971 India-Pakistan War.

Yugoslav Air Force MiG-21MF, one of more than 100 in service.

One of the few MiG-21Rs in the Czech Air Force carrying unit insignia.

Soviet Air Force MiG-21MF of a fighter regiment assigned to the Kiev Military District.

Mikoyan-Gurevich MiG-21 Fishbed/MiG-21U Mongol

MiG-21MF cutaway drawing key

1 Pitot-static boom
2 Pitch vanes
3 Yaw vanes
4 Conical three-position intake centrebody
5 "Spin Scan" search-and-track radar antenna
6 Boundary layer slot
7 Engine air intake
8 Radar ("Spin Scan")
9 Lower boundary layer exit
10 Antennæ
11 Nosewheel doors
12 Nosewheel leg and shock absorbers
13 Castoring nosewheel
14 Anti-shimmy damper
15 Avionics bay access
16 Attitude sensor
17 Nosewheel well
18 Spill door
19 Nosewheel retraction pivot
20 Bifurcated intake trunking
21 Avionics bay
22 Electronics equipment
23 Intake trunking
24 Upper boundary layer exit
25 Dynamic pressure probe for q-feel
26 Semi-elliptical armour-glass windscreen
27 Gunsight mounting
28 Fixed quarterlight
29 Radar scope
30 Control column (with tailplane trim switch and two firing buttons)
31 Rudder pedals
32 Underfloor control runs
33 KM-1 two-position zero-level ejection seat
34 Port instrument console
35 Undercarriage handle
36 Seat harness
37 Canopy release/lock
38 Starboard wall switch panel
39 Rear-view mirror fairing
40 Starboard-hinged canopy
41 Ejection seat headrest
42 Avionics bay
43 Control rods
44 Air conditioning plant
45 Suction relief door
46 Intake trunking
47 Wingroot attachment fairing
48 Wing/fuselage spar-lug attachment points (four)
49 Fuselage ring frames
50 Intermediary frames
51 Main fuselage fuel tank
52 RSIU radio bay
53 Auxiliary intake
54 Leading-edge integral fuel tank

55 Starboard outer weapons pylon
56 Outboard wing construction
57 Starboard navigation light
58 Leading-edge suppressed aerial
59 Wing fence
60 Aileron control jack
61 Starboard aileron
62 Flap actuator fairing
63 Starboard blown flap — SPS (sduva pogranichnovo sloya)
64 Multi-spar wing structure
65 Main integral wing fuel tank
66 Undercarriage mounting/pivot point
67 Starboard mainwheel leg
68 Auxiliaries compartment
69 Fuselage fuel tanks Nos 2 and 3
70 Mainwheel well external fairing
71 Mainwheel (retracted)
72 Trunking contours
73 Control rods in dorsal spine
74 Compressor face
75 Oil tank
76 Avionics pack
77 Engine accessories
78 Tumansky R-13 turbojet (rated at 14,550 lb/6 600 kg with full reheat)
79 Fuselage break/transport joint
80 Intake
81 Tail surface control linkage
82 Artificial feel unit
83 Tailplane jack
84 Hydraulic accumulator
85 Tailplane trim motor
86 Tailfin spar attachment plate
87 Rudder jack
88 Rudder control linkage
89 Tailfin structure
90 Leading-edge panel
91 Radio cable access
92 Magnetic detector
93 Tailfin mainspar
94 RSIU (radio-stantsiya istrebitelnaya ultrakorot-kykh vol'n — very-short-wave fighter radio) antenna plate
95 VHF/UHF aerials
96 IFF antennæ
97 Formation light
98 Tail warning radar

99 Rear navigation light
100 Fuel vent
101 Rudder construction
102 Rudder hinge
103 Braking parachute hinged bullet fairing
104 Braking parachute stowage
105 Tailpipe (variable convergent nozzle)
106 Afterburner installation
107 Afterburner bay cooling intake
108 Tailplane linkage fairing
109 Nozzle actuating cylinders
110 Tailplane torque tube
111 All-moving tailplane
112 Anti-flutter weight
113 Intake
114 Afterburner mounting
115 Fixed tailplane root fairing
116 Longitudinal lap joint
117 External duct (nozzle hydraulics)
118 Ventral fin
119 Engine guide rail
120 JATO assembly canted nozzle
121 JATO assembly thrust plate forks (rear mounting)
122 JATO assembly pack
123 Ventral airbrake (retracted)
124 Trestle point
125 JATO assembly release solenoid (front mounting)
126 Underwing landing light
127 Ventral stores pylon
128 Mainwheel inboard door
129 Splayed link chute
130 Twin 23-mm GSh-23 cannon installation

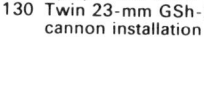

131	Cannon muzzle fairing	142	Mainwheel leg
132	Debris deflector plate	143	Aileron control linkage
133	Auxiliary ventral drop tank	144	Mainwheel leg pivot point
134	Port forward air brake (extended)	145	Main integral wing fuel tank
135	Leading-edge integral fuel tank	146	Flap actuator fairing
		147	Port aileron
136	Undercarriage retraction strut	148	Aileron control jack
		149	Outboard wing construction
137	Aileron control rods in leading-edge	150	Port navigation light
		151	Port outboard weapons pylon
138	Port inboard weapons pylon	152	"Advanced Atoll" infrared-guided AAM
139	UV-16-57 rocket pod		
140	Port mainwheel	153	Wing fence
141	Mainwheel outboard door section	154	Radio altimeter antenna

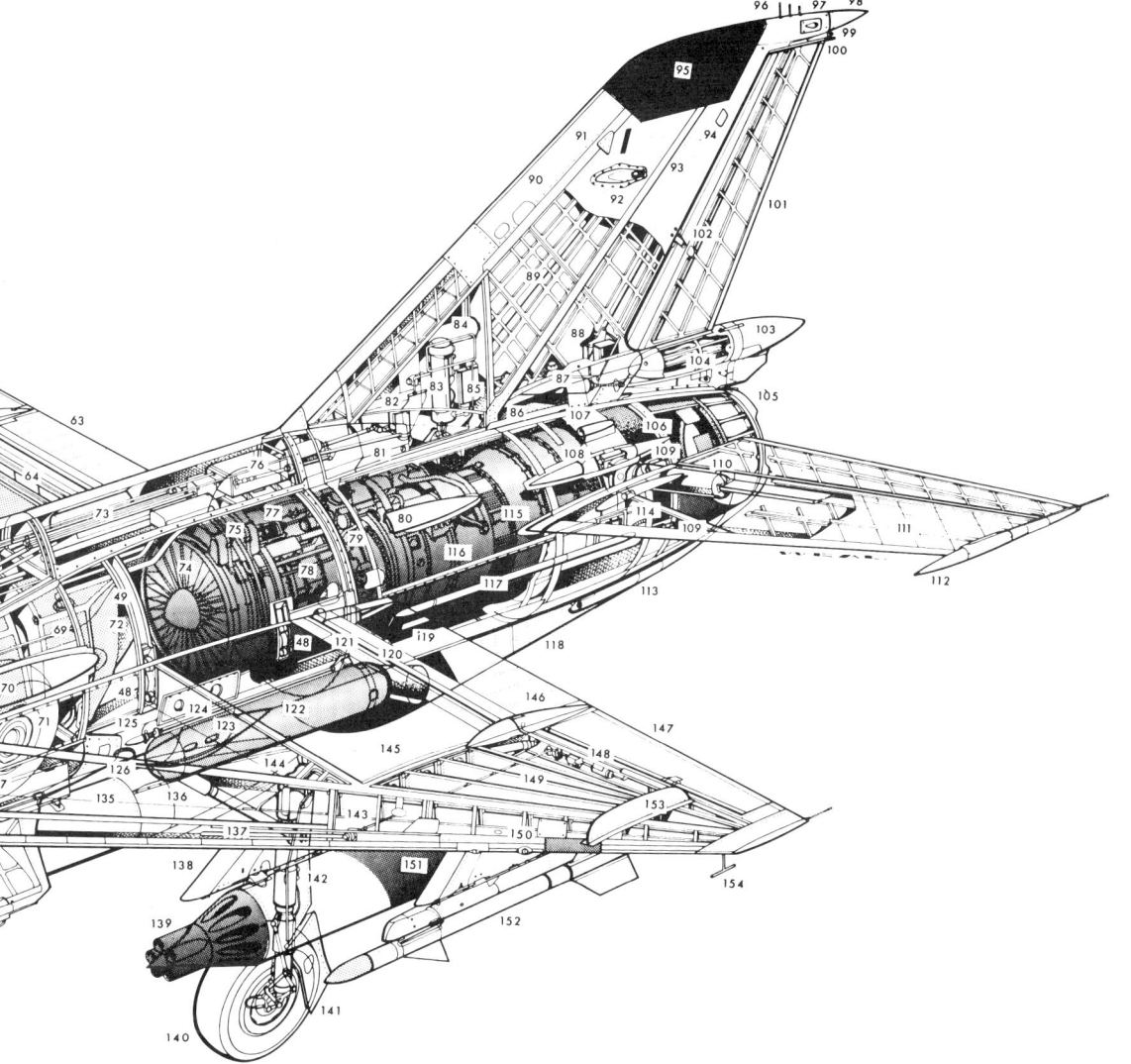

Mikoyan-Gurevich MiG-21 Fishbed/MiG-21U Mongol

Specification

Type: fighter/light strike and (MiG-21M variants) conversion trainer

Powerplant: (MiG-21bis, to which subsequent details refer) one 16,500 lb (7500 kg) Tumansky R-25 afterburning turbojet

Performance: maximum speed clean 1,320 mph (2125 km/h) or Mach 2 at 36,000 ft (11000 m); maximum speed with external stores at medium altitude 1,000 mph (1600 km/h) or Mach 1.5; maximum speed at sea level just over Mach 1; service ceiling about 50,000 ft (15000 m); hi-lo-hi combat radius about 300 miles (500 km)

Weights: empty 13,500 lb (6200 kg); maximum loaded 22,000 lb (10000 kg)

Dimensions: span 23 ft 6 in (7.16 m); length 51 ft 9 in (15.75 m); height 14 ft 9 in (4.49 m); wing area 247 sq ft (22.9 m^2)

Armament: one twin-barrel 23-mm GSh-23 cannon, plus four wing hardpoints for 3,300 lb (1500 kg) of ordnance, including up to four K-13 (AA-2 'Atoll') or AA-8 'Aphid' air-to-air missiles, AS-7 'Kerry' air-to-surface missiles or unguided

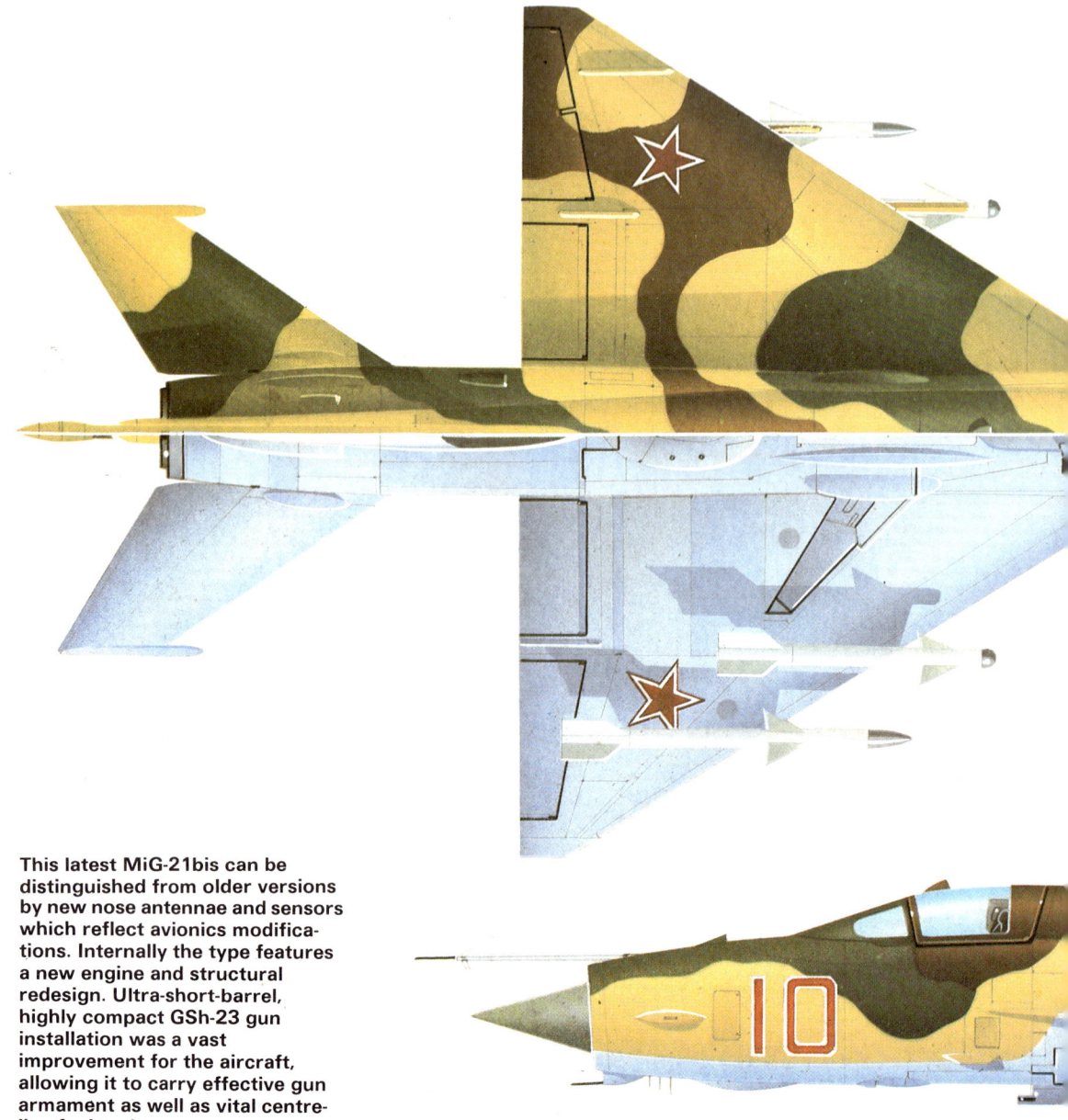

This latest MiG-21bis can be distinguished from older versions by new nose antennae and sensors which reflect avionics modifications. Internally the type features a new engine and structural redesign. Ultra-short-barrel, highly compact GSh-23 gun installation was a vast improvement for the aircraft, allowing it to carry effective gun armament as well as vital centre-line fuel tank.

rockets; outer wing pylons or centreline pylon can be used for drop tanks

Operators: Afghanistan, Albania, Algeria, Angola, Bangladesh, Bulgaria, China, Cuba, Czechoslovakia, East Germany, Ethiopia, Egypt, Finland, Hungary, India, Iraq, Laos, Malagasy, Mozambique, Nigeria, North Korea, Poland, Romania, Somalia, Sudan, Syria, Tanzania, Uganda, USSR, Vietnam, Yemen, Yugoslavia, Zambia

Small cross-section of MiG-21 is key to high performance on low power. Dorsal spine was repeatedly enlarged during development from the MiG-21F day fighter to the MiG-21MF. Even fatter fuel-carrying spine was fitted to MiG-21SMT 'Fishbed-K', but the MiG-21bis illustrated here reverts to the MiG-21MF design and 'Fishbed-K' seems to have been used in only limited numbers.

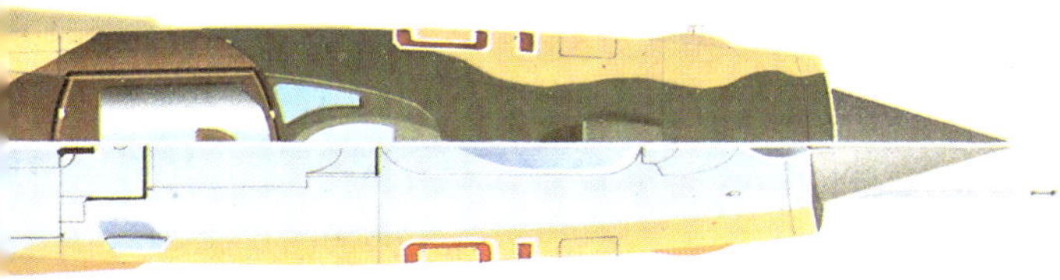

Tailed-delta shape of MiG-21 has proved highly effective in combat, remaining controllable up to high angles of attack and low airspeeds; the drawback, compared with later Western air-superiority fighters, is that high turn rates are combined with a very steep drag rise, even at low speeds, so that the MiG-21 'loses energy' at its limits and becomes vulnerable to a repeat attack. Armament includes semi-active radar-homing versions of the K-13 missile on outboard pylons; equivalent SAR version of Sidewinder was abandoned by US.

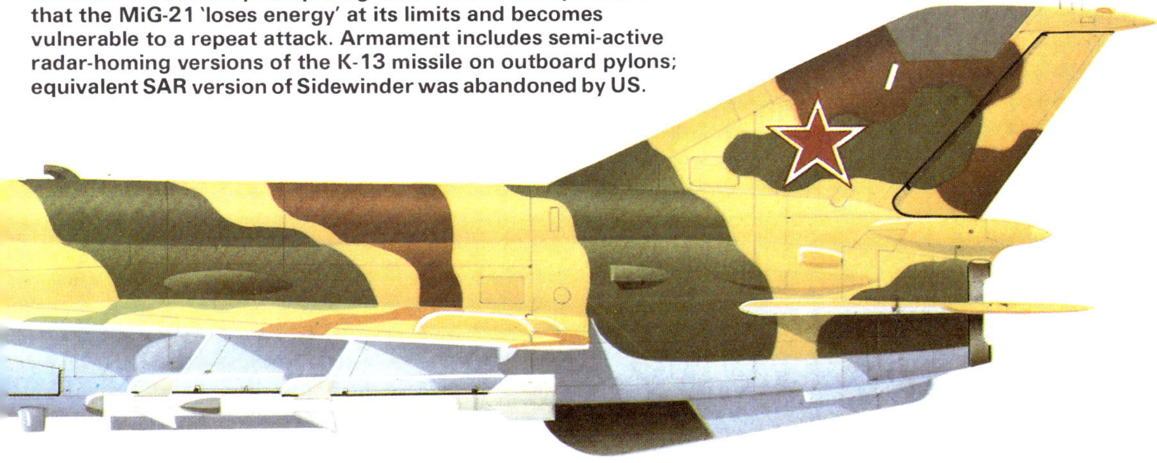

Mikoyan-Gurevich MiG-23 Flogger-A, B, C, E, G

History and notes

The Mikoyan-Gurevich MiG-23 'Flogger' is almost certainly the most important of Soviet tactical warplanes, and production of this aircraft and of its derivative the MiG-27 was reported to have attained a rate of 300 aircraft a year by 1976-77. The type has replaced many MiG-21s and Sukhoi Su-7s, and in 1978 was first deployed by the PVO air defence force. It has no direct Western equivalent, the near-contemporary Dassault-Breguet Mirage G being almost identical in concept but never put into production. The most closely comparable type in service is perhaps the Saab 37 Viggen, but the MiG-23 can probably best be likened to a 'miniaturised Phantom', later in timescale and more advanced, but intended for the same spectrum of roles. Modification fairly late in its development produced a type with better air-superiority characteristics than at first intended, but the MiG-23 cannot be compared in this respect with later specialized Western fighters. Its most significant feature, however, is that the same basic airframe serves as a dedicated air-to-ground aircraft ('Flogger D' and 'Flogger F') as well as an interceptor/air superiority fighter.

Develement of the MiG-23 was almost certainly initiated in 1963-64, before the Vietnam war and most Middle East experience of air combat. The aim was to produce for Frontal Aviation (FA) a tactical fighter which could match the payload/range of types such as the Lockheed F-104G, Republic F-105 and McDonnell Douglas F-4 Phantom without demanding massive runways. The last concern was also a feature of Western thinking at the time, leading to development of the Viggen and a short-lived NATO enthusiasm for V/STOL strike aircraft.

Even the early-production MiG-23 'Flogger-B' fighter carries an extensive array of dielectric panels and antennae around its nose, including a laser forward of the wheel well.

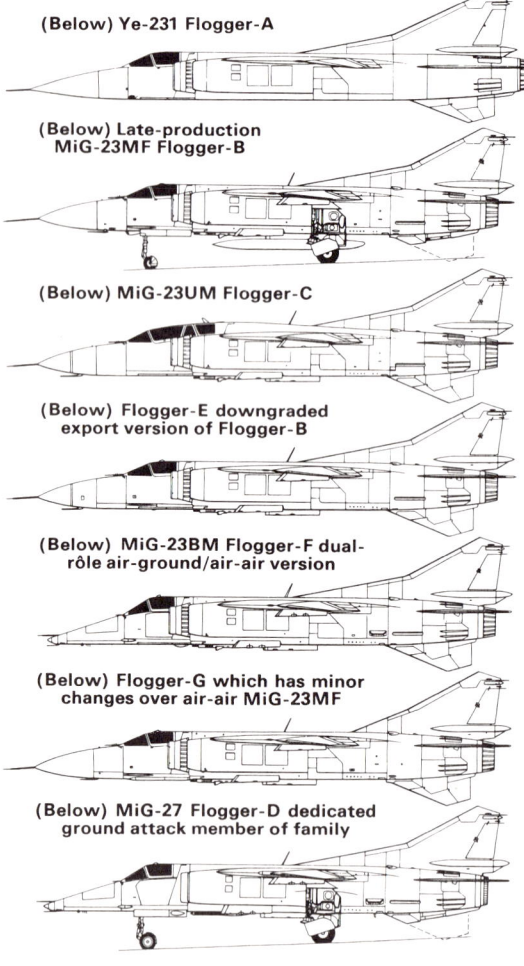

(Below) Ye-231 Flogger-A

(Below) Late-production MiG-23MF Flogger-B

(Below) MiG-23UM Flogger-C

(Below) Flogger-E downgraded export version of Flogger-B

(Below) MiG-23BM Flogger-F dual-rôle air-ground/air-air version

(Below) Flogger-G which has minor changes over air-air MiG-23MF

(Below) MiG-27 Flogger-D dedicated ground attack member of family

Mikoyan-Gurevich MiG-23 Flogger-A, B, C, E, G

The Mikoyan evaluated at least two approaches to the FA requirements: the swing-wing MiG-23 and a tailed-delta type with a battery of Kolesov lift jets amidships (the latter codenamed 'Faithless' by NATO). It is also possible that a canard type was test-flown. The swing-wing prototype was the first such aircraft to fly in the Soviet Union, as distinct from the mid-span pivot principle used on the Su-17 and Tupolev Tu-26. Both the aircraft evaluated were designed to accept the Tumansky R-27, the first Soviet afterburning turbofan for military use.

The Mikoyan prototypes were evaluated in 1966-67, and the decision to go ahead with the swing-wing type was probably taken in 1968. By that time, however, the importance of the air combat regime was being recognised; the MiG-23 may also have demonstrated generally unacceptable handling characteristics, as well as needing improvement in the air-to-air regime. In any event, although a few

Another shot of an early MiG-23 is notable for the standard K-13 'Atoll' missile-launching shoes on the belly stations and much heavier pylons on the wing roots, probably for AA-7 Apex medium-range AAMs.

aircraft basically similar to the prototype (designated 'Flogger-A' by NATO) were put into service with trials units, several years elapsed before the highly modified MiG-23S 'Flogger-B' was introduced.

Compared with the prototype, the MiG-23S features an extremely large saw-toothed leading-edge extension which increases wing area and taper, reducing the shift of aerodynamic centre with wing sweep. The planform was also altered, the tail surfaces being moved aft. Together, most of the modifications would tend to make the aircraft more stable, while the additional wing area might restore some of the manoeuvrability thus sacrificed.

The notched wing planform distinguishes the

Stemming from a trials aircraft in the MiG-27 programme is the hybrid MiG-23BM 'Flogger-F', standard-issue to non-Soviet Warsaw Pact forces. Despite a higher speed than that of the MiG-27, it is considerably less useful.

MiG-23 series from other variable-sweep aircraft. Other unusual features include a folding ventral fin and a complex but space-saving main landing gear. Movable surfaces include simple leading-edge droops on the outer sections of the moving wing panels, plain trailing-edge flaps and spoilers. The outermost of the three flap sections operate in conjunction with the four-section spoiler/dumpers and tailerons for roll control. Western testing shows strongly that variable-geometry wings should be matched with sophisticated high-lift systems.

Whereas design of the MiG-23 was biased towards the strike role, development was aimed at improving handling and manoeuvrability in the air-combat regime. No effort was made, however, to improve visibility, beyond the installation of rear-view mirrors.

Development of the MiG-23S equipment and armament went hand in hand with airframe and power-plant work. The aircraft is fitted with a radar (codenamed High Lark) considerably larger and more powerful than that fitted to the MiG-21, and is armed with specially developed medium-range and dogfighting missiles. All examples in FA service also carry a laser (or possibly infra-red) sighting or ranging aid beneath the nose.

The MiG-23S entered service in 1971-72. Early aircraft were powered by the 23,150-lb (10500-kg) Tumansky R-27, but by the time the aircraft was established in service work was under way on the more powerful R-29 engine: this was probably another example of development aimed at improving air-to-air combat capability. The R-27 is, however, still used in the MiG-23U 'Flogger-C' conversion

Mikoyan-Gurevich MiG-23 Flogger-A, B, C, E, G

Flogger-B (MiG-23MF) of the Air Force of the DDR with rocket pods on outboard fuselage pylons and AAM launching shoes on glove pylons.

Flogger-F (MiG-23BM) of the Algerian Air Force. Note that the individual aircraft number conforms with the ground line and not with the line of flight.

Flogger-E of the Libyan Arab Republic Air Force displaying the Islamic green insignia adopted in 1978 in place of the red-white-black roundels shared with Egypt. The LARAF operates both the Flogger-E and the Flogger-F, which, together with a small number of Flogger-C two-seaters, equip two squadrons. Libya was one of the two first recipients of Flogger (the other being Egypt) in the Middle East.

Flogger-G of a V-VS unit from Kubinka, 50 mls (80 km) west of Moscow, which was demonstrated in Finland and France in 1978. Essentially similar to Flogger-B, this version has an enlarged nosewheel housing containing a new nosewheel unit, and revised vertical and horizontal tail.

Flogger-F (MiG-23BM) of the Czechoslovak Air Force of a unit based at Pardubice, some 60 mls (100 km) east of Prague. The two-tone upper surface camouflage scheme with pale blue undersurfaces has now been standardised by most non-Soviet War Pac air forces.

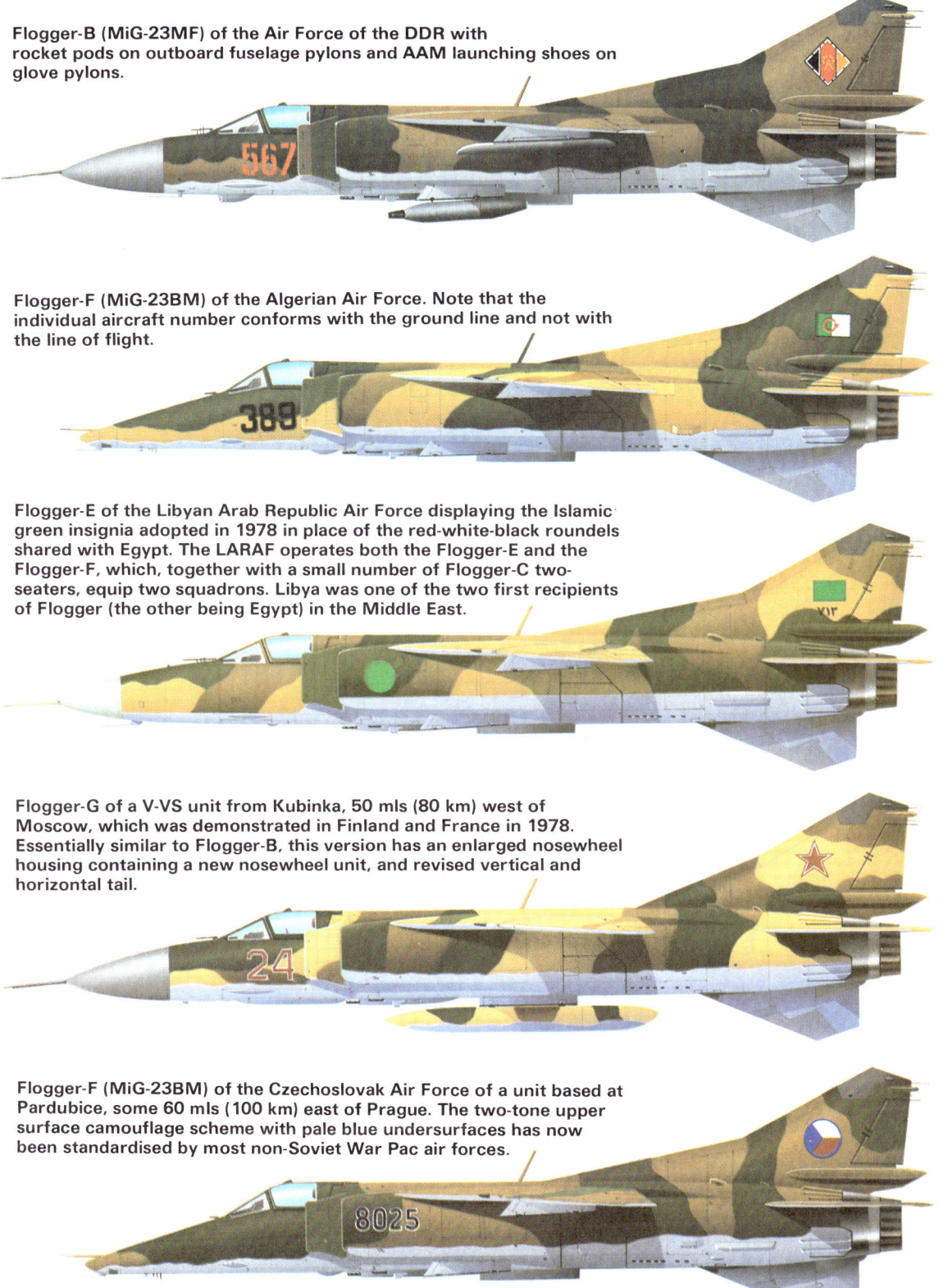

Mikoyan-Gurevich MiG-23 Flogger-A, B, C, E, G

MiG-23 'Flogger-E' in early Libyan Air Force markings as carried in early 1976. Libya was one of the first export recipients of the 'Flogger-E', which carries the radar and armament of the MiG-21bis 'Fishbed-N'.

Something of an oddity is this export-model MiG-23 'Flogger-E' in Soviet markings, with an unusual infra-red sensor beneath the nose. It may serve with a training unit.

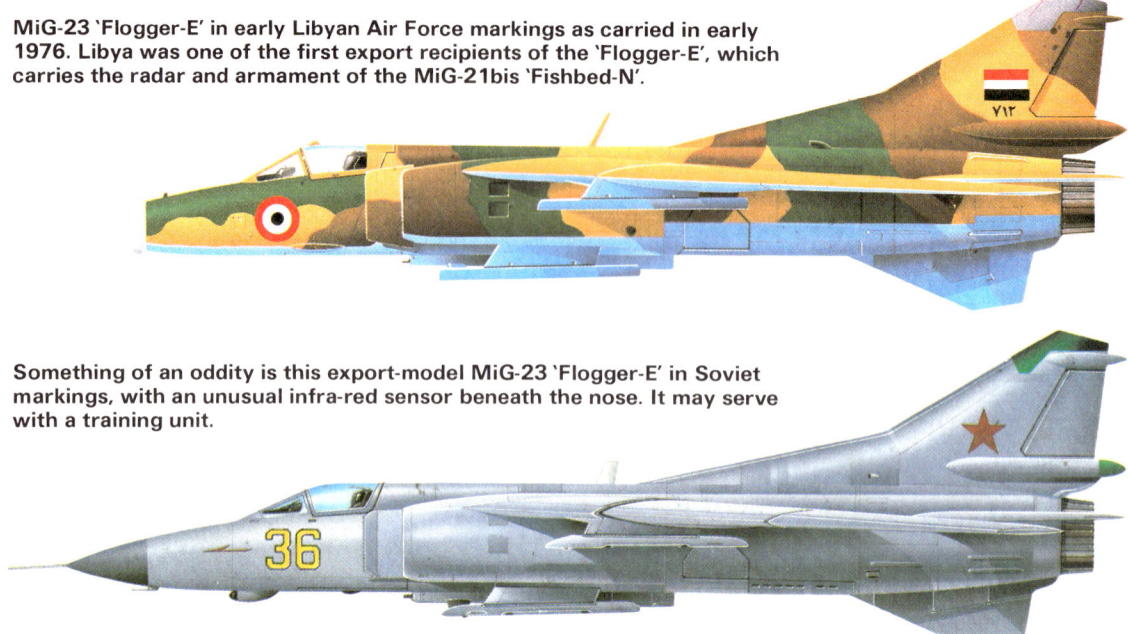

The latest known stage in MiG-23 development is 'Flogger-G' revealed to the West when the aircraft shown here and opposite visited Finland in 1978. The laser rangefinder has been deleted from these examples.

Flogger-B (MiG-23MF) in the standard air superiority overall light grey finish, the emblem on the nose indicating that the unit to which the aircraft belongs has achieved a prescribed standard of merit. Note the rocket pods on the outboard fuselage ordnance pylons and the AAM launching shoes on the glove pylons.

The export model of the MiG-23U trainer is basically similar to the 'domestic' version, neither seeming to be fitted with the full-size radar. This aircraft was delivered to Libya in early 1976.

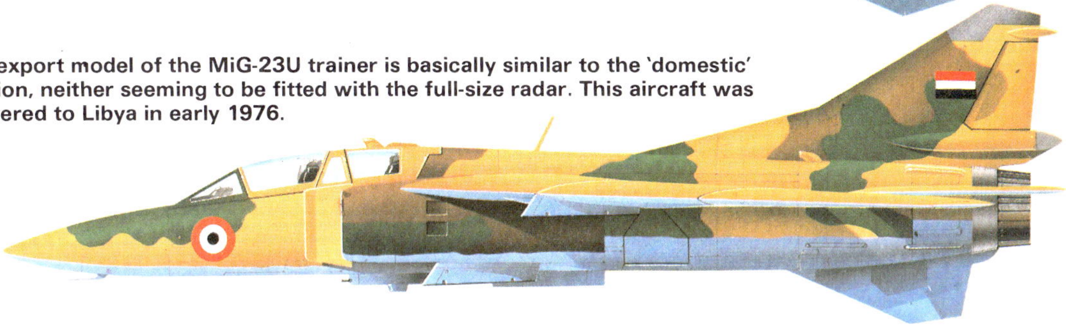

Side-view of 'Flogger-G' shows clearly the modified fin with smaller area. The MiG-23's folding ventral fin is a feature it shares with the Lockheed YF-12A experimental Mach 3 interceptor.

Mikoyan-Gurevich MiG-23 Flogger-A, B, C, E, G

trainer and the export 'Flogger-E'; the latter has a much-reduced standard of equipment, including AA-2-2 'Advanced Atoll' missiles and like the trainer, a radar apparently derived from the R2L of the MiG-21. The AA-2 'Atoll' formed the interim armament of the MiG-23S until the newly developed AA-7 and AA-8 entered service in the mid-1970s.

The current standard air defence version of the MiG-23 is identified by Nato as 'Flogger G'. Companies with examples of the 'Flogger B' type observed in 1973-74, the 'Flogger G' is distinguished externally by a smaller dorsal fin extension and the fact that the nose radome is very slightly drooped. This is in addition to a number of features which may have been phased in during the course of production rather than being specific to the 'Flogger G':

*Installation of the more powerful R-29B engine, improving acceleration, sustained turning ability and field performance

*Development of a pulse-Doppler attack radar capable of directing missiles against targets flying lower than the launching aircraft. The represents a considerable advance over the original High Lark radar, which was described by US sources as being comparable to that of the late1960s F-4J Phantom

*Provision for jettisonable overload fuel tanks on non-swivelling wing pylons

The 'Flogger G' is in production for the FA and PVO but has not been exported. Compared with aircraft now being delivered to the Western air forces, it is not a 'visual-range' fighter so much as an intercepter designed to fire at radar range, closing for cannon and short-range-missile engagement only as a second resort. It is assumed that Soviet superiority in numbers in the central region of Europe is so great that the air force is prepared to accept losses due to misidentification.

Specification

Type: air combat fighter and interceptor with secondary strike role or (MiG-23U) conversion trainer

Powerplant: (current production) one 25,350-lb (11500-kg) Tumansky R-29B afterburning turbofan

Performance: maximum speed 1,450 mph (2350 km/h) or Mach 2.2 at 36,000 ft (11000 m); maximum speed at sea level 840 mph (1350 km/h) or Mach 1.1; service ceiling 55,000 ft (17000 m); ferry range 1,750 miles (2800 km); combat radius 575 miles (930 km)

Weights: empty 25,000 lb (11300 kg); internal fuel 10,140 lb (4600 kg); normal take-off 38,000 lb (17250 kg); maximum 41,000 lb (18500 kg)

Dimensions: span (unswept) 46 ft 9 in (14.25 m); span (swept) 27 ft 2 in (8.3 m); length 59 ft 10 in (18.25 m); height 14 ft 4 in (4.35 m); wing area 400 sq ft (37.2 m^2)

Armament: one internal 23-mm GSh-23 twin-barrel cannon, two glove hardpoints for AA-7 'Apex' medium-range air-to-air missiles, or air-to-surface weapons, two belly hardpoints for AA-8 'Aphid' dogfight air-to-air missiles. The export 'Flogger-E' carries four AA-2-2 'Advanced Atoll' air-to-air missiles

Operators: Algeria, Bulgaria, Czechoslovakia, Egypt, Ethiopia, Iraq, Libya, USSR

Mikoyan-Gurevich MiG-23MF 'Flogger-G'.

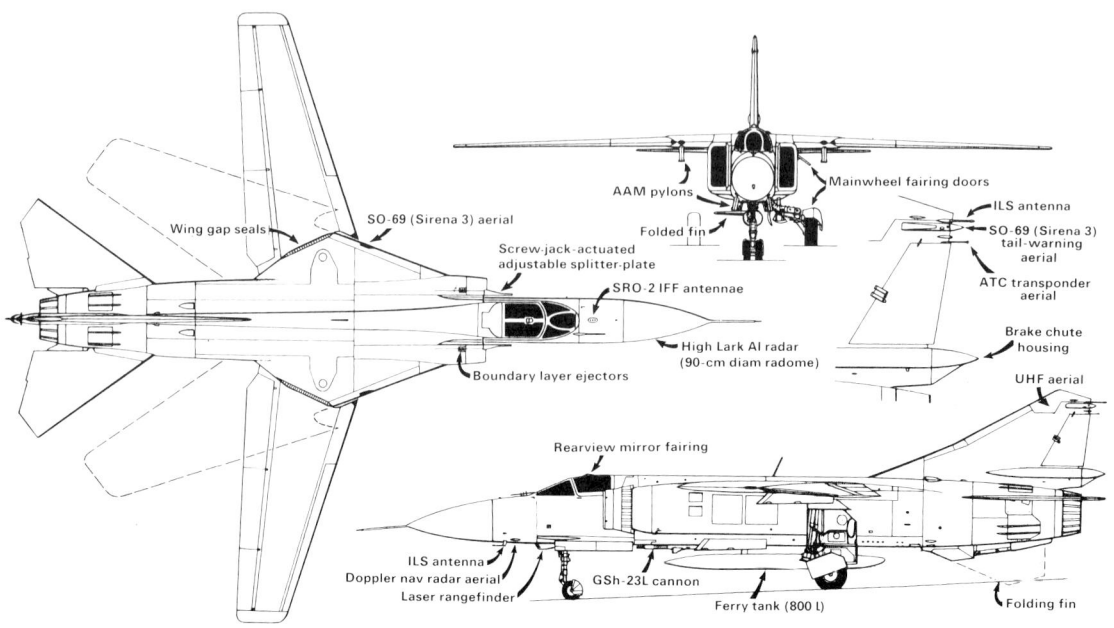

Mikoyan-Gurevich MiG-23 Flogger-A, B, C, E, G

Head-on view of a Soviet-operated MiG-23 shows the 'claws' which were added to the leading-edge of the wing after early flight tests. The tips of the claws appear to house electronic antennae.

Mikoyan-Gurevich MiG-25 Foxbat

History and notes

Unquestionably the most impressive military aircraft to appear from the Soviet Union, the MiG-25 is unique in combining spectacular speed and climb performance with simplicity and ruggedness. Only built in limited numbers, it is near to replacement in the Soviet Union but is becoming a Third World status-symbol.

In early 1979 the US Department of Defense commented that the MiG-25 'Foxbat' was being produced 'mainly for export'. At that time the only known foreign recipients were Libya and Algeria. Their MiG-25s give these nations the ability to defy all but the most sophisticated defence systems by virtue of sheer height and speed of penetration. Long ago the appearance of MiG-25s stimulated purchases of advanced weapon systems by the United States, Israel and the former Iranian regime, making the 'Foxbat' the best sales aid for McDonnell Douglas and Grumman yet devised. The type is also reported to form the basis of the Soviet Union's new air-defence system for the 1980s, but it is likely that the airframe is so highly modified for this role that a new designation will be applied.

The MiG-25 is well known to the West, because an example of the type was flown to Japan by a defec-

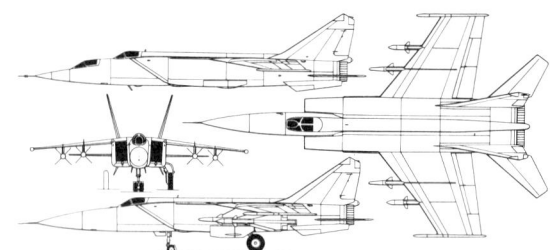

MiG-25 'Foxbat-A' and (upper side view) MiG-25U 'Foxbat-C'.

ting pilot in September 1976.

The basic design goes back to 1957-59, when it seemed possible that the US Air Force would introduce a Mach 3, 70,000-ft (21350-m) bomber (the North American B-70) by 1964. Later the Lockheed A-11, intended as a strategic reconnaissance aircraft, clearly had a strike capability. Development of a Russian Mach 3 interceptor proceeeded as a matter of urgency, the first prototype flying around 1964. By this time, however, the B-70 had been cancelled and the pace of the Russian programme slowed.

First photo to show the electronic reconnaissance 'Foxbat-D' with side-looking radar in place of the cameras of the MiG-25R 'Foxbat-B'.

Mikoyan-Gurevich MiG-25 Foxbat

The design of the E-266, as the Mikoyan bureau designated the new type, was influenced by that of the North American A-5 Vigilante. The two types both have large, thin-section shoulder wings of moderate sweep, vertical ramp inlets and identical fuselage and propulsion layouts. The main landing gear units are similar, and the twin fins of the E-266 are similar to those of the original Vigilante mock-up.

However, the Mach 3 requirement demanded a unique approach to structure and propulsion. The E-266 is constructed largely of fabricated steel sections, and the fuel tanks are of continuously welded steel sheet so that they can expand and contract with temperature without leaking. (Fuel-tank sealing proved to be a major problem with Mach 3 aircraft.) Power is provided by two extremely simple turbojets optimized for high-Mach performance; static pressure ratio is low, but at high speeds is multiplied by compression in the inlet ducts. The powerplant thus has some of the characteristics of a turbo-ramjet. At low speeds its efficiency is extremely poor, a factor exacerbated by the fact that only at high speeds is a substantial part of the lift generated by the intakes. The MiG-25 thus requires considerable nose-up trim at subsonic speeds, worsening its aerodynamic efficiency. It follows that the MiG-25 is a relatively inflexible machine, with poor loiter and mixed-profile performance, and poor manoeuvrability. It is commonly called a 'straight-line aircraft'.

The propulsion system, possibly including an early version of the electronic inlet control system, was tested on a modified Mikoyan-Gurevich I-75 interceptor, designated E-166, which is claimed to have exceeded Mach 2.8 on a 1,665 mph (2681 km/hr) official record run in 1965. However, it was not until 1967 that similar record speeds were set by E-266 development aircraft. By that time the airframe and engine appeared to be fully developed, with methanol-water injection for high-speed flight. However, it was another three years before production MiG-25s appeared in service, indicating protracted development of the offensive systems. The type received the NATO name 'Foxbat'.

There are two main versions, both deployed around 1970. The PVO air defence force operates the interceptor, possibly designated MiG-25P and known to NATO as 'Foxbat-A'. The radar and missile system is designed mainly for interceptions

Two MiG-25U 'Foxbat-C' conversion and proficiency trainers. These aircraft carry no operational equipment and are slower than the single-seaters.

Mikoyan-Gurevich MiG-25 Foxbat

A dramatic view of the MiG-25 'Foxbat A' interceptor, apparently valving fuel from points near its wingtips. Basically a straight-line aircraft, the MiG-25 has no application in normal air-to-air combat.

Mikoyan-Gurevich MiG-25 Foxbat

controlled from the ground or the Tupolev Tu-126 'Moss' AWACS aircraft. Although the 'Fox Fire' radar appears to be based on the 'Big Nose' radar of the two-seat Tu-28P, which operates with greater autonomy, the MiG-25 relies to a great extent on communication links and ground-guided trajectories rather than inertial or Doppler radar systems. Early MiG-25s carried the AA-5 'Ash' missile which arms the Tu-28P, and some may have carried the AA-3 'Anab' missile. The production-standard armament,however, appears to be the massive AA-6 'Acrid', by far the world's largest air-to-air missile and even longer than the Western Hawk surface-to-air missile. The 'Fox Fire'/AA-6 system is not thought to have any look-down/shoot-down capability or multiple-target processing.

By the time the interceptor entered service, however, the MiG-25 had found a new role as a reconnaissance aircraft, using electronic and optical sensors. Although the range and sensor capacity of the MiG-25R are markedly inferior to those of the Lockheed SR-71, the aircraft can penetrate many defence systems in safety provided that there is a safe base close at hand. MiG-25Rs have been based in Egypt for uninterceptable overflights of Israel, and have flown from Poland in missions along the East German border for Elint probing of NATO defences. Two versions of the MiG-25R appear to exist: one, designated 'Foxbat-B' by NATO, has cameras as well as Elint dielectric panels, while the 'Foxbat-D' has more extensive Elint equipment but no cameras. Both types appear to be fitted with Dop-

pler radar, and lack the compound leading-edge sweep of the interceptor. The MiG-25R has been the object of purchase enquiries by India, which may acquire a small batch of the aircraft to replace Canberras.

The third confirmed variant is the MiG-25U 'Foxbat-C' conversion trainer, with a separate second cockpit in an extended nose. It has no operational systems.

The US Department of Defense expects a 'modified MiG-25' carrying a look-down/shoot-down system based on the new AA-X-9 missile to become operational in the early 1980s, with the ability to intercept low-flying strike aircraft and to take on four targets simultaneously. However, the limitations of the MiG-25, particularly in range and subsonic loiter capability, suggest that major modifications will be needed to turn the MiG-25 into a modern air defence fighter. It is possible that the two-seat interceptor which was undergoing weapons trials in 1978 shares little more than a fixed-wing, twin-fin configuration with the MiG-25; the DoD use of the designation 'Super MiG-25' for this aircraft suggests that this possibility is appreciated, and the type is not yet identified by a NATO reporting name in the 'Foxbat' series (see introduction).

MiG-25s armed with a mix of radar-guided and IR AA-6 Acrid missiles. This picture was published in 1975, and the high-contrast colouring of the missiles suggests a trials unit. Antennae are housed in the wingtip fairings.

Mikoyan-Gurevich MiG-25 Foxbat

Mikoyan MiG-25 Foxbat-A Drawing Key

1 Ventral airbrake
2 Starboard tailplane (aluminium alloy trailing edge)
3 Steel tailplane spar
4 Titanium leading edge
5 Tail bumper
6 Fully variable engine exhaust nozzle
7 Exhaust nozzle actuator
8 Starboard rudder
9 Static dischargers
10 Sirena 3 tail warning radar and ECM transmitter
11 Transponder aerial
12 Twin brake parachute housing
13 Port engine exhaust nozzle
14 Port rudder
15 Static dischargers
16 VHF aerial
17 HF leading edge aerial
18 Port tailfin (steel primary structure)
19 Rudder actuator
20 Titanium rear fuselage skins
21 Dorsal spine fairing
22 Fireproof bulkhead between engine bays
23 Engine afterburner duct
24 Cooling air intake
25 Tailplane hydraulic actuator
26 Starboard ventral fin
27 VHF and ECM aerial housing
28 Aileron actuator
29 Starboard aileron
30 Static discharger
31 All-steel wing construction
32 Wing tip fairing
33 Sirena 3 radar warning receiver and ECM transmitter

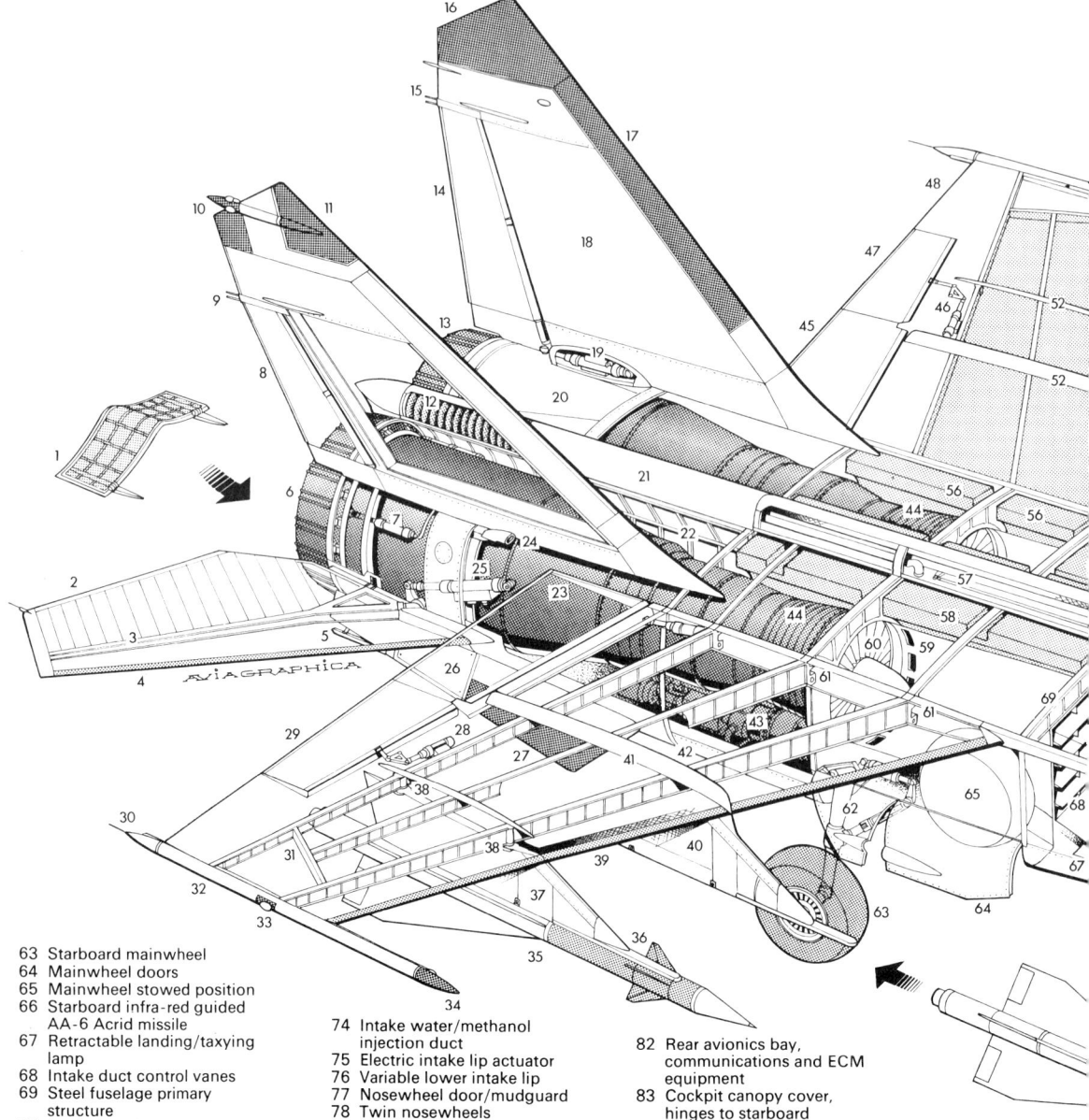

63 Starboard mainwheel
64 Mainwheel doors
65 Mainwheel stowed position
66 Starboard infra-red guided AA-6 Acrid missile
67 Retractable landing/taxying lamp
68 Intake duct control vanes
69 Steel fuselage primary structure
70 Intake bleed air outlet ducts
71 UHF communications aerials
72 Variable intake ramp doors
73 Ramp jacks
74 Intake water/methanol injection duct
75 Electric intake lip actuator
76 Variable lower intake lip
77 Nosewheel door/mudguard
78 Twin nosewheels
79 Nosewheel leg doors
80 Starboard navigation light
81 Curved intake inboard sidewall
82 Rear avionics bay, communications and ECM equipment
83 Cockpit canopy cover, hinges to starboard
84 Pilot's ejection seat
85 Cockpit rear pressure bulkhead
86 UHF communications aerial

34 Continuous wave target illuminating radar
35 AA-6 Acrid semi-active radar guided air-to-air missile
36 Missile launching rail
37 Outboard missile pylon
38 Pylon attachments
39 Wing titanium leading edge
40 Inboard pylon
41 Wing fence
42 Engine access panels
43 Engine accessory gearbox
44 Tumansky R-31 single shaft afterburning turbojet engine

45 Port flap
46 Aileron hydraulic actuator
47 Port aileron
48 Fixed portion of trailing edge
49 Sirena 3 radar warning receiver and ECM transmitter
50 Continuous wave target illuminating radar
51 Titanium leading edge
52 Port wing fences
53 AA-6 Acrid semi-active radar guided air-to-air missile
54 Infra-red guided AA-6 Acrid missile

55 Stainless steel wing skins
56 Intake flank fuel tanks
57 Controls and systems ducting
58 Main fuel tanks (welded steel integral construction) total system capacity 31,575 lb (14 322 kg), nitrogen pressurised
59 Intake bleed air ducts, engine bay cooling
60 Engine compressor face
61 Wing spar attachments
62 Main undercarriage leg strut

87 Radar altimeter
88 Pilot's side console panel
89 Control column
90 Instrument panel shroud
91 Standby visual sighting system for infra-red missiles

98 Scanner tracking mechanism
99 Radar scanner dish, 2 ft 9½ in (85 cm) diameter
100 Radome
101 "Swift-rod" ILS antenna
102 Pitot tube

103 MiG-25U Foxbat-C training variant
104 Student pilot's cockpit enclosure
105 Instructor's cockpit
106 MiG-25R Foxbat-B reconnaissance variant
107 Reconnaissance cameras, one vertical and four oblique

92 Windscreen panels
93 "Odd-rods" IFF aerials
94 Pitot tube
95 Forward avionics compartment, radar and navigation equipment
96 "Fox-Fire" fire control radar system
97 Angle-of-attack probe

108 Sideways-looking radar aperture (SLAR)
109 Ground mapping and Doppler radar antennae
110 "Jay-Bird" radar

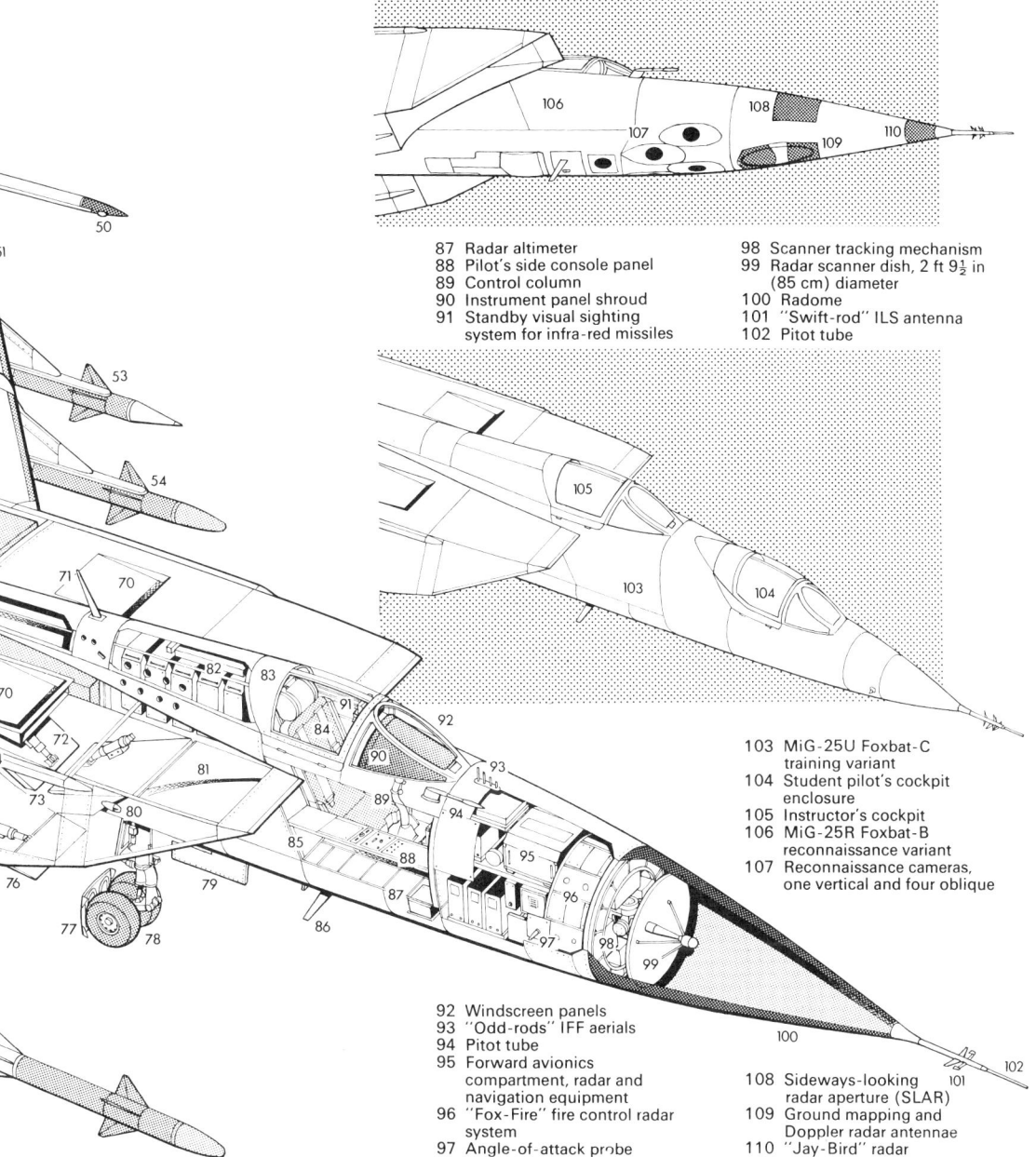

Mikoyan-Gurevich MiG-25 Foxbat

The ultimate 'hot fighter', the MiG-25 was designed to counter the threat of US supersonic-cruise technology by carrying a powerful radar and four heavy missiles— each large enough to disable a heavy bomber—up to 500 miles to an intercept line in little more than 20 minutes.

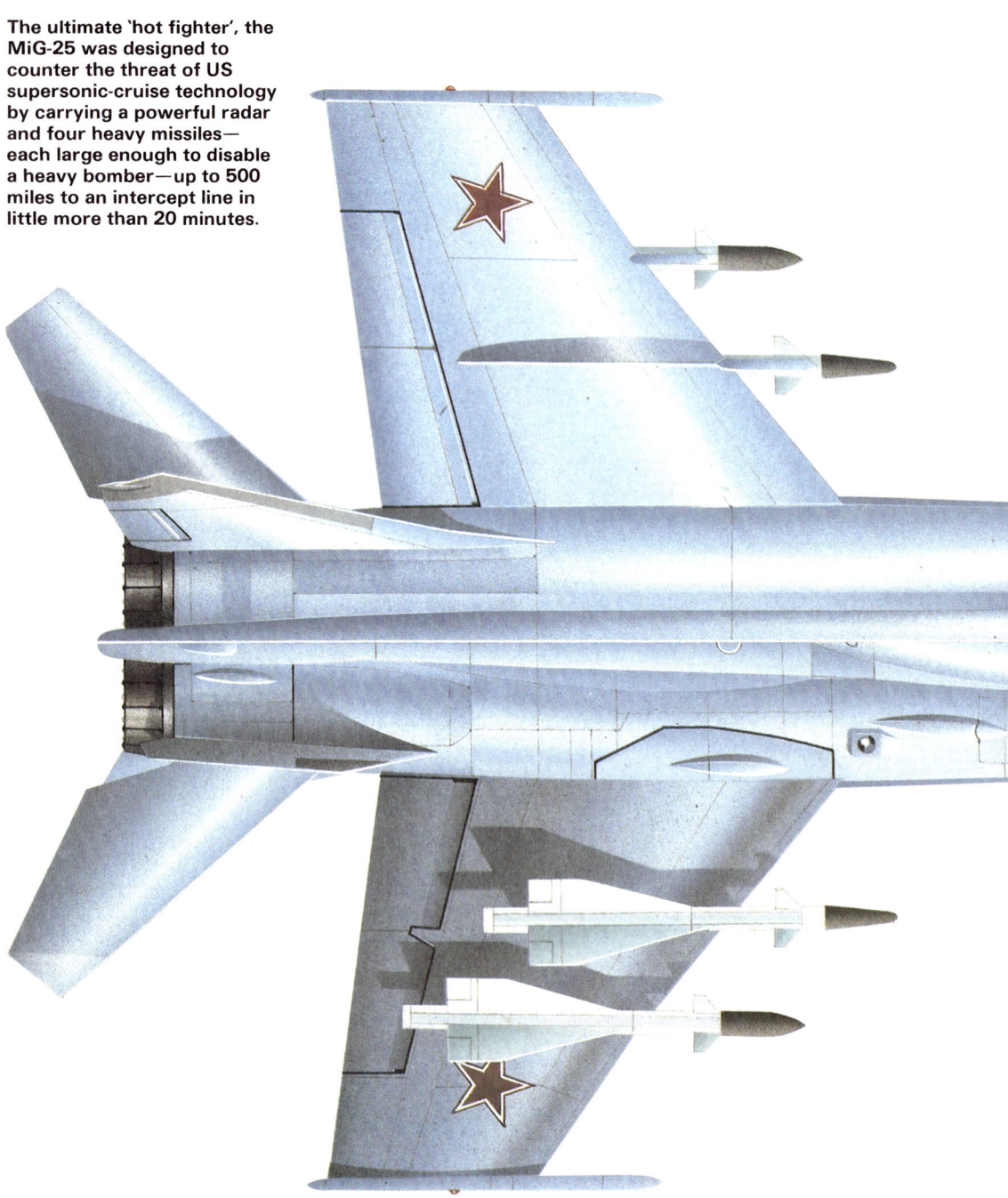

The wing of the MiG-25 is set well aft compared with those of slower aircraft. At high speeds, the necessary trim download on the tailplane is reduced by lift from the intakes; in low-speed air combat, the MiG-25 would be virtually useless.

In front view, the MiG-25 consists of a slim fuselage flanked by vast inlet ducts for the supersonic-dash-optimised Tumansky engines. Development of the inlet system was one of the more remarkable achievements in the design of the aircraft.

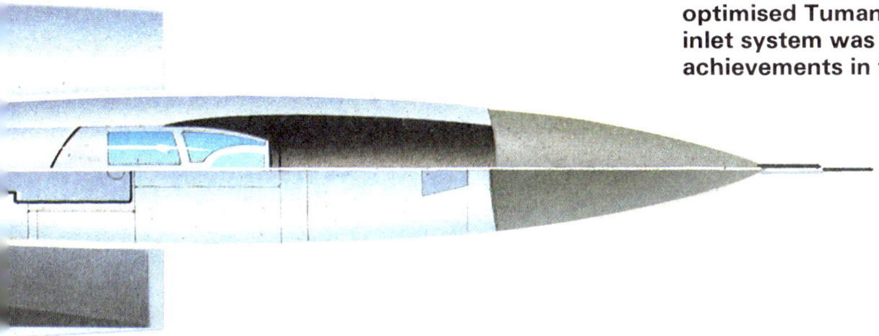

Specification

Type: interceptor and reconnaissance aircraft

Powerplant: two 27,000-lb (12250-kg) Tumansky R-31 afterburning turbojets

Performance: maximum speed (clean) Mach 3.0, equivalent to just under 2,000 mph (3200 km/h) at medium and high altitudes; maximum speed with external stores Mach 2.8; maximum sustained altitude 75,000 ft (23000 m); typical intercept radius 460 miles (740 km); range at Mach 3 900 miles (1500 km); initial climb rate 30,000 ft (9000 m) per minute

Weights: empty 44,000 lb (20000 kg); maximum take-off 82,500 lb (37500 kg)

Dimensions: (interceptor) span 46 ft (14 m); length 73 ft 2 in (22.3 m); height 18 ft 6 in (5.64 m); wing area 605 sq ft (56.2 m^2)

Armament: up to four AA-6 'Acrid' air-to-air missiles (two radar and two infra-red) plus optional ventral gunpack probably containing GSh-23 cannon

Operators: Algeria, Libya, Syria, USSR

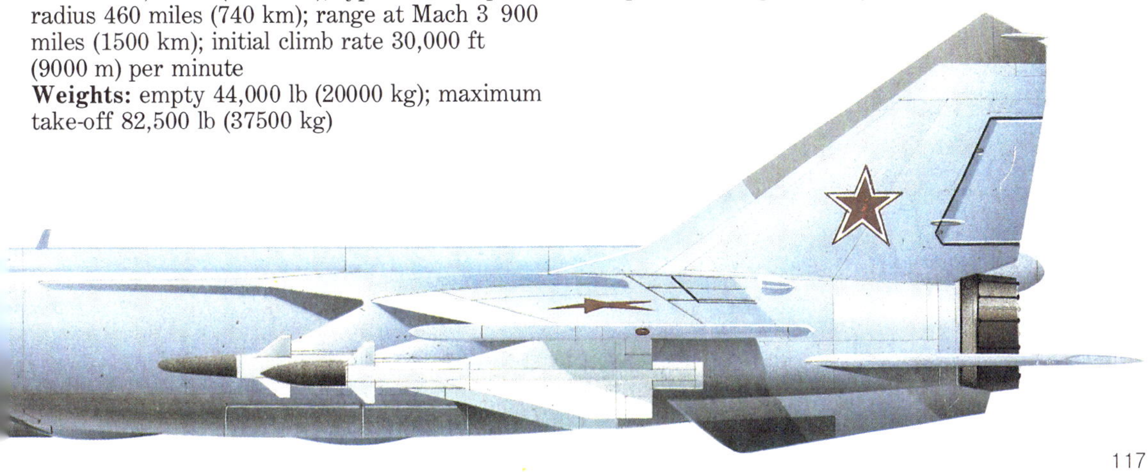

Mikoyan-Gurevich MiG-27 Flogger-D, F

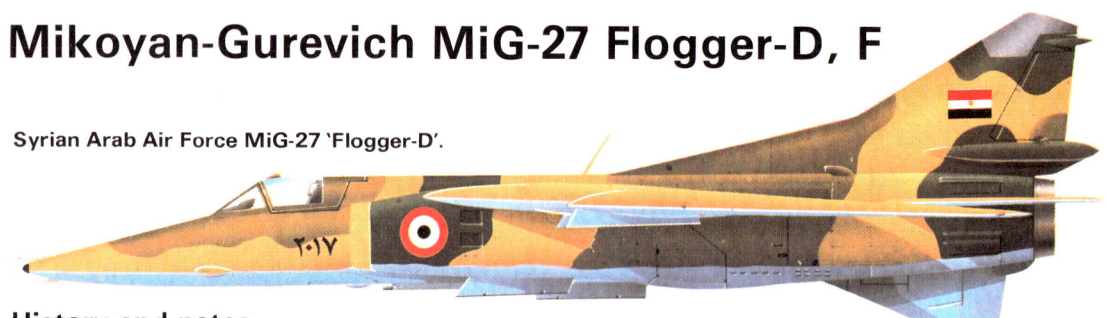

Syrian Arab Air Force MiG-27 'Flogger-D'.

History and notes

With the increasing optimization of the Mikoyan-Gurevich MiG-23 for the air-to-air role, it became increasingly attractive to develop a specialized version of the type for strike duties rather than employing the type as a multi-role aircraft as had been intended. This was the rationale behind the MiG-27, known to NATO as the 'Flogger-D', which presumably flew in 1972-73 (development having been initiated once the MiG-23 was reasonably well settled in service) and entered service with the Soviet Union's 16th Air Army in East Germany in 1975.

The main difference between the MiG-23 and the MiG-27 lies in the forward fuselage. The MiG-27 dispenses with the nose radar and has a slimmer nose giving a much better downward view. The nose cap houses a simple ranging radar; aft of this is a small window for a laser ranger, a radome which may cover a terrain-avoidance radar, and a Doppler aerial. Several other aerials appear on the leading edge of the wing gloves and on either side of the forward fuselage.

In order to save weight the variable inlets of the MiG-23 are dropped in favour of simple fixed structures; the medium-altitude high-speed performance thus sacrificed is not needed by the MiG-27 in any case. The secondary power nozzle of the engine is also simplified, probably to balance the weight saved in the forward fuselage. Weapon pylons are installed beneath the inlet ducts, rather than on the fuselage underside as on the MiG-23. The quoted weapon load is small by comparison with smaller Western aircraft, but represents an operating standard rather than the all-out "Christmas-tree" figure used in Western brochures. The twin-barrel GSh-23 gives way to a much harder-hitting six-barrel weapon, probably of 23-mm calibre although some reports claim that it is a 30-mm gun. The mainwheel tyres are fatter, to cope with greater weights, and the type can be fitted with auxiliary RATO (rocket-assisted take-off) units on rear-fuselage racks.

Interestingly, it is the specialised ground-attack version of the MiG-23 that has been chosen for export to the Soviet Union's satellites in Eastern Europe. This export model, the 'Flogger F', has the F-4-style ramp inlets and variable nozzle of the air-defence 'Floggers', which presumably endow it with a considerably higher top speed than the FA's 'Flogger D'; however, this performance is academic because it can only be used for air-to-air combat, for which purpose the export aircraft is quite useless due to its lack of air-intercept (AI) radar. The nose is

Mikoyan-Gurevich MiG-27 'Flogger-D'.

similar to that of the FA strike aircraft, but the export types lack some of the 'domestic' model's antannae and dielectrics. The cannon of the export model is the fighter's twin-barrel GSh-23, while the underfuselage pylons are located under the belly (as on the fighter) rather than under the inlet ducts, probably precluding ASM armament. The export aircraft have RATO attachments. All in all, the 'Flogger F' seems to be less well optimised for the strike role than the 'Flogger D' and although it has been seen in service with Soviet units it is basically a downgraded version. It is probably powered by the R-27.

There is no direct trainer equivalent to the MiG-27, conversion being carried out on MiG-23Us despite the different propulsion systems. Some MiG-23Us have similar aerials to those of the MiG-27, suggesting that they are used for MiG-27 weapons training.

The closest Western equivalent to the MiG-27 is the smaller Jaguar, and like the Western aircraft it is probably intended for the medium-depth strike role rather than close-support duties or interdiction. However, with the aid of jetisonable drop tanks and rocket-assisted take-off, the MiG-27 can threaten a considerable area of Europe from dispersed forward bases in East Germany, being vastly more effective in payload range terms than its predecessors.

Weapons developed for the MiG-27 include cluster and fuel-air munitions as well as laser-guided and electro-optical 'smart' glide bombs. It is the first Soviet type to be seen with multiple stores racks: tandem racks can be fitted to both centreline and wing stations. The number of aerials on the airframe bear witness to an extensive internal ECM suite, augmented by external pods.

Mikoyan-Gurevich MiG-27 Flogger-D, F

Apparent in this view of four MiG-27 'Flogger-D' strike aircraft are launching shoes for air-to-surface missiles, attached beneath the standard glove and belly pylons. They probably carry the missile known to Nato as AS-7 'Kerry' which is associated with the devices on the wing leading edge above the pylons.

Mikoyan-Gurevich MiG-27 Flogger-D, F

The Mikoyan-Gurevich MiG-27 'Flogger-D' represents a remarkable rework of the basic MiG-23 to optimise it for the strike role. However, high commonality has been maintained and the aircraft have basically similar structures. This view shows the range of wing sweep from 16° to 72°, the saw-toothed leading-edge and relatively simple high-lift devices.

The new front fuselage and redesigned windscreen give the MiG-27 pilot a better view than is available from the MiG-23MS with its bulky nose radar. The under-fuselage stores pylons are situated under the inlet ducts to give clearance for air-to-surface missiles as well as free-fall bombs.

Specification

Type: tactical attack fighter
Powerplant: one 25,350-lb (11500-kg) Tumansky R-29B afterburning turbofan
Performance: maximum speed 1,050 mph (1700 km/h) or Mach 1.6 at 36,000 ft (11000 m); maximum speed (clean) at sea level 840 mph (1350 km/h) or Mach 1.1; service ceiling 55,000 ft (17000 m); ferrry range 1,750 miles (2800 km); combat radius 575 miles (930 km)
Weights: empty 24,000 lb (11000 kg); internal fuel 10,100 lb (4600 kg); normal take-off 39,500 lb (18000 kg); overload take-off 44,300 lb (20100 kg)
Dimensions: span (spread) 46 ft 9 in (14.25 m); span (swept) 27 ft 2 in (8.3 m); length 58 ft (17.7 m); height 14 ft 4 in (4.35 m); wing area 400 sq ft (37.2 m²)
Armament: one six-barrel rotary cannon, two multiple weapon points under each inlet duct and two multiple racks under gloves for maximum external weapon load estimated at 6,600 lb (3000 kg), including air-to-surface missiles.
Operators: (MiG-27) Cuba, Egypt, Iraq, Syria, USSR

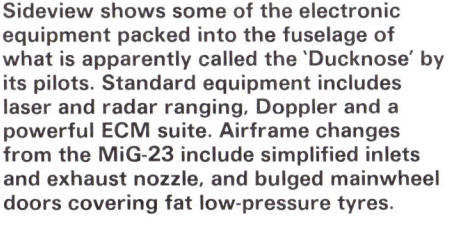

Sideview shows some of the electronic equipment packed into the fuselage of what is apparently called the 'Ducknose' by its pilots. Standard equipment includes laser and radar ranging, Doppler and a powerful ECM suite. Airframe changes from the MiG-23 include simplified inlets and exhaust nozzle, and bulged mainwheel doors covering fat low-pressure tyres.

Mil Mi-1 Hare

History and notes

By 1947 it had become clear to the Soviet leadership that helicopters would be necessary for many military and civil tasks, and a specification for a three-seat general-purpose helicopter was issued. One of three design bureaux asked to produce helicopter designs was that of Mikhail I. Mil, whose last previous design had been the A-15 autogiro of 1938. The first prototype, designated GM-1, flew in autumn 1948 and was the first Soviet production helicopter of the classic single-rotor layout. It was selected for production rather than the twin-rotor Bratukhin competitor and single-rotor Yakovlev Yak-100, and the Russian air force demonstrated the type for the first time in 1951 as the Mi-1 'Hare'.

Float-equipped (Mi-1P) and trainer (Mi-1U) versions of the basic versions were produced in quantity, in addition to Russian air force and navy co-operation and liaison aircraft. The overhaul life of critical components such as the transmission and rotor head was substantially improved during the production run, from 100 hours in 1951, to 500-600 hours in 1956, and to 1,000 hours in 1960.

The Mi-1 also started the record-breaking tradition which has typified Soviet helicopter development, setting up a variety of class records in the late 1950s. Long-distance records of up to 760 miles (1224 km) were set, as well as a speed of 87 mph (141.2 km/h) on a 621-mile (1000 km) closed circuit.

Production of the Mi-1 in the Soviet Union tailed off in 1956-58, being gradually transferred to the Polish state aircraft factory, WSK-Swidnik. Both the airframe and engine were licence-built in Poland, WSK-manufactured aircraft being designated SM-1. About 150 SM-1s were delivered to the Soviet Union, and manufacture of the type paved the way for Polish production of the later Mi-2.

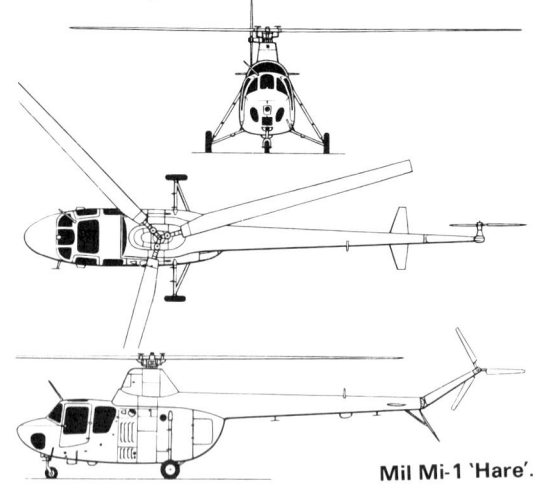

Mil Mi-1 'Hare'.

Specification

Type: utility and training helicopter
Powerplant: one 575-hp (429-kW) Ivchenko AI-26V seven-cylinder radial piston engine
Performance: maximum speed 125 mph (205 km/h); cruising speed 85 mph (140 km/h); range 370 miles (590 km); hovering ceiling 6,500 ft (2000 m)
Weights: empty 3,900 lb (1760 kg); normal loaded 5,300 lb (2400 kg); maximum loaded 5,650 lb (2550 kg)
Dimensions: main rotor diameter 47 ft 1 in (14.346 m); fuselage length 39 ft 4½ in (12.0 m); height 10 ft 10 in (3.3 m); main rotor disc area 1,739 sq ft (161.56 m²)
Operators: Albania, Bulgaria, China, Cuba, Czechoslovakia, East Germany, Finland, Iraq, Romania, Syria, USSR

The Mil Mi-1 is one of the older Soviet types that remain in service with allied forces.

Mil (PZL) Mi-2 Hoplite

History and notes

The Mi-2 'Hoplite' was developed in the early 1960s by the Mil bureau as a straightforward turbine-powered version of the Mi-1, the availability of the shaft-turbine engine having revolutionised the design of the helicopter. The twin turbines develop 40% more power than the Mi-1's piston engine for barely half the dry weight, more than doubling the payload. The fuselage of the Mi-2 is completely different from that of its progenitor, carrying the engines above the cabin. Although some of the points of commonality between the Mi-1 and the Mi-2 were eliminated during development, the overall dimensions of the two types remain closely similar.

The Mi-2 was flown in 1962, but never put into production in the Soviet Union. Instead responsibility for the type was assigned to WSK-Swidnik now (PZL) in Poland as part of a Comecon rationalization programme, becoming the only Soviet-designed helicopter to be built solely outside the Soviet Union. Production in Poland started in 1965, and continues with more than 3,000 delivered.

The Mi-2 is now the standard training helicopter of the Soviet Union, and has also been seen armed with anti-tank guided weapons. Its role, however, may be as a weapons trainer rather than an attack helicopter, as its slow speed and relatively old-technology rotor system (which limits its manoeuvrability for low-level 'nap-of-the-earth' flying) would render it vulnerable to defences. It is therefore more likely that pilots and weapon operators learn their skills on the Mi-2 before proceeding to the Mi-24 'Hind'.

PZL has developed a slightly enlarged version of the Mi-2, designated Mi-2M, but this 10-seat aircraft appears to be aimed mainly at the civil market. A reported version with a lighter skid landing gear (the only use of such a feature on a recent Warsaw Pact helicopter) has not been proceeded with, but efforts are being made to sell a US-engined version of the Mi-2, the PZL Taurus, in the United States. PZL has

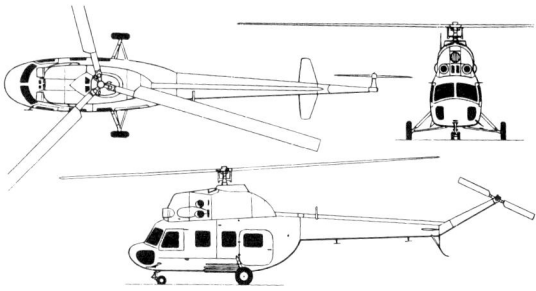

Mil Mi-2 'Hoplite'.

also developed a larger helicopter called the Sokol (Falcon) with technical assistance from Mil. It has similiar engines to the Ka-25.

Specification

Type: eight-passenger transport attack and training helicopter
Powerplant: two 400-shp (298-kW) Isotov GTD-350 turboshafts
Performance: maximum speed at sea level 130 mph (210 km/h); cruising speed 125 mph (205 km/h); maximum range 370 miles (590 km); range with eight passengers 150 miles (240 km); service ceiling 13,100 ft (4000 m)
Weights: empty 5,255 lb (2384 kg); maximum slung load 1,750 lb (800 kg); maximum take-off 8,160 lb (3700 kg)
Dimensions: main rotor diameter 47 ft 7 in (14.5 m); fuselage length 39 ft 2 in (11.94 m); height 12 ft 3½ in (3.75 m); main rotor disc area 1,727.6 sq ft (160.5 m²)
Armament: up to four AT-3 'Sagger' (possibly AT-5) anti-tank guided weapons or a combination of rocket pods and gun pods
Operators: Bulgaria, Czechoslovakia, Egypt, Hungary, Iraq, Jugoslavia, Poland, Romania, USSR

All production Mi-2s have been built in Poland, which is a major operator of the type.

Mil Mi-4 Hound

History and notes

Developed to flight-test status in only seven months following a personal edict from Stalin, the Mil Mi-4 'Hound' was at first considered to be a Soviet copy of the Sikorsky S-55 until it was realised that it was considerably larger than the later S-58. It was thus the first of a long line of large Mil helicopters.

The first prototype Mi-4 was completed in April 1952. It shared the basic layout of the S-55, with the powerful radial engine in the nose and quadricycle landing gear, but added a pair of clamshell loading doors capable of admitting a small military vehicle or most light infantry weapons such as anti-tank guns. It was thus a far more capable military transport than its Western contemporaries, and several thousand of the type were built.

The Mi-4 entered service in 1953. Early production aircraft had wooden-skinned rotor blades of very short life, but later aircraft had all-metal blades. Special versions include an amphibious development tested in 1959. The Mi-4V was developed for high-altitude operations with a two-stage supercharger fitted to the ASh-82FN engine and became a standard production version. The Mi-4 was also put into production at the Shenyang plant in China, as the Whirlwind-25 or H-5. One of these aircraft has been fitted with a Pratt & Whitney Canada PT6T-3 Twinpac engine.

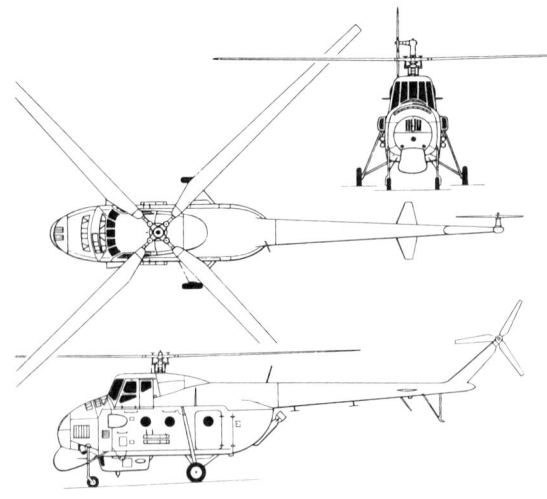

Mil Mi-4MA 'Hound-B'.

The Mi-4 has been one of the most important helicopters in service with the Soviet armed forces. At the 1956 Tushino air display, a formation of 36 Mi-4s demonstrated their ability to land a sizeable and well-equipped infantry force; later, the type became the Soviet Union's first armed helicopter,

The Mil Mi-4, seen here in service with the Czechoslovak air arm (CL), was one of the world's largest transport helicopters at the time of its entry into service.

Mil Mi-4 Hound

Larger than its Western contemporaries, the Mi-4 was one of the few contemporary helicopters to feature a rear-loading door. This example is in the Finnish Air Force service.

with a machine-gun in the nose of the navigator's gondola and rocket pods on outriggers from the fuselage. This version was introduced as an interim armed helicopter with the expansion of the Soviet tactical air forces in the late 1960s. More recently, Mi-4s have been equipped with prominent aerials for communications jamming equipment. This version is known to Nato as 'Hound-C'.

With the rise of the Soviet navy, the Mi-4 found another new role: a number of the type were fitted with search radar beneath the nose and used as anti-submarine warfare aircraft in the Black Sea and Baltic areas. Other ASW equipment includes a magnetic anomaly detector (MAD) installed in a 'bird' towed behind the helicopter, and the type presumably also carries dunking sonar. The Mi-4 ASW variant paved the way for the later introduction of the Mi-14 'Haze'.

Specification

Type: 12-seat transport and anti-submarine warfare helicopter

Powerplant: one 1,700-hp (1268-kW) Shvetsov ASh-82V two-row radial piston engine

Performance: maximum speed 130 mph (210 km/h) at 5,000 ft (1500 m); cruising speed 100 mph (160 km/h); normal range 370 miles (590 km); ceiling 19,700 ft (6000 m); hovering ceiling 6,500 ft (2000 m)

Weights: empty 11,800 lb (5356 kg); maximum internal payload 3,840 lb (1740 kg); maximum take-off 17,200 lb (7800 kg)

Dimensions: main rotor diameter 68 ft 11 in (21.0 m); fuselage length 55 ft 1 in (16.79 m); height 14 ft 5¼ in (4.4 m); main rotor disc area 3,724 sq ft (346 m²)

Armament: 7.62-mm machine-gun in ventral gondola, and rocket or gun pods; (ASW) depth charges or torpedoes

Operators: Afghanistan, Albania, Algeria, Bulgaria, China, Cuba, Czechoslovakia, East Germany, Egypt, Finland, Hungary, India, Iraq, Mali, Mongolia, North Korea, Poland, Romania, Somalia, Syria, USSR (AF and Navy), Vietnam, Yemen

Mil Mi-6 Hook/Mi-10 Harke

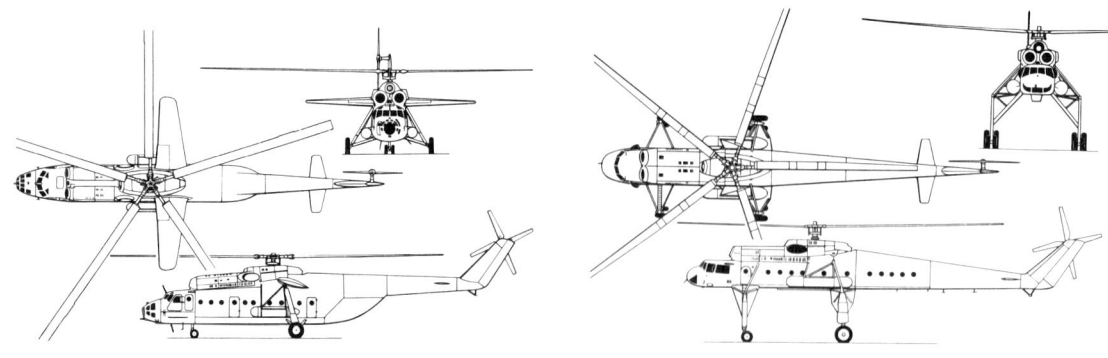

Mil Mi-6 'Hook'.

Mil Mi-10 'Harke'.

Mil Mi-6 Hook/Mi-10 Harke

History and notes

When the first of five prototypes of the Mil Mi-6 'Hook' was flown in September 1957, it was by far the largest helicopter in the world; what is more surprising is that with one exception (the same design bureau's abortive Mi-12) it has retained that distinction up to the appearance of its 1980s descendant, the Mil 'Halo' (see introduction).

The Mi-6 was the result of a joint military and civil requirement for a massive helicopter that would not only bring a new dimension to mobile warfare, with the ability to transport light armoured vehicles, but would also help in the exploitation of previously uncharted areas of the Soviet Union. Thus the requirement was not only demanding in terms of payload, calling for a disposable load half as great again as

the fully loaded weight of the Mi-4, but also in terms of range.

The requirement was met by the first use of turbine power in a Soviet helicopter, and also by the provision of variable-incidence wings, first fitted in 1960 to the 30 pre-series aircraft, which carry 20% of the weight of the aircraft in cruising flight. Unusually the Mi-6 can make a rolling take-off at a weight greater than that at which it can take-off vertically. The engineering problems were formidable — the R-7 gearbox and rotor head alone weigh 7,055 lb (3200 kg), more than both the engines.

Like the Mi-4, the Mi-6 has clamshell doors at the rear of the cabin and can accommodate small armoured vehicles. Even larger loads can be lifted by the specialized flying-crane derivative of the Mi-6, the Mi-10 'Harke'; this features a much shallower fuselage than the Mi-6, and in its initial version is fitted with a vast quadricycle landing gear which allows it to straddle and lift loads as large as a motor-coach or a prefabricated building. The later Mi-10K has a shorter, lighter landing gear and rear-facing gondola beneath the nose for a crewman to direct lifting operations.

The Mi-6 and Mi-10 are not as widely used as the Mi-8 by the Soviet armed forces, possibly because such large helicopters are vulnerable in combat. However, they were used to carry heavy weapons in support of Soviet-backed forces in Africa in 1978.

Specification

Type: heavy transport helicopter and (Mi-10) crane helicopter (specification Mi-6)
Powerplant: two 5,500-shp (4103-kW) Soloviev D-25V turboshafts
Performance: maximum speed 186 mph (300 km/h); crusing speed 155 mph (250 km/h); range with 26,500-lb (12000-kg) payload 125 miles (200 km); range with 8,800-lb (4000-kg) payload 620 miles (1000 km); service ceiling at maximum gross weight 14,500 ft (4400 m); hovering ceiling 8,200 ft (2500 m)
Weights: empty 60,050 lb (27240 kg); maximum internal payload 26,500 lb (12000 kg); normal take-off 89,300 lb (40500 kg); maximum vertical take-off 93,700 lb (42500 kg)
Dimensions: main rotor diameter 114 ft 10 in (350 m); fuselage length 108 ft 10¼ in (33.18 m); wing span 50 ft 2½ in (15.3 m) height on ground 30 ft 1 in (9.16 m); main rotor disc area 10,356.8 sq ft (962 m²)
Armament: in tactical role, one machine-gun in nose compartment
Operators: Algeria, Bulgaria, Egypt, Ethiopia, Iraq, Libya, Peru, Syria, USSR, Vietnam

An antediluvian monster among helicopters, the Mi-6 has retained its title of the world's largest practical helicopter for nearly a quarter-century.

Mil Mi-6 Hook/Mi-10 Harke

A feature of the Mi-6 is the vast size of the rotor and power train compared to the cabin, visual evidence of the fact that the giant is relatively inefficient. Given that the design is 25 years old, however, it was a feat on the part of the designers to make it fly at all. This aircraft is one of five supplied to the Fuerza Aerea del Peru in 1978.

Mil Mi-8 Hip

History and notes

The Mil Mi-8 'Hip' relates to the earlier, piston-engined Mi-4 'Hound' as the Mi-2 'Hoplite' relates to the Mi-1 'Hare'. As in the case of the smaller helicopter, development started as a turbine-powered adaptation of the original design and proceeded to a point where there was little if any commonality between the new helicopter and its predecessor.

The first prototype of the Mi-8 was flown in 1961, with the four-blade rotor of the Mi-4 and a single Soloviev turboshaft of 2,700-shp (2014-kW). In 1962, however, the second prototype flew with the production standard twin-engine installation, and in 1964 a five-blade rotor was added. It was this version which went into production as the standard Warsaw Pact medium transport helicopter in about 1967.

The Mi-8 is widely used by the Soviet air force and other Warsaw Pact forces, apparently by the tactical units rather than by the VTA military transport force. It is broadly comparable with the land-based transport versions of the Sikorsky S-61 family, although there is so far no evidence that the type is used in the long-range rescue role as are the US Air Force's HH-3s. Its usefulness in military service is increased by its rear-loading doors, which allow the full width of the cabin to be used for bulky or awkward loads. The Mi-8 can, for instance, accommodate small military vehicles or infantry weapons such as anti-tank guns. Another standard feature is a four-axis (roll, pitch, yaw and altitude) autopilot.

The data apply to the basic Mi-8T utility version, which has been offered for export for civil operators in the West. Defects of the civil design, which must add to the type's vulnerability in combat, include a fuel system which could be rendered inoperative by a single leak. However, it was reported in 1978 that an improved version of the Mi-8 was under development. About 6,000 of the basic version had been built by 1980.

Most military Mi-8s in Warsaw Pact service are armed, usually carying two weapon pylons on outriggers on each side of the fuselage. These are generally used for carrying rocket pods. Machine-guns do not seem to be permanently installed on the Mi-8, but it is reported that Soviet airborne troops are trained to fire their own small-arms from pivoted mountings in the windows. The current standard version is Hip E, with attachments for up to six rocket pods, surmounted by four launchers for AT-2 Swatter anti-tank guided weapons. The export Hip F carries six AT-3 Sagger ATGWs. Some Mi-8s also feature an oblong housing under the tailboom; it is possible that this is the electrical battery, moved aft for centre-of-gravity considerations, rather than a doppler radar as reported elsewhere. Later versions of the helicopter may use the 2,200-shp (1640-kW) TV-3 engine.

The Mi-8's armament is presumably intended for self-defence in the form of fire suppression during

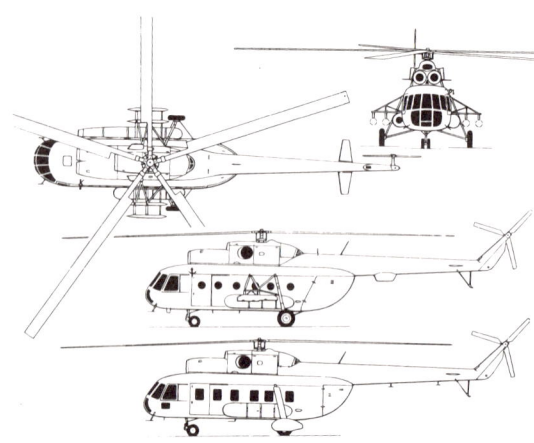

Mil Mi-8 'Hip' and (lower side-view) civilian Mi-8P.

landings in hostile territory. The type is too large for aggressive use in combat, its size and conventional rotor system making it less manoeuvrable than a specialized attack helicopter. However, a salvo of unguided rockets may prove effective in keeping the defenders' heads down while the helicopters land and unload their cargoes, by far the most dangerous point of a mission.

A specialized role in which the Mi-8 has been seen is minesweeping, a number of aircraft of this type having been ferried to Egypt in 1974 to assist in the clearing of the Suez Canal. It is not known whether this was an entirely *ad hoc* operation, or whether the Mi-8, rather than its amphibious relative the Mi-14 'Haze', is the Soviet navy's standard minesweeping helicopter. The Mi-8, however, does not appear to be operable at sea, the aircraft used in the Egyptian operation being carried shrouded on the deck of a helicopter carrier. More recently, the type has been reported as an overland mine-layer.

Development of the Mi-8 started as a simple turbine-powered aircraft using the Mi-4 rotor system. However, evolution has eliminated any resemblance between the two aircraft.

Mil Mi-8 Hip

Finland uses half-a-dozen of the standard commercial export Mi-8P passenger helicopter for military transport duties. The Ilmavoimat engineers have added weather radar, which the Soviet aircraft lack.

Specification

Type: twin-engined medium transport helicopter
Powerplant: two 1,500-shp (1119-kW) Isotov TV-2-1117A turboshafts
Performance: maximum speed 145 mph (230 km/h); cruising speed 125 mph (200 km/h); range with 6,500-lb (3000-kg) payload 265 mph (425 km); hovering ceiling 14,765 ft (4500 m)
Weights: empty 15,780 lb (7420 kg); maximum payload 8,800 lb (4000 kg); maximum take-off (VTO) 26,500 lb (12000 kg)

Dimensions: main rotor diameter 69 ft 10¼ in (21.29 m); fuselage length 60 ft 1 in (18.31 m); height 18 ft 4½ in (5.6 m); main rotor disc area 3,828 sq ft (355 m²)
Armament: normally, up to four 16×57-mm rocket pods on fuselage pylons
Operators: Afghanistan, Bangladesh, Czechoslovakia, East Germany, Egypt, Ethiopia, Finland, Hungary, Iraq, North Korea, Libya, Pakistan, Peru, Poland, Romania, Somalia, South Yemen, Syria, USSR, Vietnam, Yugoslavia

Egypt's 70 Mi-8s are being supplemented by Anglo-American Westland Commandos.

Mil Mi-14 Haze

History and notes

It is not surprising that the Soviet Navy's land-based anti-submarine warfare (ASW) helicopter, the Mil Mi-14 'Haze' should be derived from the Mi-8 'Hip'; what is surprising, however, is that its development should have taken so long to come about. Once the requirement was formulated, the evolution of the type was fairly rapid; the prototype, designated V-14, was reported to be flying in 1973, and the operational version was seen in service in 1977. It is steadily replacing such aircraft as the ASW version of the Mi-4 'Hound' (possibly designated Mi-4MA), while the Kamov Ka-25 'Hormone' will probably continue to be the Soviet navy's standard shipboard helicopter.

The powerplant, rotor system and much of the airframe of the Mi-14 appear closely similar to those of the Mi-8, the structural difference between the two types being confined mainly being found in the lower part of the fuselage. The Mi-14 has a flying-boat-type bow, a watertight hull, and rear-set sponsons carrying stabilising floats. Unlike that of its land-based progenitor, the undercarriage of the Mi-14 is retractable. The Mi-14 is clearly capable of water landings, although like the closely comparable Sikorsky SH-3 series it may be designed for water landings only in an emergency. This is also suggested by the location of the search radar under the nose; repeated immersion in salt water is hardly calculated to extend the life of electronic equipment, while the radome would not improve stability on the water. The tail bumper of the Mi-8 is retained, and carries a small pontoon to prevent the tail rotor from

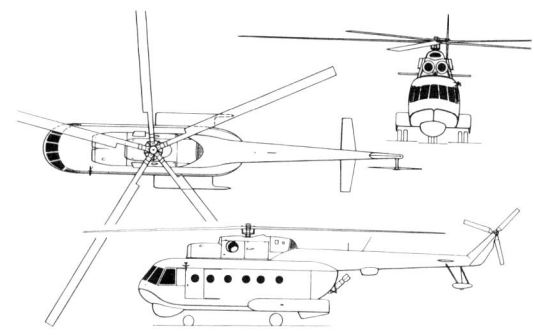

Mil Mi-14 'Haze'.

striking the water. The sponsons presumably contain fuel, supplanting the side-mounted tanks of the land-based aircraft.

Externally visible operational equipment includes the search radar beneath the nose and a magnetic anomaly detector "bird" carried on the rear of the pod. The "bird" is towed on a long cable when in use, well away from the magnetic disturbances produced by the airframe of the helicopter. It is likely

Apparently a fairly simple derivative of the Mi-8, the Mi-14 antisubmarine warfare helicopter is in the same class as the Western Sikorsky SH-3/Westland Sea King. The radar could well be identical to that of the Kamov Ka-25.

Mil Mi-14 Haze

Mil Mi-14 'Haze' of the AVMF (Soviet Naval Aviation).

that, like the SH-3, the Mi-14 carries a "dunking sonar" in the fuselage, and that the helicopter can lower this into the water while hovering. Weapons can presumably be carried on the lower fuselage sides forward of the sponsons, close to the centre of gravity.

The effectiveness of the Mi-14 is difficult to assess, depending as it does on the quality of its sensors and the data-processing equipment installed. It is likely that the systems are similar to those of the Ka-25, with the addition of extra processes, displays and crew positions, and that both aircraft will be steadily updated and improved in service. The main advantage of the larger helicopter over the Ka-25 is its greater range, and its ability to strike targets without the assistance of a surface vessel.

Specification

Type: Amphibious (?) anti-submarine warfare (ASW) helicopter. Powerplant, weights, performance and dimensions not known, but generally assumed to be similar to Mi-8
Armament: Offensive stores almost certainly include mines, depth charges and homing torpedoes
Operator: Soviet Navy

Despite the boat hull of the Mi-14, it is probably not designed for routine operations from water. Like similar Western aircraft, it is probably able to land on water in an emergency.

Mil Mi-24 Hind

History and notes

One of the most significant developments in the Soviet Union's tactical air power recently has been the development of a powerful force of heavily armed helicopters. The Mil Mi-24 'Hind' is a large and intimidating armed helicopter, and has been a cause for controversy and a source of puzzlement in the West since it was first observed in 1973. At first it was thought to be a straightforward armed version of the Mi-8, but it soon became clear that the new helicopter was rather smaller than its predecessor, although apparently using the same engines. The early 'Hind-A' appeared to be a conventional squad-carrying helicopter, with the addition of rocket pods and missile rails. This sort of combination had been experimentally used by the US Army in Vietnam, but had led to the development of specialized armed helicopters with automatic turreted armament and small silhouette, designed to escort the troop carriers, while other helicopters armed with guided weapons took on the enemy armour. The 'Hind-A', however, appeared to combine all three elements into one unwieldy package: a troop carrier with guns for self-defence, but equipped with rockets for

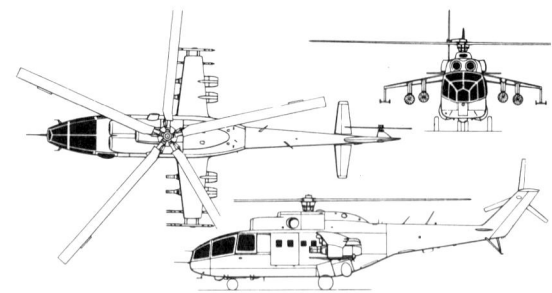

Mil Mi-24 'Hind-A'.

defence suppression and anti-tank missiles for attacking enemy armour.

The conundrum of how the Mi-24 was to be used became even more perplexing with the arrival in 1975 of the 'Hind-D', adding to the earlier versions' armament a highly complex nose gun installation. The 'Hind-D' and the similar 'Hind-E' and 'Hind-F,' also feature a more heavily protected cockpit, considerably less spacious than that of its predecessor.

'Hind-A' was the original service version of the Mi-24, with lighter gun armament and less all-weather capability than later versions.

Mil Mi-24 Hind

'Hind-D' introduced a completely new forward fuselage with gunner and pilot in tandem under blown canopies, a turret-mounted gun and an array of sensors. 'Hind-F' is similar but carries the AT-6 missile.

One fear was that the gun armament is intended for use against NATO's own anti-tank helicopters in Western Europe. By early 1980 it had been estimated that more than 1,000 'Hinds' were in service, both 'Hind-A' and '-C' and later variants being in volume production at a total rate of 30 units a month. The 'Hind-C' lacks provision for anti-tank guided weapons, while the 'Hind-B' was an early variant which does not appear to have entered service.

The Mi-24 seems to combine the powerplant and transmission of the Mi-8 with a smaller rotor and airframe, retaining the fan-cooled transmission characteristic of large Mil turbine helicopters. The cabin is considerably smaller than that of the 28-seater Mi-8, but should be able to accommodate a 12-man infantry section without difficulty, off-loading them via a large side door forward of the anhedralled stub wings. The latter carry missiles on downward tip extensions, presumably to allow easy reloading from ground level while carrying the wing spar above the cabin. The rough-field landing gear is retractable.

The forward fuselage of the 'Hind-A' comprises a spacious 'greenhouse' canopy for the crew of three. Access to the flight-deck is via two large sliding windows, which can be opened in flight and may be used for defensive machine-guns. Visible avionic equipment includes a small blister under the forward fuselage (probably a missile sight) and an electro-

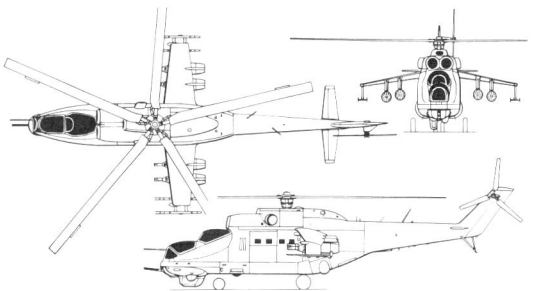

Mil Mi-24 'Hind-D'.

optical head on the left inner pylon.

The 'Hind-D' forward fuselage features two tandem blown canopies on separate cockpits, reducing the chance of both crewmen being disabled with one hit. The windscreens are made of flat armour glass. In the extreme nose is a turret mounting a four-barrel gun; early models carried a 12.7-mm weapon, but a 23-mm cannon is fitted to current aircraft. Aft of the turret are two installations: a blister very similar to that under the nose of the 'Hind-A' and a larger installation which appears to contain a sensor slaved in elevation to the gun. This may be an assisted gunsight (either infra-red or TV). A large low-airspeed probe juts from the forward (gunner's) windscreen.

Now entering service on a version of the helicopter

Mil Mi-24 Hind

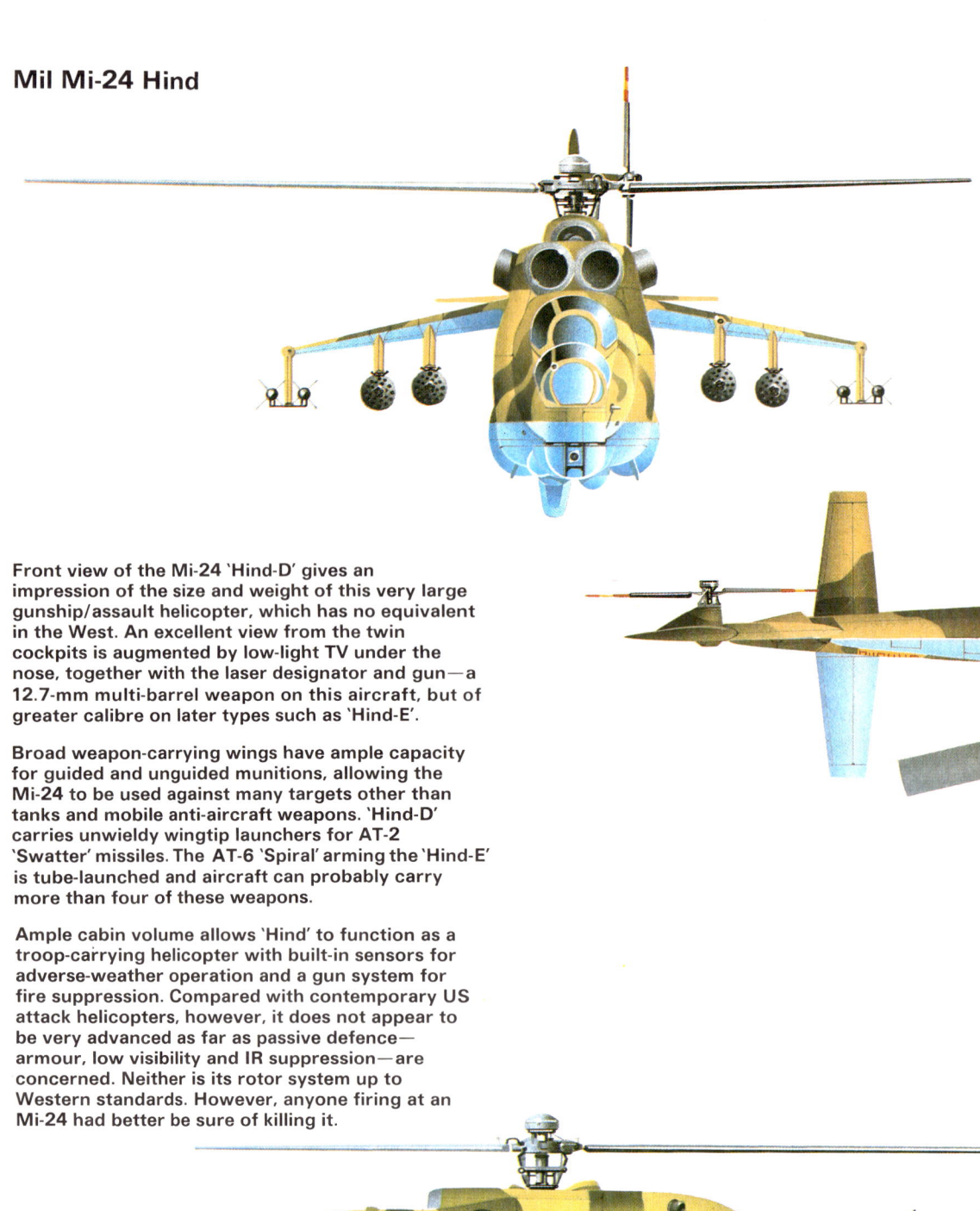

Front view of the Mi-24 'Hind-D' gives an impression of the size and weight of this very large gunship/assault helicopter, which has no equivalent in the West. An excellent view from the twin cockpits is augmented by low-light TV under the nose, together with the laser designator and gun—a 12.7-mm multi-barrel weapon on this aircraft, but of greater calibre on later types such as 'Hind-E'.

Broad weapon-carrying wings have ample capacity for guided and unguided munitions, allowing the Mi-24 to be used against many targets other than tanks and mobile anti-aircraft weapons. 'Hind-D' carries unwieldy wingtip launchers for AT-2 'Swatter' missiles. The AT-6 'Spiral' arming the 'Hind-E' is tube-launched and aircraft can probably carry more than four of these weapons.

Ample cabin volume allows 'Hind' to function as a troop-carrying helicopter with built-in sensors for adverse-weather operation and a gun system for fire suppression. Compared with contemporary US attack helicopters, however, it does not appear to be very advanced as far as passive defence— armour, low visibility and IR suppression—are concerned. Neither is its rotor system up to Western standards. However, anyone firing at an Mi-24 had better be sure of killing it.

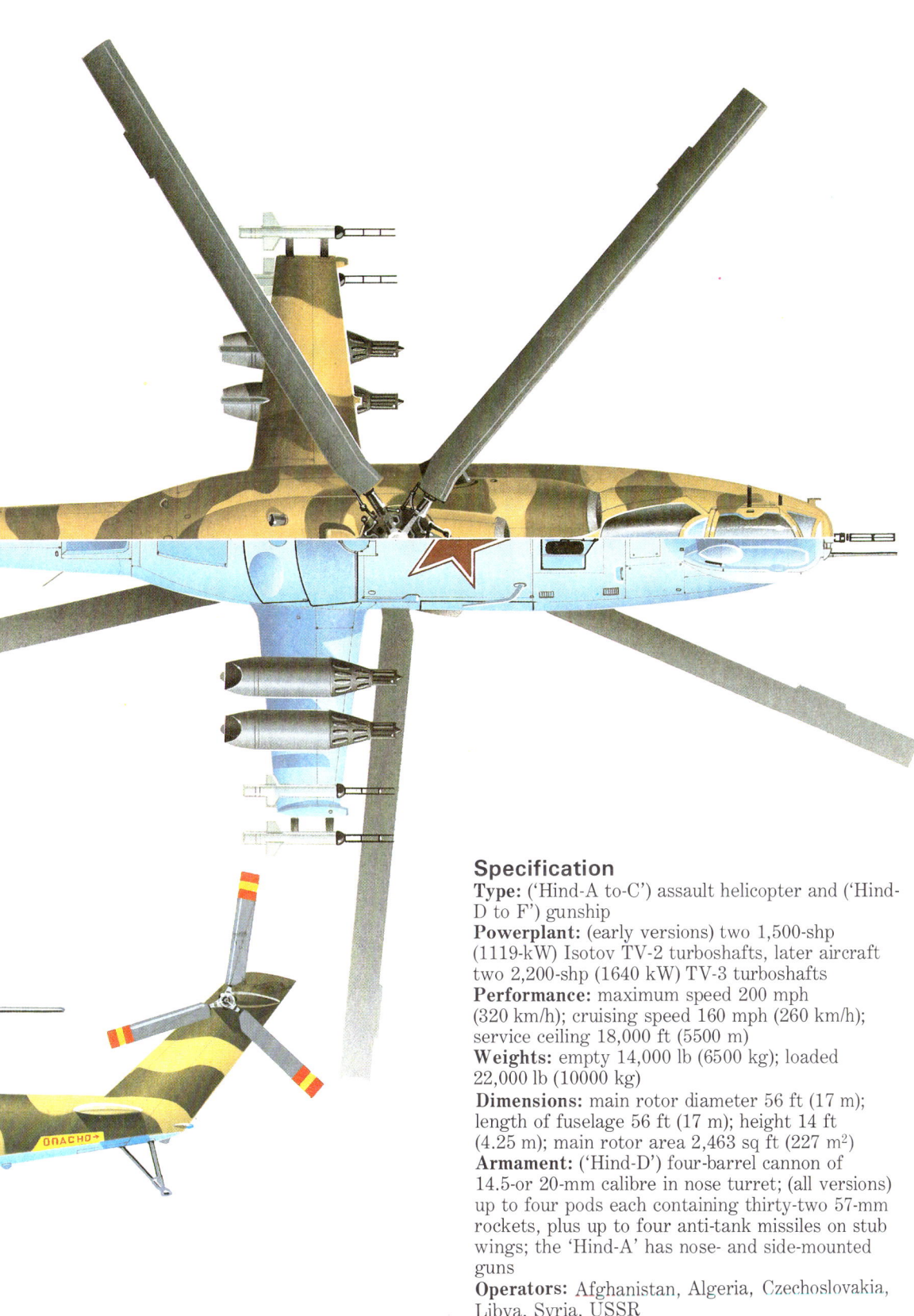

Specification

Type: ('Hind-A to-C') assault helicopter and ('Hind-D to F') gunship

Powerplant: (early versions) two 1,500-shp (1119-kW) Isotov TV-2 turboshafts, later aircraft two 2,200-shp (1640 kW) TV-3 turboshafts

Performance: maximum speed 200 mph (320 km/h); cruising speed 160 mph (260 km/h); service ceiling 18,000 ft (5500 m)

Weights: empty 14,000 lb (6500 kg); loaded 22,000 lb (10000 kg)

Dimensions: main rotor diameter 56 ft (17 m); length of fuselage 56 ft (17 m); height 14 ft (4.25 m); main rotor area 2,463 sq ft (227 m²)

Armament: ('Hind-D') four-barrel cannon of 14.5-or 20-mm calibre in nose turret; (all versions) up to four pods each containing thirty-two 57-mm rockets, plus up to four anti-tank missiles on stub wings; the 'Hind-A' has nose- and side-mounted guns

Operators: Afghanistan, Algeria, Czechoslovakia, Libya, Syria, USSR

Mil Mi-24 Hind

Mi-24 'Hind-D' helicopters of Frontal Aviation. Prominent in this photograph is the curious saucepan-shaped object atop the rotor mast; its purpose is not clear, but it could form a part of an electronic surveillance measures (ESM) system.

identified as 'Hind-E' is a new heavy anti-tank missile designated AT-6 'Spiral' by NATO, possibly weighing as much as 200 lb (90 kg) per round and with a 6-mile (10-km) range. It is likely to be laser-guided, with semi-active seeking, rather than wire/infra red guided like the AT-2 'Swatter' previously carried by 'Hind-D'. It is also believed to be tube-launched, and it is possible that more than four could be carried on one helicopter. Export customers get a downgraded gunship known as 'Hind-E', armed with wire-guided AT-3 'Sagger' missiles.

Performance figures for the Mi-24 are difficult to assess, but records established by Soviet women pilots in a helicopter known as the 'A-10' may give a clue. Given that the Mi-24 has as much power as the larger Mi-8, the performance of the 'A-10' — including top speed of 228.9 mph (368.4 km/h) — is roughly what might be expected. However, its power/weight ratio is considerably less than that of the latest US armed helicopters, and with its relatively old-technology rotor system (similar to that of the Mi-8) the Mi-24 is not likely to be agile. Its

large size compared with the Western ideal of a combat helicopter will also make it vulnerable to hostile fire. A surprising feature of the design, which will adversely affect its survivability, is its complete lack of infra-red signature suppression; the exhausts are open from all aspects. Counter-attack rather than stealth seems to be the key to survivability.

The Mi-24 has been described as a 'helicopter battle-cruiser' and this may not be too bad a summing-up of what the machine does. Its main advantage is its ability to fight in several different ways: by dropping an anti-tank platoon, complete with missiles, while defending itself against ground fire with the nose gun (or in the case of the 'Hind-A', with side guns); by acting as its own escort on troop-carrying flights; by acting as a tank-killer pure and simple, with a vast capacity for even the heaviest reload rounds; or by carrying a squad of troops armed with man-portable surface-to-air missiles. An inevitable corollary of this 'combination of all arms' in a single aircraft, however, is that the vehicle's size and weight rule out evasive flying, and render it difficult to escape alert and well-equipped defences.

Mil/PZL V-3 Sokol

History and notes

Although developed, tested, produced and marketed by PZL in Poland, the Sokol (Falcon) helicopter clearly stems from a design produced by the Mil bureau, and as such is highly interesting because it is the only new civil helicopter to appear from the Mil bureau since the early 1960s.

Design of the Sokol is reported to have started in May 1974. It bears a close family resemblance to the PZL-Mil Mi-2 but is nearly twice as heavy. Its engines are the same as those of the Kamov Ka-25 Hormone anti-submarine helicopter; both shaft-turbine and turboprop versions of the basic Glushenkov engine (the latter being used in the PZL-built An-28) are in production in Poland.

The most significant innovation in the design of the Sokol is the use of glass-fibre-reinforced plastic (GFRP) composite material in the construction of the rotor blades, which both save weight and allow the rotor designer more freedom in choosing the most efficient section for the blade. The head of the Sokol rotor is, however, a traditional fully articulated design.

As the Warsaw Pact's most modern light helicopter, the Sokol is likely to be employed for military operation. However, its lack of armament will probably relegate it to a second-line role. Production is expected to start in mid-1982.

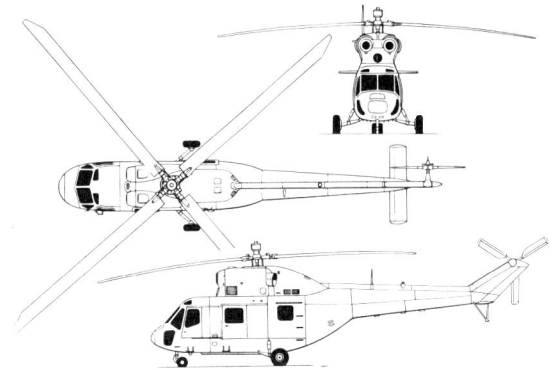

PZL V-3 Sokol.

Specification

Type: light transport helicopter (up to 14 seats)
Powerplant: two 860/990 shp (640/735-kW) PZL-10W turboshaft engines (licence-built Glushenkov)
Performance: max speed 160 mph (260 km/h); cruise speed 137 mph (220 km/h); range with standard fuel 340-375 miles (550-600 km)
Weights: max slung payload 3,300 lb (1500 kg); max take-off 13,300 lb (6000 kg)
Dimensions: rotor diameter 51 ft 6 in (15.7 m); length overall with rotor turning 66 ft 8 in (18.8 m); height 13 ft 5 in (4.1 m).

The most recent design from the Mil bureau is the V-3, designed from the outset for production in Poland. A military derivative may well be produced. Unlike earlier Mil helicopters, it has glass-fibre blades.

Myasishchev M-4/201 Bison

History and notes

One of the Soviet Union's most underestimated air-craft, the Myasishchev bomber usually known as the M-4 'Bison' has probably been at least as important to the development of Long-Range Aviation (DA) and the AVMF (Soviet Naval Aviation) as the better known Tupolev Tu-95 'Bear'. The type is often dismissed as a near-failure, partly because it was not appreciated for many years that what had been iden-tified as a special record-breaking version was in fact the difinitive production model of the aircraft.

The availability of the massive Mikulin AM-3 tur-bojet made it a logical step to incorporate four of these engines in a heavy bomber, as well as using them in the twin-engined Tu-16 'Badger'. The Myasishchev bureau was formed in 1951 to build such an aircraft, and the first prototype flew in early 1953, shortly after its US contemporary, the Boeing B-52 Stratofortress. However, by that time it was clear that the original version would have inade-quate range, and it appears that only a few of the AM-3-powered aircraft (designated 'Bison-A' by NATO) went into service. The heavier and con-siderably more powerful Myasishchev 201M 'Bison-B' flew in early 1955. Among other changes, two of the five gun turrets fitted to the original aircraft were removed to save weight.

The 'Bison-B' was one of the first Soviet types to carry a flight-probe, and many of the old 'Bison-As' were converted to tankers with a hose-reel in the bomb bay. With the rise of the Soviet navy, many of the 'Bison-Bs' were transferred to the AVMF as long-range reconnaissance aircraft, and a later development, the 'Bison-C', carried a large search radar in an extended nose. All 'Bisons' have ventral radar installations and observation blisters, and some appear to be equipped for electronic in-telligence (Elint) operations. Most AVMF aircraft have now been retired, but the M-4 remains in service as a bomber and tanker with the DA.

The 201M established a series of impressive world records in 1959, although at that time the designa-tion was thought to apply to the M-52 supersonic bomber; only in 1967 was it realised that the 201M was a 'Bison' variant. One aircraft attained 638 mph (1028 km/h) on a 1000-km (621-mile) closed circuit with a 59,525-lb (27000-kg) payload, simultaneously setting a record for zero payload over the same course. The 201M lifted a 121,275-lb (55000-kg) payload to 43,036 ft (13121 m), a record unmatched by any aircraft until the appearance of the Lockheed C-5A.

The 201M has not been seen with air-to-surface missiles, possibly because its twin-bogie under-carriage design results in a lower ground clearance than that of the Tu-95. As a free-fall bomber, it was probably obsolete almost as soon as it entered ser-vice, the increasing performance of interceptors and missile systems rendering it a relatively easy target. As far as is known, the 'Bison' has never been con-

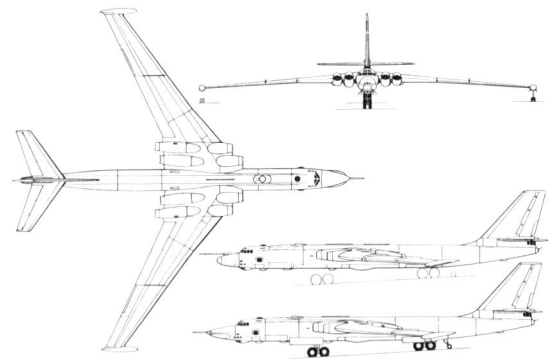

Myasishchev M-4 'Bison-C' and (upper side-view) 'Bison-B'.

verted for low-level attack as have the B-52 and BAe Vulcan. It is most unlikely that any of the 201Ms are still equipped as bombers, serving instead as tankers and reconnaissance aircraft. The old AM-3-powered 'Bison-As' have probably all been retired.

The powerplants of the 201M were identified as D-15s on the occasion of the record attempts; although D stands simply for 'engine', this system of designation was associated with the Soloviev bureau in the late 1950s and early 1960s, and the designa-tion D-15 fits in with the numerical series of Soloviev engines. The D-20 flew in the Tu-124 'Cookpot' in 1960, and as the D-20 was an early low-bypass-ratio turbofan, it is possible that it is a scaled-down ver-sion of the 201M.

Specification

Type: strategic bomber, tanker and maritime reconnaissance aircraft (specification for Myasishchev 201 'Bison-C')
Powerplant: four 28,500 lb (13000 kg) Soloviev D-15 (almost certainly bypass) turbojets
Performance: maximum speed 680 mph (1100 km/h) or Mach 0.95 at 10,000 ft (3000 m); cruising speed 560 mph (900 km/h); service ceiling 56,000 ft (17000 m); range with 11,000-lb (5000-kg) weapon load 11,200 miles (18000 km)
Weights: empty 198,500 lb (90000 kg); normal take-off 365,000 lb (165000 kg); overload take-off 463,000 lb (210000 kg)
Dimensions: span 172 ft 2 in (52.5 m); length 175 ft 2 in (53.4 m); wing area 3,440 sq ft (320 m²)
Armament: Six 23-mm NR-23 cannon in dorsal, ventral and tail barbettes, and up to 33,000 lb (15000 kg) of internal stores
Operators: USSR

Myasishchev M-4/201 Bison

Surviving version of the M-4 is the much-improved, high-gross-weight 'Bison-B', from which the now-retired maritime-reconnaissance 'Bison-C' is believed to have been developed. The 'Bison-C', pictured above and below, differs from the bomber/tanker 'Bison-B' in possessing a large nose radar.

Sukhoi Su-7 Fitter

History and notes

The standard strike fighter of Soviet Air Force Frontal Aviation from the early 1960s to the introduction of the Mikoyan-Gurevich 'Flogger-D' MiG-27 and Sukhoi Su-17 'Fitter-C' and '-D' in the early 1970s, the Sukhoi Su-7 'Fitter-A' has earned a reputation as a reliable and dependable warplane in action in the Middle East and the Indian subcontinent. Its radius of action and warload, however, are not what might be expected of so large an aircraft, and in general it carries fuel or weapons, but not both. The type also relies to a great extent on visual weapon-aiming, which limits its effectiveness.

The Sukhoi bureau had been disbanded for some years before it was re-formed to produce a new supersonic fighter designed around an afterburning version of the Lyulka AL-7 turbojet. The Lyulka bureau had been developing high-powered turbojets based on wartime German research since 1945; the AL-7 was the first of these to enter production.

The Sukhoi and Mikoyan bureaux were each apparently directed by the TsAGI (the Central Hydrodynamic Institute) to develop two alternative fighter designs: one with a wing not dissimilar to that of the MiG-19 'Farmer', then showing great

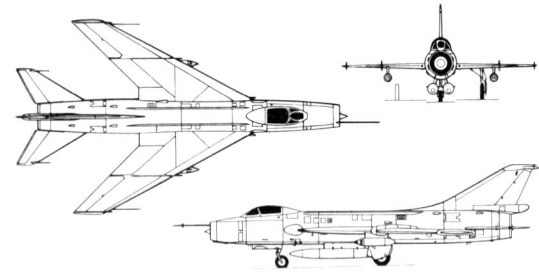

Sukhoi Su-7BM 'Fitter-A'.

promise, and the other with the newly developed tailed-delta configuration. All four prototype designs shared the mid-wing and circular-section fuselage of earlier Soviet jet fighters, leading to problems for Western intelligence analysts as they tried to determine which of the new types had gone into service.

Both Sukhoi types were ordered in quantity. The Su-7, the swept-wing version, was selected as the strike fighter for Frontal Aviation, and built in large

Sukhoi Su-7BMK at an Egyptian base in early 1975. The type served with some distinction in various Middle East conflicts, pilots commenting favourably on its ruggedness and generally good handling.

Sukhoi Su-7 Fitter

Sukhoi Su-7B of Soviet Frontal Aviation, late 1970s.

Carrying full external fuel, a SU-7BM of the Czechoslovak CL.

Egyptian Air Force Su-7U conversion trainer; back-seat view is poor.

Egyptian Air Force Su-7BMK strike aircraft are being refitted with British nav-attack systems.

Sukhoi Su-7 Fitter

The Su-7 shown here typifies two features of the
aircraft: the need to carry external fuel tanks for
virtually any mission, due to the inadequate internal
fuel capacity, and the heavy and effective cannon
permanently installed in the wing roots. The nose air
intake is ringed with blow-out doors which relieve
excess air pressure at high speed.

Sukhoi Su-7 Fitter

Sukhoi Su-7MBK Fitter-A
Cutaway Drawing Key

1 Pitot tube
2 Pitch vanes
3 Yaw vanes
4 Engine air intake
5 Fixed intake centre-body
6 Radome
7 Ranging radar scanner
8 ILS aerial
9 Radar controller
10 Weapon release ballistic computer
11 Retractable taxiing lamp
12 SRO-2M 'Odd-rods' IFF aerials
13 Intake suction relief doors
14 Intake duct divider
15 Instrument access panel
16 Su-7U 'Moujik' two-seat operational training variant
17 Armoured glass windscreen
18 Reflector sight
19 Instrument panel shroud
20 Control column
21 Rudder pedals
22 Control linkages
23 Nose undercarriage wheel well
24 Nosewheel doors
25 Torque scissor links
26 Steerable nosewheel
27 Low pressure 'rough-field' ture
28 Hydraulic retraction jack
29 Cockpit pressure floor
30 Engine throttle
31 Pilot's side console panel
32 Ejection seat

33 Canopy release handle
34 Parachute pack headrest
35 Rear view mirror
36 Sliding cockpit canopy cover
37 Instrument venturi
38 Radio and electronics equipment bay
39 Intake ducting
40 Air conditioning plant
41 Electrical and pneumatic systems ground connections
42 Cannon muzzle
43 Skin doubler/blast shield
44 Fuel system components access
45 Main fuel pumps
46 Fuel system accumulator
47 Filler cap
48 External piping ducts
49 Starboard main undercarriage leg pivot fixing
50 Shock absorber pressurization charging valve
51 Gun camera
52 Starboard wing integral fuel tank
53 Starboard wing fence
54 Outer wing panel dry bay
55 Wing tip fence
56 Static discharger
57 Starboard aileron
58 Flap guide rail
59 Starboard fowler flap
60 Flap jack

61 Fuselage skin plating
62 Fuselage fuel tank
63 Wing/fuselage attachment double frame
64 Engine compressor face
65 Ram air intake
66 Engine oil tank
67 Bleed air system 'blow-off' valve
68 Fuselage break point, engine removal
69 Lyulka AL-7F-1 turbojet
70 Afterburner duct
71 Fin root fillet
72 Autopilot controller
73 Starboard upper airbrake, open
74 Rudder power control unit
75 Artificial feel unit
76 Tailfin construction
77 VHF/UHF aerial fairing
78 RSIU (very short wave figher radio) aerial
79 Tail navigation light
80 Sirena-3 tail warning radar
81 Rudder
82 Brake parachute release tank
83 Brake parachute housing
84 Parachute doors
85 Engine exhaust nozzle
86 Port all-moving tailplane

87 Static discharger
88 Tailplane anti-flutter weight
89 Tailplane construction
90 Pivot mounting
91 Tailplane limit stops
92 Variable area exhaust nozzle flaps
93 Nozzle control jacks
94 Fin/tailplane attachment fuselage frame
95 Afterburner cooling air intak
96 Rear fuselage frame and stringer construction
97 Insulated tailpipe
98 Airbrake housing
99 Hydraulic jack
100 Tailplane power control uni
101 'Odd-rods' IFF aerials
102 Port lower airbrake, open
103 Engine accessories
104 Jettisonable JATO bottle
105 Port fowler flap
106 Port wing integral fuel tank
107 Aileron control rod
108 Port aileron construction
109 Static discharger
110 Wing tip fairing

111	Port navigation light	130	Retractable landing lamp
112	Wing tip fence	131	Ammunition tank (70 rounds per gun)
113	Pitot tube		
114	Wing rib and stringer construction	132	30-mm NR-30 cannon
		133	Cannon pressurization bottle
115	Port outer stores pylon	134	Ventral gun gas venting intake
116	UV-16-57 rocket launcher pack	135	Radar altimeter
		136	Fuselage pylon, port and starboard
117	Auxiliary fuel tank, inner pylon		
118	Port mainwheel	137	Twin fuselage mounted auxiliary fuel tanks
119	Low-pressure 'rough-field' main undercarriage		
		138	551-lb (250 Kg) concrete piercing bomb
120	Inner stores pylon		
121	Port wing fence	139	1,102-lb (500 Kg) HE bomb
122	Mainwheel doors		
123	Main undercarriage leg strut		
124	Leg shortening link		
125	Hydraulic retraction jack		
126	Wing fuel tank filler cap		
127	Port mainwheel bay		
128	Main undercarriage up-lock		
129	Aileron power control unit		

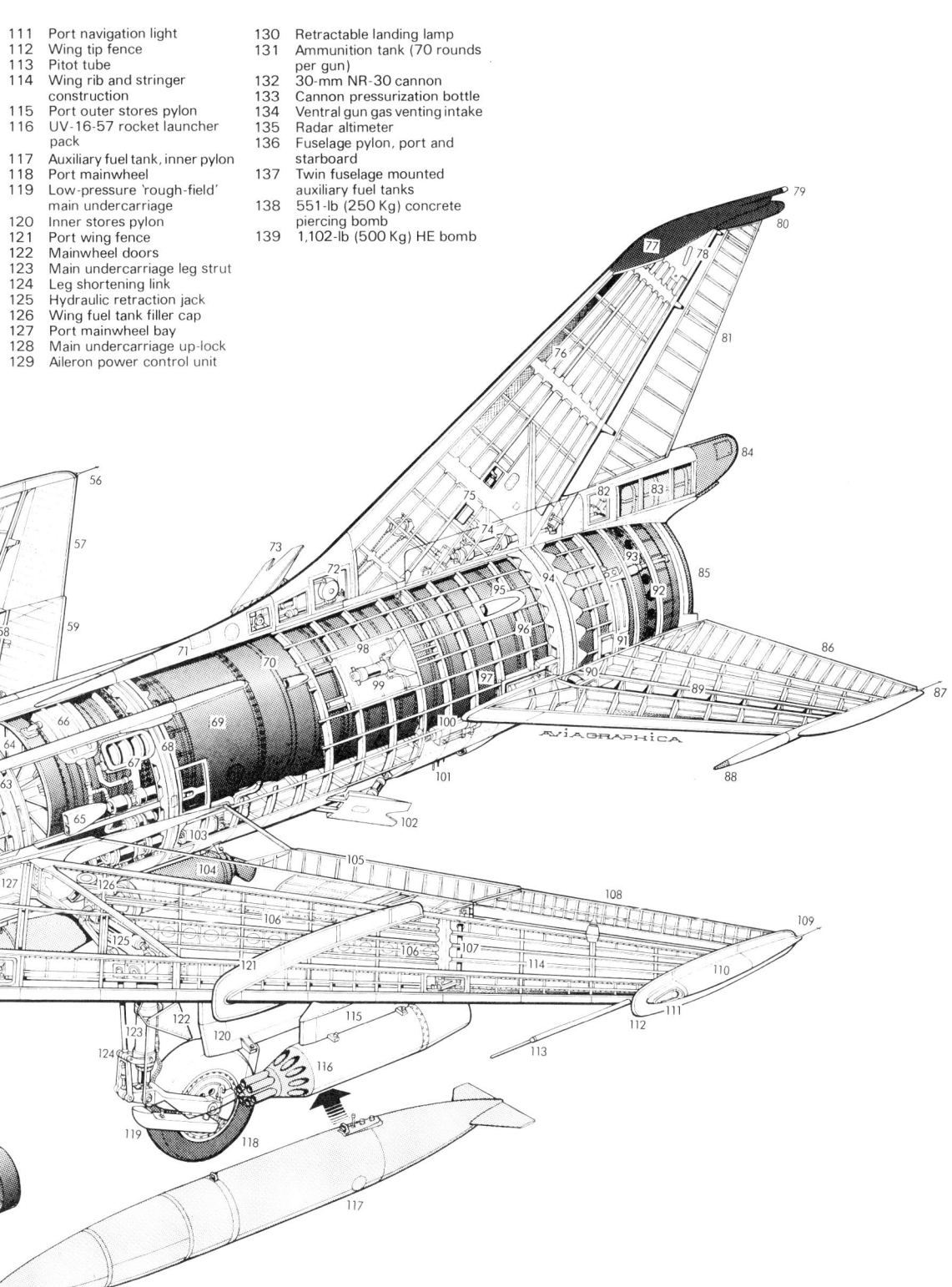

AVIAGRAPHICA

Sukhoi Su-7 Fitter

One of many Middle East users of the Su-7 is Algeria.

India has used the Su-7 in combat.

numbers. Points in its favour for this role included reasonable, if not outstanding, field performance; unlike that of the MiG-19, the swept wing of the Su-7 is furnished with area-increasing trailing-edge flaps. Like the definitive MiG-19, the Su-7 has an all-moving tailplane.

The Su-7 was clearly not designed from the same sort of deep interdiction role that was foreseen for contemporary Western strike aircraft, being more of the traditional fighter-bomber. The type has never been seen even with simple air-to-air missiles, indicating that its role is exclusively air-to-ground, using rockets, bombs and its heavy cannon against ground targets. Its endurance is limited, because the general arrangement of a circular-section fuselage and long inlet ducts drastically limits available fuel capacity. In service, Su-7s are seldom seen without their twin ventral fuel tanks, precluding the carriage of weapons on the fuselage pylons.

Operational equipment includes a ranging radar in the intake centre-body. The nose pitot boom carried yaw and pitch sensors, presumably feeding a simple ballistic computer for weapon-aiming.

Early production Su-7Bs, delivered from 1959, probably had early 20,000-lb (9000-kg) versions of the AL-7. The Su-7BM has the more powerful engine described below, while the later BMK version has low-pressure tyres and twin brake parachutes. Some Su-7BMKs are equipped for take-off rocket boost. Many have been seen operating from rough fields during manoeuvres. Also in service is the Su-7U conversion trainer.

The Su-7BMK is the standard export model, and often mounts two extra pylons aft of the mainwheel wells. Some aircraft of the type have been seen with

up to six underwing stations. Egyptian pilots have described their Su-7s as the best aircraft available to them for high-speed combat at low level, where the type is tractable despite the high air loads in such conditions; losses against strong AAA and missile fire in the October 1973 war were remarkably low. The main problems were the lack of efficient navigation and weapon-aiming systems (possibly being rectified by British avionics, though this has yet to be confirmed) and the lack of range and endurance. Just over 1,000 Su-7s were built before production switched to the Su-17 series in 1971-72.

Specification

Type: fighter-bomber

Powerplant: one 15,400-lb (7000-kg) dry or 22,000-lb (10000-kg) afterburning Lyulka AL-7F-1 turbojet

Performance: maximum speed at altitude 1,050 mph (1700 km/h), or Mach 1.6; maximum speed (clean) at sea level Mach 1.1; service ceiling 49,700 ft (15150 m); range with two drop tanks 900 miles (1450 km)

Weights: empty 19,000 lb (8620 kg); maximum loaded 30,000 lb (13600 kg)

Dimensions: length (including probe) 57 ft (17.37 m); span 29 ft 3½ in (8.93 m); height 15 ft 5 in (4.7 m)

Armament: two 30 mm NR-30 cannon in wing roots, plus four wing and two ventral stores pylons, all capable of carrying weapons (rocket pods and bombs form main armament)

Operators: Afghanistan, Algeria, Czechoslovakia, Egypt, Hungary, India, Iraq, North Korea, Poland, Romania, Syria, USSR, Vietnam

Sukhoi Su-9/11 Fishpot

History and notes

Never as widely used or as well known as the contemporary Mikoyan-Gurevich MiG-21 'Fishbed' or Su-7 'Fitter-A', the Sukhoi bureau's delta-wing prototype of 1955-56 nevertheless led to the Su-9 'Fishpot-B' the most numerous supersonic interceptor in the PVO (Air Defence Forces) fleet for many years. The type was supplanted by the Su-15 'Flagon' on the production lines in the late 1960s, but some 600 remain in service.

The Su-9 was designed as an all-weather fighter based on the same tailed-delta configuration as the MiG-21. Entering service in 1958-59, it typified Soviet practice in that it combined a new engine and airframe with an existing weapon, the K-5M 'Alkali' air-to-air missile already in service on the MiG-19P 'Farmer'. The small radar fitted quite simply into the nose of the Su-9, which was closely similar to that of the Su-7. However, the all-weather capability of the Su-9 is fairly limited, as this radar lacks search range. In practice, the type presumably operates in close co-operation with ground control.

An Su-9 development aircraft was probably the type which, under the designation T-405, established a 100-km (62-mile) closed-circuit speed record of 1,299 mph (2091 km/h) in May 1960. This was probably close to the ultimate 'clean' maximum speed of the early type, which like early production Su-7s was powered by a 20,000-lb (9000-kg) engine.

The 1961 Tushino air display, however, saw the appearance of a new derivative of the basic type, featuring a longer and less tapered nose. The inlet diameter was considerably larger, and there was a

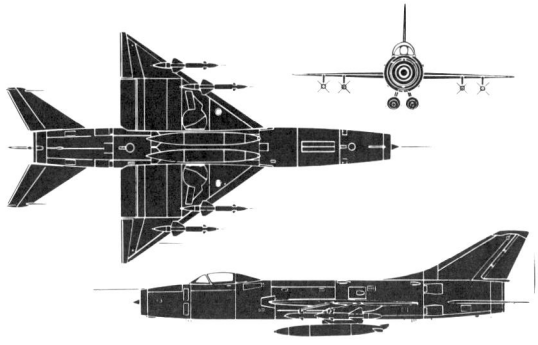

Sukhoi Su-9 'Fishpot-B'.

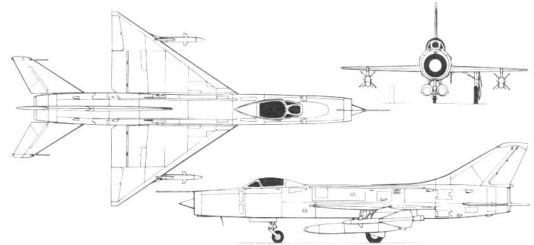

Sukhoi Su-11 'Fishpot-C'.

First supersonic interceptor in the Soviet inventory with limited-all-weather capability was the Sukhoi Su-9. It was replaced in production by the Su-11 by 1962-63.

Sukhoi Su-9/11 Fishpot

The Su-9 was replaced by the Su-11, with a more efficient intake, more engine power and a more effective radar/missile system.

proportionate increase in the size of the centre-body radome to accommodate a new and more powerful radar known to NATO as 'Skip Spin'. The new type replaced the Su-9 on the production lines, and was designated Su-11, with the codename 'Fishpot-C'; it appears to be Sukhoi practice to apply new designations to reflect relatively minor changes, the Su-11 being no more different from its predecessor than contemporary MiG-21 versions differed from the MiG-21F.

It is possible that the aircraft designated T-431, which established a series of records in 1959-62, was an Su-11 development aircraft. The T-431's performance suggests that Western estimates of the Su-11's performance may be on the conservative side; its records include a sustained altitude of 69,455 ft (21170 m) and a speed of 1,452 mph (2337 km/h) round a 500-km (311-mile) closed circuit. The improved performance of the Su-11 can probably be attributed to greater power and more efficient inlet design.

A measure of the comparative worth of the 'Alkali' and later 'Anab' missiles is the fact that the Soviet air force was prepared to accept two of the more potent later weapons on the Su-11 in place of four 'Alkalis' on the Su-9. It is probable that, like many first-generation missile systems, the performance of the K-5M Izumrud system was barely good enough for operational clearance. The 'Anab' has clearly been more successful, and has remained in service and under development for many years.

Like most Soviet interceptors, the Su-9/11 series has never been exported, even to the Warsaw Pact. The Su-11 is closely comparable to the British Aerospace Lightning, lacking the British fighter's combat performance but possessing radar-guided missiles. It presented a credible defence against the high-flying bomber armed with free-fall weapons, but is increasingly an anachronism in the age of low-level aircraft armed with stand-off weapons, as it lacks the range for long-range patrols. Its importance in combat units, together with that of the Su-9U trainer variant, is likely to decline rapidly in the late 1970s and early 1980s.

Specification

Type: all-weather interceptor
Powerplant: one 22,000-lb (10000-kg) afterburning Lyulka AL-7F turbojet
Performance: maximum (clean) 1,400 mph (2250 km/h), or Mach 2.1; maximum speed with two AAMs and external fuel tanks 1,000 mph (1600 km/h) or Mach 1.5; service ceiling 65,000 ft (20000 m); range about 700 miles (1125 km)
Weights: empty 20,000 lb (9000 kg); maximum loaded 30,000 lb (13500 kg)
Dimensions: span 27 ft 8 in (8.43 m); length (including instrument boom) 60 ft (18.3 m); height 15 ft (4.9 m)
Armament: (Su-9) four K-5M (AA-1 'Alkali') beam-riding air-to-air missiles on wing pylons; (Su-11) two AA-3 'Anab' semi-active bombing (almost certainly) AAMs
Operators: USSR

Sukhoi Su-15 Flagon

History and notes

The Sukhoi Su-15 'Flagon' interceptor is a demonstration of the Soviet Union's practice of constantly improving a basic design over a period of many years to produce a highly effective definitive production aircraft. It is now the main interceptor in service with the PVO air-defence force, some 850 being reported to be operational. However, PVO re-equipment needs are now being met partly by the Mikoyan-Gurevich MiG-23S, and with the next generation of interceptor likely to enter service in the early 1980s the importance of the Su-15 could soon decline.

The Su-15 traces its origin back to a requirement issued in the early 1960s for a supersonic interceptor with better radar and speed than the Su-11 then under development.

The Mikoyan bureau produced its E-152, which was demonstrated at Tushino is 1961 but not put into service. The Su-15 appears to have evolved rather later, and as flown in 1964-65 appears to have combined the Tumansky R-11 engines, 'Skip Spin' radar and AA-3 'Anab' missiles of the Yakovlev Yak-28P with the delta wing and tail of the Su-9/-11 (almost completely unchanged) and a new fuselage. The two engines were fed by variable-geometry side inlets with auxiliary inlet doors. The Su-15 thus represented a very low-risk development, making use of a large proportion of components from existing aircraft, though it evolved with an uncharacteristically low power-loading and high wing-loading.

A pre-series batch of Su-15s made their appearance at the 1967 Domodedovo air display, but this basic type does not appear to have been built in quantity, probably because it did not represent enough of an advance over the Su-11 to warrant replacement of the single-engined type. Development of the Su-15 was already under way, as indicated by the presence at Domodedovo of an experimental version known to NATO as the 'Flagon-

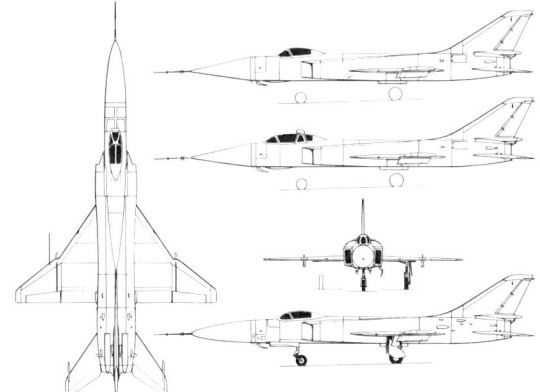

Sukhoi Su-15VD 'Flagon-F' with (top side-view) 'Flagon-D' and (centre side-view) Su-15U 'Flagon-C'.

B' (the designation 'Flagon-A' being allotted to the basic aircraft). The 'Flagon-B' was a reduced-take-off-and-landing (RTOL) aircraft similar to the Mikoyan 'Faithless', with three Kolesov lift jets installed in the centre fuselage. The sweep of the outer wing panels was reduced, possibly in order to allow the ailerons to be extended; one of the problems of such RTOL prototypes was the difficulty of control in partially jetborne flight. Although the Soviet Union abandoned research into such aircraft, the wing planform of the 'Flagon-B' foreshadowed the compound sweep of the later Su-15 variants.

The first major production version of the Su-15 is reported to have been the 'Flagon-D', which entered service in the late 1960s or early 1970s. Retaining the radar and missiles of the 'Flagon-A', the 'Flagon-D' probably introduced more powerful engines and compound sweep on the outer wings, separated by a short unswept section from the inner wing. This curious 'soft dog-tooth' is reminiscent of that fitted to the wing of the Ilyushin Il-62 airliner,

Latest 'Flagon-F' photographed by Swedish fighter over the Baltic Sea. Designation of this type is reported as Su-15VD.

Sukhoi Su-15 Flagon

Specification

Type: interceptor

Powerplant: two 16,000-lb (7500-kg) Tumansky R-13 afterburning turbojets

Performance: maximum speed Mach 2+ at medium altitude, equivalent to 1,320 mph (2120 km/h) at 36,000 ft (11000 m); maximum speed at sea level 680 mph (1100 km/h) or Mach 0.9; service ceiling 55,000 to 60,000 ft (17000 to 18000 m); combat radius 400 miles (650 km)

Weights: empty 27,500 lb (12500 kg); normal loaded 40,000 lb (18000 kg); maximum loaded 45,000 lb (20000 kg)

Dimensions: span 34 ft 6 in (10.5 m); length 70 ft 6 in (21.5 m); height 16 ft 6 in (5 m); wing area 385 sq ft (35.7 m^2)

Armament: two air-to-air missiles, normally AA-3-2 'Advanced Anab'; guns have been reported, but are unconfirmed

Operator: USSR

Originally designed as an evolutionary development of the Su-9/11 family with a more capable radar, the Su-15 has grown into a much larger and heavier aircraft. Weight increases have been accompanied by modifications to the wing design to increase lift at low speeds; the 'soft notch' is noteworthy. However, the wing loading of the Su-15 is too high for any worthwhile air-combat capability.

The variable-geometry air inlets of the Su-15 are canted outwards in side view, and the internal volume of the fuselage is larger than a first glance might suggest. Indeed, 'Flagon' is almost the only Soviet fighter which does not habitually carry external fuel. The afterburner-cooling scoops are prominent.

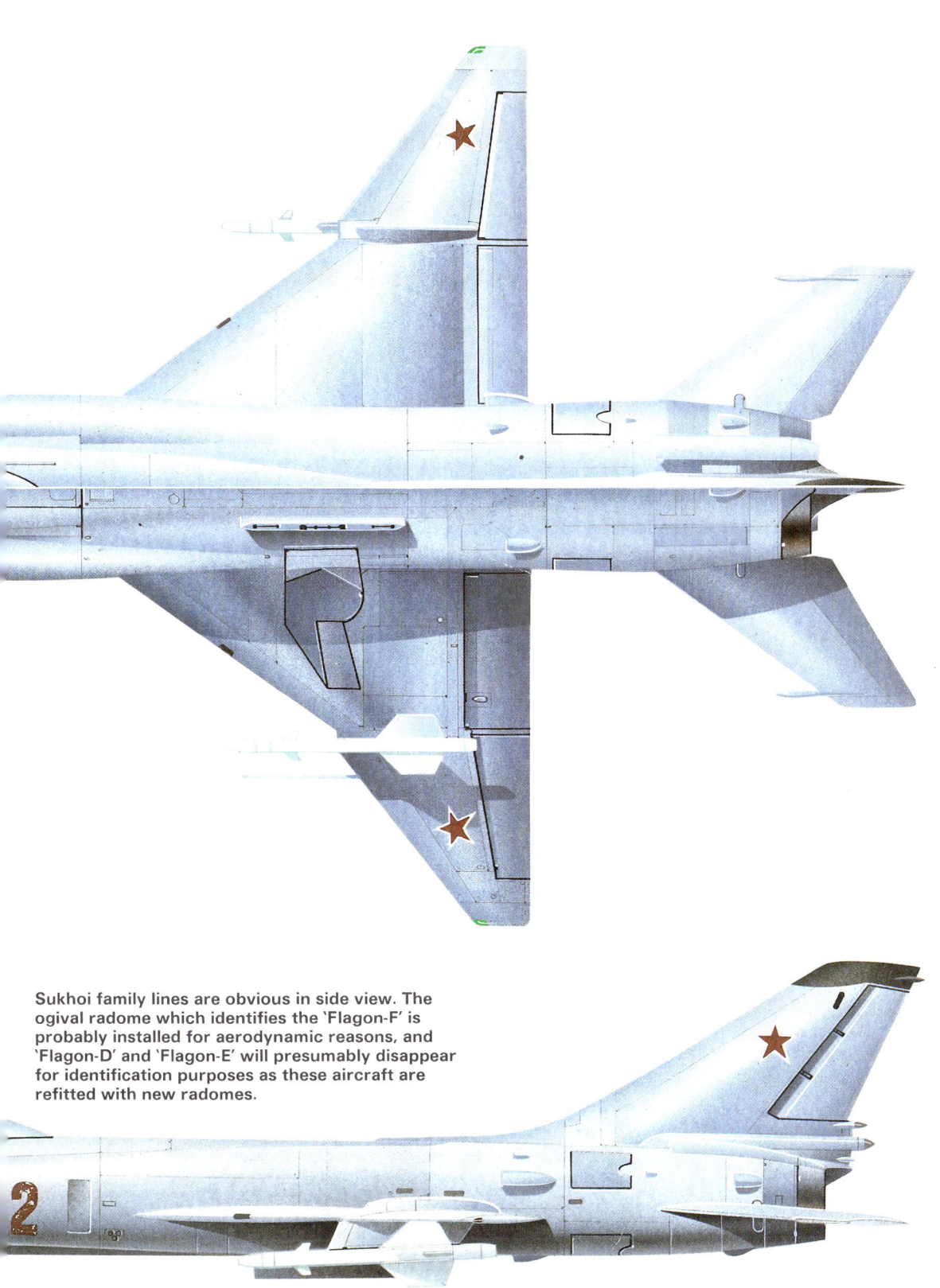

Sukhoi family lines are obvious in side view. The
ogival radome which identifies the 'Flagon-F' is
probably installed for aerodynamic reasons, and
'Flagon-D' and 'Flagon-E' will presumably disappear
for identification purposes as these aircraft are
refitted with new radomes.

Sukhoi Su-15 Flagon

the only other type to display such a feature. It is likely that the modification to the Su-15 wing is intended to improve low-speed handling and to reduce landing speeds; these were very high on the earlier sub-types, which are considerably heavier than the Su-11 despite having a similar wing area.

The 'Flagon-E', with more powerful R-13 engines, is said to be the most important production version so far. According to the US Department of Defense, it has improved electronics, but these do not appear to have advanced so far as to make the aircraft useful against low-flying targets; this capability was not credited to any PVO aircraft until the introduction of the MiG-23S. Neither are there any firm reports of Su-15s carrying the AA-7 'Apex' missile which arms the MiG-23S, although any new radar fitted to the later 'Flagons' could be the equal of the MiG-23S equipment.

The latest production version of the Su-15 is identified as the 'Flagon-F' by NATO, and is distinguished by a new radome which may be able to accommodate a larger aerial than the unusual conical radome of earlier versions, although it is more likely that the modification has been made for aerodynamic reasons.

Persistent reports that the Su-15 was to be equipped with cannon appear to have been in error. The type seems to be confined to the high-altitude interception role, which it shares with the MiG-25. Like other single-seat Soviet interceptors, it operates under close ground control. There appears, for instance, to be no HUD display, suggesting that the pilot need never see the target except on head-down radar and flight-director displays. In its primary role, the Su-15's attributes include speed and respectable fuel capacity; just how much space there is in the airframe can be judged by the fact that the fuselage of the 'Flagon-B' was little if any wider than standard, despite the battery of lift engines. The engines are tried and proven as is the AAM system.

Su-15 'Flagon-E' of the Soviet PVO air-defence forces shows off its unique notched-delta planform. The less-efficient conical radome is being replaced by an ogival type.

Sukhoi Su-17/Su-20/Su-22 Fitter C to H

History and notes

The Sukhoi Su-17/-20/-22 'Fitter' family of close-support fighters stems from what was apparently a research aircraft, and the three types are the only examples of production variable-sweep aircraft derived from a fixed-geometry design. They reflect the Soviet industry's traditional reluctance to terminate production of an established design, and its talent for filling an operational requirement in a manner which may appear crude but is nonetheless effective. Pending the emergence of a specialized close-support type, the Su-17 and its derivatives continue to fill an important role in the Soviet armoury.

It appears that the development of the Su-17 was a matter of chance. Soviet designers became absorbed in the study of variable sweep in the early 1960s, and discovered the same fundamental problems as had plagued Western designers. Among them was the tendency for the aerodynamic centre to move aft with increasing sweep, causing trim difficulties. The answer, it was discovered, was to set the pivots outboard, but only in the Soviet Union, however, was this trend continued to produce a 'semi-variable-geometry' layout, in which only the outer panels move. This was adopted by the Tupolev bureau for a

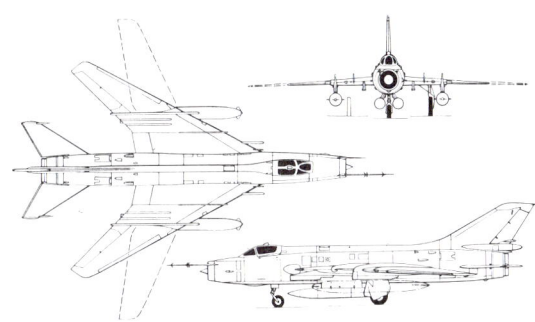

Sukhoi Su-17 'Fitter-C'.

Above, Poland was the first export recipient of the Su-20 export model of the Su-17; below, a line-up of Soviet Frontal Aviation Su-17s.

Sukhoi Su-17/Su-20/Su-22 Fitter C to H

Specification

Type: close-support attack

Powerplant: one 24,250-lb (11000-kg) Lyulka AL-21F afterburning turbojet

Performance: maximum speed at 36,000 ft (11000 m) 1,200 mph (1925 km/h) or Mach 1.8: maximum speed at sea level (clean) 830 mph (1340 km/h) or Mach 1.1; maximum speed at sea level with external fuel (almost invariably carried) 650 mph (1050 km/h) or Mach 0.88; service ceiling 55,000 ft (17000 m); ferry range 1,100 miles (1760 km); tactical radius 300 miles (480 km)

Weights: empty 22,000 lb (10000 kg); maximum external load about 7,500 lb (3500 kg); maximum take-off about 37,500 lb (17000 kg)

Dimensions: span (swept) 34 ft 6 in (10.5 m); span (spread) 45 ft (14 m); length (including probe) 58 ft (17.6 m); height 15 ft (4.6 m)

Armament: two wing-root 30-mm NR-30 cannon, plus a total of six (some Su-17s have eight) hardpoints for rockets, air-to-surface missiles or fuel tanks, although 250-Imperial gallon (1130-litre) auxiliary tanks are nearly always carried on outer pylons; some aircraft are fitted to carry AA-2 'Atoll' air-to-air missiles

Operators: Egypt, Peru, Poland, Syria, USSR

Perhaps the only test-bed aircraft ever to make it into service, the swing-wing 'Fitter' family—this is an Egyptian Air Force Su-20 'Fitter-C'—are also the only swing-wing aircraft to be derived from a fixed-wing forebear. The movable wing sections are almost solely a take-off and landing aid, the aircraft being otherwise similar to a standard Su-7 in its control system. The Su-20 has two belly pylons, while some Su-17s have four.

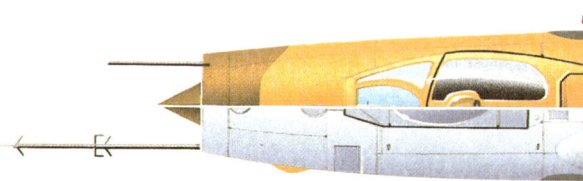

This Su-20 is in long-range strike configuration, with four out of six stores stations occupied by fuel tanks. However, the aircraft still has two wing pylons and its heavy 30mm cannon. Nose and tail fins on the underwing tanks, similar to those carried by Su-24 'Fencer' bombers, ensure clear separation.

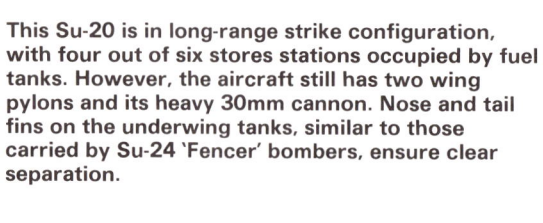

The swing-wing 'Fitters' differ from the Su-7 in areas other than the wing, featuring a dorsal spine and a clamshell canopy in place of a rearward-sliding hood. Weapon-aiming, however, is similarly based on radar ranging and pitch/yaw sensors on the nose boom, at least in early versions.

Frontal Aviation Su-17 'Fitter-C'; this aircraft may well have been brought up to 'Fitter-D' standard or converted to a later version. It has only two belly pylons, while others have four.

supersonic bomber in 1965-66, and a Sukhoi Su-7 was apparently modified as a test-bed. This modified aircraft made its public debut at the Domodedovo air display in 1967, and was codenamed 'Fitter-B' by NATO. However, the improvement over the Su-7 was so great that it was decided to place this testbed in production. The first were observed in service in 1970-71.

The basic Su-17 is thought to be powered by the higher-powered AL-21F, while the Su-22 and possibly the Su-20 may have the older AL-7. The Su-17 differs from the Su-7 and the 'Fitter-B' in having a more advanced weapon-aiming system using a complex array of aerodynamic sensors on the nose boom. Control runs are relocated in a dorsal spine, possibly to improve maintainability.

Compared with the Su-7, the Su-17 offers a slight increase in maximum speed in clean condition, but the main advantage comes in weight-lifting and runway capability. The outer wing sections are fitted with slats and trailing-edge flaps, allowing the Su-17 to take off at least 7,500 lb (3500 kg) heavier than the Su-7 from a shorter runway. Two of the pylons, attached to the massive wing fences, are nearly always occupied by large tanks, but even so the Su-17 can still lift more weapons than an Su-7.

The Su-17 is not in the class of the Mikoyan-Gurevich MiG-27, despite its similar thrust, because of its much smaller internal fuel capacity (demanding the carriage of drag-causing external tanks), its less optimized unswept configuration, and its less efficient engine. However, it remains an effective close-support aircraft. At low level with tanks it is probably subsonic, and would use the afterburner only for take-off.

Poland was the first country to take delivery of the Su-20, the initial export model. Some sources suggest that the Su-20 has the AL-7 engine, and it has only two ventral pylons. One possible explanation is that the Poles, lacking MiG-27s, operate their Su-20s as long-range strike aircraft with four tanks, while Russian aircraft are used in the close-support role exclusively, for which wing tanks are adequate.

The second export version is the Su-22, the first Soviet combat aircraft in South America when delivered to Peru in 1977. The Su-22 carries AA-2 'Atoll' missiles, but otherwise is equipped to a very basic standard, lacking radar-warning systems and other items. Peru has had great difficulty in turning the type into an efficient weapon platform.

The Soviet forces, by contrast, are now taking delivery of an even more advanced version, the 'Fitter-D'. First reported in 1977, this appears to have a new weapon-aiming system with an electro-optical device or laser in the centrebody and radar beneath the nose, probably matched with 'smart' weapons similar to those arming the MiG-27. The reporting names 'Fitter G' and 'Fitter H' have also been quoted, implying that at least four more variants (E to H) have been identified. 'Fitter H' is a reconnaissance aircraft carrying a massive ventral reconnaissance pod. The Su-17 derivatives seem to have proved an unexpected windfall for Soviet close-support units, and a highly successful interim type pending deployment of a specialised close-support fighter such as the RAM-J (see introduction).

Sukhoi Su-24 Fencer

History and notes

Backing up the front-line Mikoyan MiG-27s of Frontal Aviation is an increasing force of the heavily-armed, all weather Sukhoi Su-24 strike aircraft. The Nato code-name 'Fencer' applied to these aircraft is something of a misnomer, because the Su-24 (commonly referred to as the Su-19 until the use of the Su-24 designation by the Department of Defense in 1980) has no air-to-air capability to speak of. It is the first Soviet aircraft designed specifically for tactical air-to-ground operations to be put into production since the 1939-45 war, and as such represents an important weapon in the armoury of Frontal Aviation.

Development of the Su-24 presumably got under way shortly after 1965, consequent on the decision to develop Frontal Aviation to the point where it could match and surpass Nato's non-nuclear tactical air capability. It was accepted that operations at night or in adverse weather dictated a two-seater aircraft with avionics systems rather more advanced than those planned for the strike version of the MiG-23, and that this aircraft would have to be generally larger than the single-engined Mikoyan fighter.

The Su-24 made its maiden flight in the early years of the decade and was first observed in 1971-72. Operational units were worked up by mid-1977, and in early 1980 there were eight or nine regiments operational in the Western Soviet Union (equivalent to a total of 280-310 aircraft) and other aircraft of the type were deployed near the Chinese border. Its range, particularly at high altitude, is sufficient for the aircraft to be based in the Western USSR rather than in the more vulnerable (and rather crowded) locations of Eastern Europe. The Su-24 can fly nearly as far in Western Europe on a hi-lo-hi profile from these more secure bases as it could fly lo-lo-lo from Eastern Europe. This explains the fact that the aircraft has not joined the 16th Air Army units in East German; so far the type has been camera-shy, Western Intelligence getting its first clear shots of the aircraft in late 1979.

The development of Fencer was an echo of mid-1950s Soviet design practice in that the wing/tailplane planform was chosen basically similar to that of the MiG-23 'Flogger A'; the modifications applied later to improve the manoeuvrability of the Mikoyan fighter proved unnecessary for the specialised strike bomber, so Fencer lacks the leading-edge extension and claw of the definitive MiG-23/27, and its tailplane tips align with the sweptback wingtips as on the 'Flogger A'. The development process is highly reminiscent of the development of the MiG-21 and Su-9/11, both of which appear to have stemmed from a common basic planform.

The Su-24 is about 50 per cent bigger than the MiG-23/27, but has a longer range due to an 80 per cent greater internal fuel capacity. The crew of two are seated side-by-side in what must be a fairly

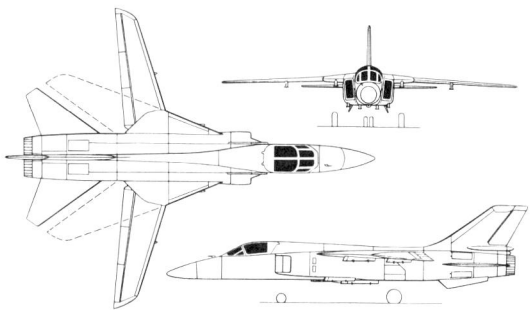

Sukhoi Su-24 'Fencer'.

cramped cockpit given the width of the forward fuselage. The nose appears to house radar equipment for terrain-following, and possibly, target tracking and weapon aiming, but the aircraft is not considered to be in the same league for nav/attack capability as the considerably bigger General Dynamics F-111 or the much later Panavia Tornado IDS. Some of the early aircraft may have been fitted with an interim limited all-weather avionics suite similar to that of the MiG-27 'Flogger D'. Internal ECM is probably comprehensive. The proportions of the Su-24 powerplant installation seem to suggest reheated turbofan engines significantly smaller than the Tumansky R-29B, corresponding to no known Soviet engine.

Armament of the Su-24 includes a GSh-23 twin-barrel cannon offset to starboard under the fuselage. Other weapons are carried on two swivelling wing pylons, two hardpoints under the wing gloves (which have been seen carrying large external fuel tanks) and three belly pylons. Apart from the range of ordnance carried by the MiG-27, the Su-24 is also expected to carry the longer-range AS-9 anti-radiation missile.

The Su-24 is not regarded as a "deep interdiction" aircraft; in any event, such an aircraft would not fit in with the FA's primary task of contributing directly to the land war. The Su-24 is more accurately

Released in 1977, this is the photograph from which the drawing overleaf was derived.

Sukhoi Su-24 Fencer

classified as an all-weather back-up to the MiG-27, with greater load-carrying capacity but aimed at the same targets: Nato military installations, particularly air bases, in Western Europe. additionally, the Su-24 can strike air bases in Eastern England, but probably not from its normal quarters in the Western USSR. In numbers in service and production rate the type is never likely to match the cheaper and simpler MiG-23/27, but its capability is nevertheless significant to the Frontal Aviation forces.

Specification

Type: two-seat all-weather interdiction/strike aircraft
Powerplant: two unidentified afterburning turbofans, each rating about 19,500 lb (8800 kg) with afterburner
Performance: maximum speed at 36,000 (11000 m) 1,320 mph (2120 km/h) Mach 2; maximum speed at sea level (clean) 900 mph (1450 km/h), Mach 1.2; cruising speed at sea level 600 mph (980 km/h); ferry range 3,750 miles (6000 km); combat radius 700 miles (1100 km) on hi-lo-hi profile
Weights: empty 37,500 lb (17000 kg); maximum normal external load 12,500 lb (5700 kg); normal take-off 65,000 lb (30000 kg); overload take-off 70,000 lb (32000 kg)
Dimensions: span (spread) 56 ft 10 in (17.3 m); (span swept) 32 ft 8 in (10 m); length 72 ft 10 in (22.2 m); height 18 ft (5.5 m); wing area (swept) 485 sq ft (45m^2)
Armament: one fixed twin-barrel 23-mm Gsh-23 cannon, up to 12,500 lb (5700 kg) of guided and unguided weapons on two swivelling wing pylons and five other hardpoints under wing gloves and fuselage
Operator: USSR

This drawing depicts the basic layout of the Su-24. Both this aircraft and the MiG-23 appear to have been developed to a common basic design, but the Su-24 seems to have been developed without the aerodynamic modifications needed by the MiG-23 and its planform is that of the prototype 'Flogger-A'.

The *raison d'etre* of the Su-24 is all-weather capability, which the otherwise extremely capable MiG-27 lacks. Essential to this are the two-man crew, seated side-by-side in a cramped cockpit, and the nose radar installation, presumably housing terrain-following and attack radars.

The side profile of the Su-24 is distinctly Sukhoi, despite the design's common origins with the MiG-23. Weapons and auxiliary fuel tanks are carried on glove, wing and belly stations.

Tupolev Tu-4 Bull

History and notes

If the US Department of Defence is to be believed, this ancient bomber is still in limited service with the Chinese air arm. It was in fact reported to be the carrier for the first Chinese nuclear weapons in the late 1960s.

Faced in 1945 with a series of failures in the Soviet industry's attempts to build a modern heavy bomber, the Soviet leadership decided to produce a carbon copy of the Boeing B-29 Superfortress, several of which had force-landed in Siberia during 1945 after raids on Japan. The Tupolev and Myasishchev bureaux were assigned the task of copying the airframe, while the Shvetsov team worked on producing a copy of the Wright R-3350 Cyclone 18 engine. Other teams copied the many complex systems of the American bomber, including its system of low-drag remotely controlled gun turrets. The formidable task of copying an aircraft so far in advance of anything previously seen in the Soviet Union was accomplished with remarkable speed; the first aircraft of the type to fly, in the spring of 1948, was not a true prototype but the first of 20 pre-series aircraft, and production deliveries started in 1949. The main difference between the US and Soviet aircraft was the latter's heavier defensive armament, 23-mm cannon replacing the 0.5-in machine-guns of the Boeing B-29.

About 1,200 Tu-4s were built, of which some 400 were supplied to China. The type was replaced as a first-line bomber by the end of the 1950s in the Soviet Union, but continued to be used for the development of flight-refuelling techniques and for maritime reconnaissance.

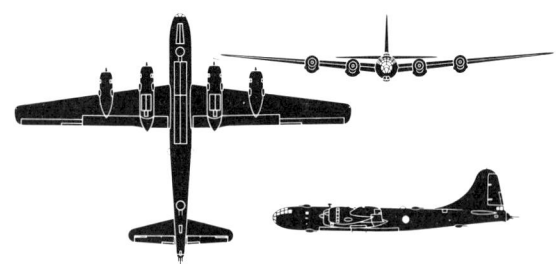

Tupolev Tu-4 'Bull'.

Specification

Type: strategic bomber, tanker and reconnaissance aircraft
Powerplant: four 2,300-hp (1716-kW) Shvetsov ASh-73TK 18-cylinder radial piston engines
Performance: maximum speed 360 mph (580 km/h) at 33,000 ft (10000 m); range with 11,000-lb (5000-kg) bomb load 3,050 miles (4900 km); ceiling 36,750 ft (11200 m)
Weights: empty 75,000 lb (34000 kg); normal loaded 105,000 lb (47600 kg)
Dimensions: span 141 ft 4 in (43.08 m); length 99 ft 1 in (30.19 m); wing area 1,680 sq ft (156 m^2)
Armament: up to 11,000 lb (5000 kg) of bombs in two internal bays; five remote-controlled turrets (tail, two dorsal and two ventral) each mounting two 23-mm NS cannon
Operators: China (and formerly USSR)

Copied from the World War II Boeing Superfortress bomber, the Tu-4 must be one of the oldest designs in active service. Chinese designation is not known.

Tupolev Tu-16 Badger

History and notes

The development in the early 1950s of the Mikulin bureau's massive AM-3 turbojet marked the end of the Soviet Union's dependence on Western technology in engines. Rated at 18,000 lb (8200 kg) in its initial version, the AM-3 made possible the design of new bombers with fewer engines than their Western counterparts, being twice as powerful as most contemporary Western engines.

Known as the Tupolev Tu-88 or Samolet N, the prototype of the Tu-16 'Badger' was flown in 1952; it was thus a contemporary of the British V-bombers rather than the American Boeing B-47. Like many Soviet aircraft designs, it was a mixture of the radically new and the conservative in its design philosophy. The fuselage was generally similar to that of the Tu-4, and the defensive armament, structure and systems were all based on the Tu-4. The wing set the pattern for future Tupolev aircraft, with a high degree of sweep and a bogie landing gear

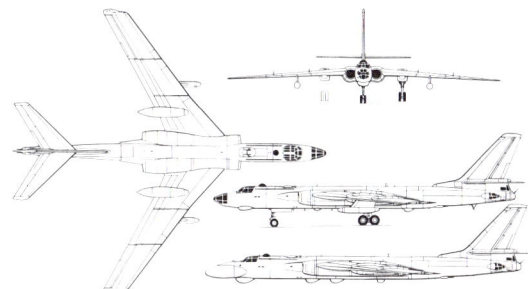

Tupolev Tu-16 'Badger-F' and (lower side-view) 'Badger-D'.

Egypt's missile-armed 'Badger-B' bombers were the most potent striking force in the Middle East until their destruction during the Israeli Air Force's pre-emptive strike in June 1967.

Specialised reconnaissance versions of the Tu-16 such as this 'Badger-F' are still the workhorses of the Soviet naval air force (AVMF).

Tupolev Tu-16 Badger

Evidence of increasing AVMF use of jet aircraft came early in the 1960s, as Tu-16s engaged in close visual reconnaissance of Western warships.

Tupolev Tu-16 Badger

retracting rearwards into trailing-edge pods. The layout offered a sturdy and simple gear, left the centre-section free for weapon stowage and offered wide track; in addition, the pods helped to delay the transonic drag-rise. An apparent anomaly was the fixed forward-firing gun, retained to the present day.

The Tu-88 was ordered into production for the DA (Long-Range Aviation) and entered service in 1955. Later versions were equipped with the uprated AM-3M, and most of the type were eventually fitted with flight-refuelling equipment. The system fitted to Tu-16s so far seen is unusual, involving a tip-to-tip connection; other Soviet aircraft have nose probes. Some Tu-16s were completed as specialized tankers with a tip-hose or belly hose-reel.

Soviet production of the Tu-16 probably gave way to the Tu-20 and Tu-22 in the late 1950s, but in 1968 the type was put back into production (as the B-6) in China, as a replacement for the Tu-4. The Tu-16 also formed the basis for the Tu-104, the first Soviet jet airliner.

A new lease of life for the Tu-16 came with the rising power of the Soviet navy in the early 1960s. Tu-16s were steadily transferred from the DA to the AVMF (Soviet Naval Aviation), and became that service's first missile-carriers. The first missile-armed variant, the 'Badger-B', of 1961, carried two turbojet-powered AS-1 'Kennel' missiles under the wings; these aircraft appear to have been converted into 'Badger-Gs' with the more advanced AS-5 'Kelt' missile, and a number of these were delivered to Egypt in the late 1960s and early 1970s. The 'Badger-C' also seen in 1961, carries a single super-

Versions of the Tu-16 assigned to electronic reconnaissance and countermeasures are distinguished by small ventral radomes.

Tu-16s in AVMF service practise a unique wingtip-to-wingtip refuelling system. The tanker aircraft, with its hose stowage neatly concealed in the starboard wingtip, is nearer the camera.

Tupolev Tu-16 Badger

The subsonic AS-5 'Kelt' anti-ship missile is a slightly modernised version of the first generation AS-1 'Kennel'.

sonic AS-2 'Kipper' missile, with a large radar installation replacing the glazed nose. A similar radar is featured by the 'Badger-D' maritime reconnaissance aircraft, together with an array of radomes indicating an electronic surveillance capability. The 'Badger-E' and 'Badger-F' are generally supposed to be specialized electronic intelligence (Elint) aircraft, with glazed noses and a plethora of aerials. 'Badger H' is an electronic warfare platform with a specialised role as a chaff dispenser; 'Badger J' carries active jamming equipment while 'Badger K' is an Elint platform.

About 400 Tu-16s are still in service with AVMF, including tankers as well as strike aircraft. The reconnaissance and Elint aircraft are likely to be replaced in first-line service by the better-optimized turboprop Ilyushin Il-38 and Il-18 while the missile-armed variants are being replaced by Tu-26s. However, there is life in the 'Badger' yet, as is shown by the re-equipment of some 'Badger-Gs' with a single AS-6 'Kingfish' missile under one wing.

Specification

Type: strategic bomber, missile platform, reconnaissance aircraft, Elint aircraft and flight-refuelling tanker

Powerplant: two 19,200-lb (8700-kg) Mikulin AM-3M turbojets

Performance: maximum speed 620 mph (1000 km/h) or Mach 0.91; cruising speed 530 mph (850 km/h or Mach 0.8; service ceiling 46,000 ft (14000 m); maximum range 4,000 miles (6400 m)

Weights: empty 80,000 lb (36000 kg); maximum take-off 158,500 lb (72000 kg)

Dimensions: span 113 ft 3 in (34.54 m); length 120 ft (36.5 m); height 35 ft 6 in (10.8 m); wing area 1,820 sq ft (170 m²)

Armament: ('Badger-B') two AS-1 'Kennel' ASMs (no longer in service); ('Badger-C') one AS-2 'Kipper'; ('Badger-G') two AS-5 'Kelt'. Bomber versions have provision for 13,000 lb (6000 kg) of internal stores. All versions have seven 23-mm NR-23 cannon: one fixed in forward fuselage, two in tail turret and two each in ventral and dorsal barbettes

Operators: China, Iraq, Indonesia (in storage), Libya, USSR

Tupolev Tu-22 Blinder

History and notes

Often considered a failure, the Tupolev Tu-22 'Blinder' appears in fact to be a workmanlike design, and limited production appears to be a consequence of changing requirements and political factors rather than a technical decision. The figures below reflect the compiler's latest estimates, and in some respects contradict earlier information; the range quoted for the aircraft, for example, has generally been closer to the all-supersonic range capability of the type, rather than reflecting its normal operating profile.

Development of the Tu-22, under the Tupolev bureau designation Tu-105, was initiated in 1955-56. By that time it was clear that the effectiveness of Western air-defence systems was improving rapidly, and that supersonic, missile-armed all-weather interceptors and medium/high-altitude SAMs would be in large-scale service by the end of the decade. The Tu-16, with its modest cruising altitude and defensive gun turrets, was already obsolescent for penetration of hostile territory. The design objectives of the Tu-105 were to produce an aircraft with

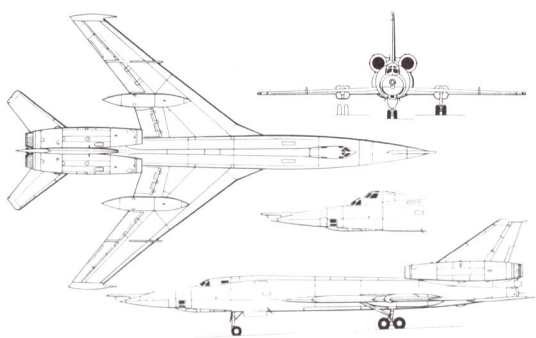

Tupolev Tu-22 'Blinder-A' with (scrap view) Tu-22U 'Blinder-D'.

performance generally comparable with the Tu-16, but with greatly increased penetration altitude and speed.

The Tu-105 was thus designed to incorporate supersonic dash at high altitude without excessively penalizing subsonic efficiency. The engines were mounted high on the rear fuselage in slim cowlings to avoid the weight and drag penalties of long inlet ducts. Sweep was increased relative to that of the Tu-16, but a compound-sweep layout was chosen for minimum subsonic and low speed penalty. The fuselage, wing, landing-gear pods and engine nacelles were positioned and designed in strict accordance with the area rule. The elimination of defensive armament except the tail cannon saved weight and volume and the crew was reduced to three, seated in tandem downward-ejecting seats. For the first time in a Soviet aircraft, bombing/navigation radar displaced the glazed nose.

The source of the engines has long been a mystery, but it appears they are Kolesov VD-7s, similar to the engines fitted to the Myasishchev M-50. The nacelles are fitted with plain inlets; production Tu-22s have narrower inlets than early aircraft, and the lips slide forwards to open an auxiliary annular aperture at low speeds.

The Tu-105 probably flew in 1959, in time for 10 (including one with a missile) to be demonstrated at Tushino in 1961. The type's debut was a complete surprise to Western intelligence, but progress in defence systems had come to the point where a supersonic dash and better cruise altitude were in practice not much of an advantage over the subsonic Tu-16. In addition, the decision to rely solely on missiles for strategic attack had already been taken, leading to the temporary cessation of bomber development, and transfer of many aircraft to the Soviet naval air arm (AVMF).

There was, however, a continuing role for the Tu-22 in the precision strike and missile-carrying role, and about 170 of the type were delivered to Long-Range Aviation (DA) units from about 1964. These were of the variant known to NATO as

The dramatically area-ruled shape of the Tu-22, chosen to permit supersonic dash with as little penalty in terms of subsonic performance as possible, is apparent in this view of a 'Blinder-B'.

Tupolev Tu-22 Blinder

'Blinder-B', with a bomb-bay modified to accept the AS-4 'Kitchen' air-to-surface missile, as well as free-fall weapons. The designation 'Blinder-A' was applied to the nine non-missile aircraft seen at Tushino in 1961. The AS-4 is the Soviet equivalent of the defunct British Hawker Siddeley Blue Steel, rocket-powered and with a 200-mile (320-km) range.

The main AVMF variant of the Tu-22 in current service is the maritime-reconnaissance Elint 'Blinder-C'. The 'Blinder-B' and the AS-4 do not appear to be in AVMF service. In the reconnaissance role, the 'Blinder-C' offers payload and flight-refuelled endurance similar to those of the Tu-16, but less space for the crew. Only some 50 are in AVMF service. Both the DA and AVMF operate a few 'Blinder-D' (probably Tu-22U) conversion trainers, with a separate second cockpit above and behind the standard (pupil's) cockpit.

Although the Tu-22 is far from being the failure it has been considered in the West, it has not found an important niche in the Soviet forces. Its main role in the late 1960s and early 1970s was strike in the European region, but its importance in this role has diminished with the introduction of the Sukhoi Su-19 into the FA, and the Tu-26 'Backfire' into the DA and AVMF. The small batches of 'Blinder-Bs' supplied to Libya and Iraq (without AS-4 missiles or nuclear weapons) were probably surplus to DA requirement. The Iraqi aircraft have been used in action against Kurdish insurgents, and one Libyan machine at least against Tanzania, in support of Uganda. The Tu-22 has thus become one of very few large bombers conceived since 1945 to drop bombs in anger. A second batch was delivered to Libya in 1979.

In 1974 it was reported that Tu-22s were being converted to the interceptor role to replace Tu-28Ps, but this report has not been substantiated.

When the Tu-22 entered service its engines—probably Kolesov VD-7s—were the most powerful in the world. The rear engines eliminate the need for long inlet ducts and minimise engine-out handling problems.

Tupolev Tu-22 Blinder

A Tu-22 'Blinder-B' bomber/missile carrier takes off. A competent design according to its lights, the Tu-22 was never fully exploited because its performance advantage over the Tu-16 was rendered insignificant by Western Mach 2 interceptors.

Tupolev Tu-22
Blinder

Called on to produce a supersonic successor to the Tu-16, the Tupolev bureau chose a thin compound-sweep wing and a high degree of area-ruling. Removable panels ahead of the twin conventional bomb-bays permit rapid conversion to a carrier for the AS-4 missile.

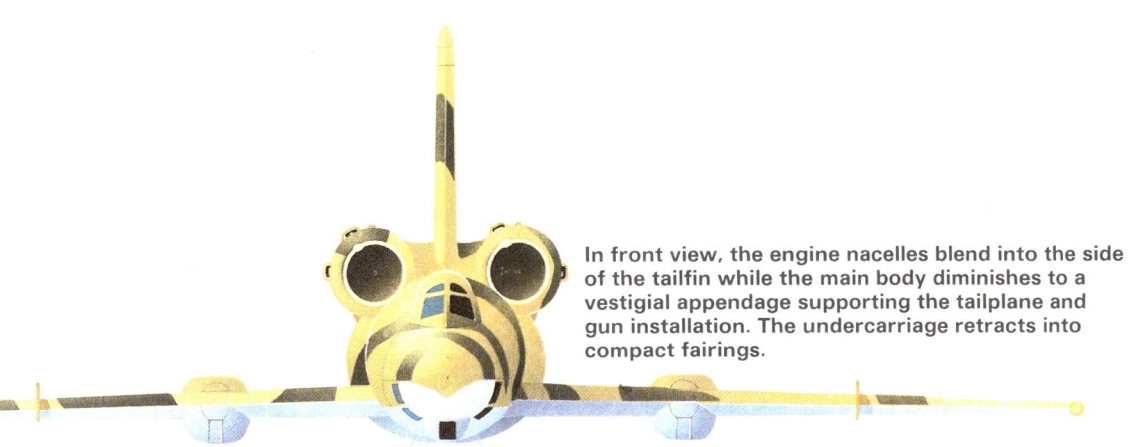

In front view, the engine nacelles blend into the side of the tailfin while the main body diminishes to a vestigial appendage supporting the tailplane and gun installation. The undercarriage retracts into compact fairings.

Specification

Type: bomber, reconnaissance and maritime-strike aircraft

Powerplant: probably two 31,000-lb (14000-kg) Kolesov VD-7 afterburning turbojets

Performance: maximum speed at 36,000 ft (11000 m), 1000 mph (1600 km/h) Mach 1.5; cruising speed 36,000 ft (11000 m) 560 mph (900 km/h) or Mach 0.85; service ceiling 60,000 ft (18000 m) with afterburning, 50,000 ft (15000 m) without; maximum range (subsonic) 4,000 miles (6500 km); unrefuelled tactical radius with 250 miles (400 km) supersonic dash 1,750 miles (2800 km)

Weights: empty 90,000 lb (40000 kg); internal fuel 80,000 lb (36000 kg); maximum take-off 190,000 lb (85000 kg)

Dimensions: span 94 ft 6 in (28.8 m); length 136 ft 9 in (41.7 m); height 28 ft 2 in (8.6 m); wing area 1,650 sq ft (155 m^2)

Armament: one 23-mm cannon in radar-directed tail barbette, and about 17,500 lb (8000 kg) of internal stores or ('Blinder-B') one AS-4 'Kitchen' cruise missile

Operators: Iraq, Libya, USSR

Scarcely a straight line mars the side profile, an indication of the care taken to follow the area-rule in the design of the aircraft. Automated, radar-aimed tail gun, used for the first time on a Soviet aircraft, saved weight and drag.

Tupolev Tu-26 Backfire

History and notes

Few contemporary combat aircraft have been the subject of as much controversy as the Tupolev bureau's swing-wing bomber, codenamed 'Backfire' by NATO and referred to as the Tu-26 by the US Department of Defense. The Soviet Union has quoted the designation Tu-22M, but this is not universally believed to be the actual service designation of the type. Throughout the Strategic Arms Limitation Talks (SALT) negotiations, the Soviet Union has maintained that the 'Backfire' is intended for maritime and European strike missions rather than long-range strike against the USA; US negotiators, on the other hand, have consistently argued that the aircraft has strategic range, and there have been accusations that some estimates of 'Backfire' performance have been deliberately suppressed to suit the political line. However, the aircraft is now regarded as a 'peripheral' system, and unless it is equipped with long-range cruise missiles (allowing it to fly its entire mission to the launch point at subsonic speed, while still threatening a large proportion of the USA) it is not seen as a true strategic system. However, it still presents a very serious threat to Western Europe, the North Atlantic and above all to China, which completely lacks the air-defence capability needed to intercept the 'Backfire' at any altitude. Its potential in the maritime strike role is also significant; in the 1980 US Department of Defence annual report its was suggested that "the Backfire threat . . . will exceed the menace of Soviet attack submarines."

'Backfire' development started in 1964-65, to meet a joint Soviet Naval Aviation (AVMF) and Long-Range Aviation (DA) requirement for a Tu-22/Tu-16 replacement. It is questionable whether or not, by that time, the decision to abandon the bomber as a strategic weapon had been reversed. It was inevitable that any bomber developed with variable sweep and turbofans would have very long subsonic range, and thus some strategic potential, as a corollary of improved low-level and loiter performance.

The design of the 'Backfire' (reported bureau designation is Tu-116, but this is not confirmed) was typically evolutionary, combining elements from a number of designs. The NK-144 engines were already well developed for the Tu-144 supersonic airliner, while the general arrangement of the aircraft was similar to that of the Tu-102/28, with long inlet ducts and a low-set wing. The Tupolev bureau decided to accept the performance penalties of the unique semi-variable-geometry layout, with pivot points at one-third span, rather than take the much greater risks of a fully variable configuration, as used on the Rockwell B-1. In addition, the initial design retained the waisted fuselage and podded landing gear of the Tu-28. High-lift devices were apparently conventional, with slats on the outer wings, Fowler flaps and (possibly) a droop on the glove leading edge.

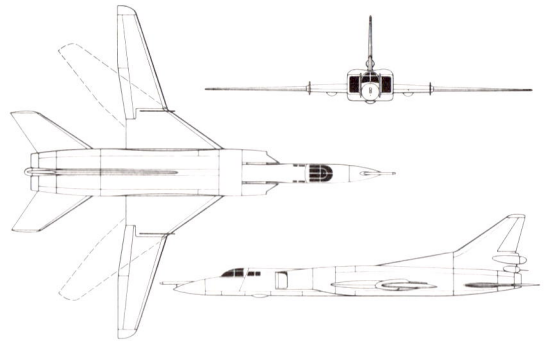

Tupolev Tu-26 'Backfire-B'.

The first prototype, representative of the aircraft known as 'Backfire-A' to NATO, flew in 1969 and demonstrated a considerable range deficiency as a result of excessive drag, probably affecting low-level performance most severely. It was therefore decided to modify the aircraft radically. The 'Backfire-B' features new outer wings of increased span, with a distinctive double-taper on the trailing edge, and a new landing gear, which retracts inwards into the fuselage. There may have been other changes, but the nose and tail were little altered. The first trials unit started working up in 1975.

Tupolev Tu-26 Backfire

Production has been reported to be running at a rate of 35 aircraft a year, but this is hard to square with the US Defence Department's statement that only 100 aircraft were in service in early 1980, suggesting an average production rate of 20 ships/year.

With refuelling, the 'Backfire-B' does sustain a one-way threat to the continental USA, but its main role (particularly in view of the long-range bomber anticipated in early 1979) is in the European and maritime theatres. In Europe, the 'Backfire' remains the only aircraft in the Soviet inventory which can cover the whole of the NATO region at low level from a 'starting line' on the Eastern bloc border, operating on a hi-lo-hi profile from secure bases in the western Soviet Union.

An equally serious threat is posed by AVMF 'Backfires', with their capability to launch long-range strikes from the North Cape area over much of the Atlantic. The 'Backfire' force thus menaces NATO's vital resupply route; NATO's main counter seems to be to close the gap between Scotland and Iceland with AWACS aircraft (BAe Nimrod AEW.3) and long-range interceptors (Panavia Tornado F.2). Another potential use of the 'Backfire' is as a long-range 'air interdictor', armed with a heavy load of air-to-air missiles for use against transatlantic freight aircraft carrying priority reinforcements.

Missile armament of the 'Backfire' is an area of uncertainty. The Mach 3 AS-6 'Kingfish anti-shipping missile was reported to be under development for the 'Backfire', and at one stage it was thought that two of these weapons might be carried. However, as seen in late 1977 the weapon appears to be larger than first reported, and is more suited to a single installation like that of the AS-4, on the Tu-22. Armament of the 'Backfire' on long-range missions is likely to comprise a single AS-4 or AS-6 at present, but a new 750-mile (1200-km)-range weapon has been test-fired from a Tu-26; it is believed to exist in surface- and air-launched versions. The internal ECM suite of the Backfire is comparable to that of a specialised ECM Tu-16.

In early 1979 the US journal *Aviation Week* reported that a 'Backfire' development with MiG-25-type ramp inlets was under test. Such a version — possibly identified a 'Backfire C' — might be marginally faster at medium altitude, but this would make little difference to its effectiveness. It is expected that about 450 'Backfires' will be delivered to the AVMF and DA, and deliveries to date appear to have been shared roughly equally between the two sub-types.

The best photographs of the 'Backfire' seen so far have been taken by Swedish Air Force aircraft over the Baltic Sea.

Front view of Backfire is dominated by the massive intakes and trunks for the afterburning turbofan engines. Ventral fin of the AS-4 'Kitchen' missile—an early-1960s rocket-powered weapon closely comparable with the contemporary British Hawker Siddeley Blue Steel—folds to starboard when the missile is carried. Underwing fairings house undercarriage-retraction mechanism.

Specification

Type: medium-range bomber and maritime strike/reconnaissance aircraft

Powerplant: two 45,000-lb (20500-kg) Kuznetsov NK-144 afterburning turbofans

Performance: maximum speed at 36,000 ft (11000 m) 1,200-1,320 mph (1930-2120 km/h) or Mach 1.8-2.0; cruising speed 560 mph (1900 km/h)

The 'Backfire' has a basically slender fuselage blended into the big intake tunnels. Internal bombs may be carried in place of the AS-4. Other stores may be carried on pylons under the inlet ducts. What appear to be multiple stores racks have been seen, although there is some feeling that they may be antennae of some sort.

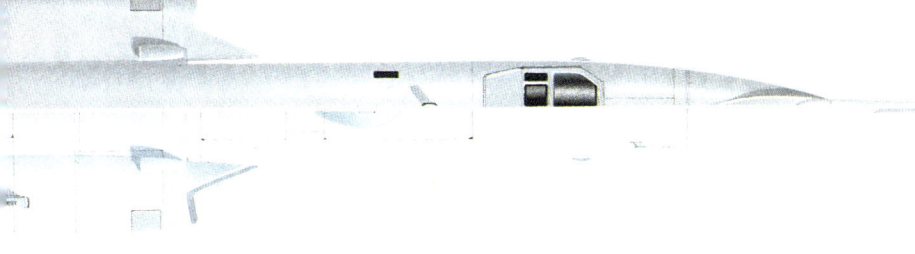

at 33,000 ft (11000 m); maximum speed at sea level 650 mph (1050 km/h); cruising speed at sea level 500 mph (800 km/h); service ceiling 55,000 ft (17000 m); range 5,000 miles (8000 km); hi-lo-hi combat radius 1,600 miles (2600 km); sea-level combat radius 850 miles (1400 km)

Weights: empty 110,000 lb (50000 kg); internal fuel 105,000 lb (47500 kg); maximum take-off 245,000 lb (11000 kg)

Dimensions: span (unswept) 113 ft (34.5 m) span (swept) 86 ft (26.2 m); length 132 ft (40.2 m); height 30 ft (9.1 m); wing area 1,785 sq ft (166 m²)

Armament: two 23-mm cannon in radar-directed tail barbette, plus one or two AS-4 'Kitchen', or AS-6 'Kingfish' missiles recessed into fuselage or under wings; other stores may be carried in internal weapons bay, for a total stores capacity estimated at 17,500 lb (8000 kg)

Operators: USSR

Side view of 'Backfire' is dominated by the massive fin, which houses a considerable quantity of fuel in addition to extensive electronics and the tail gun installation. Plethora of aerials and radomes indicates the formidable internal ECM equipment carried by Backfire, which can expect to be a priority target.

Tupolev Tu-28 Fiddler

History and notes

Originally developed as the Soviet Union's counter to missile-carrying subsonic bombers in the late 1950s and early 1960s, the Tupolev Tu-28 'Fiddler' remains the largest fighter in the world. Most of the aircraft of this type appear to be deployed along the northern edge of the Soviet Union; in that sense, their opposite numbers are the fighters of the Canadian Armed Forces, with a vast periphery to protect an inhospitable territory beneath them.

The Tu-28P appears to have entered service rather later than the Tu-22, but the design is earlier in origin and carries the bureau designation Tu-102. It represented a development of one of the most publicised but least used of Soviet aircraft, the Tupolev Tu-98 'Backfin'. It is difficult to work out the characteristics of the Tu-98, because in 1956-60 it was the object of a vast amount of speculation in the West, by intelligence and press sources alike. Some of this appears to have been picked up by Eastern European sources and 're-transmitted'. This speculation was aroused by the inclusion of the Tu-98 among a collection of (mostly cancelled) Soviet aircraft demonstrated to the US Air Force in the summer of 1956 at Kubinka near Moscow. The Tu-98 was then ascribed by the West to the Yakovlev bureau, and even designated Yak-42.

In fact the Tu-98 had been flown in 1955, as a light transonic tactical bomber intended as a successor to the Ilyushin Il-28. Like the contemporary Il-54, it was powered by two Lyulka AL-7F afterburning

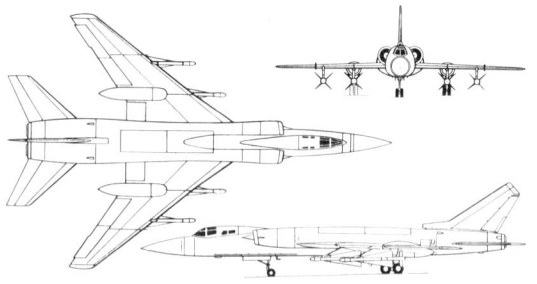

Tupolev Tu-28P 'Fiddler'.

turbojets of 20,000-lb (9000-kg) thrust. Unlike the Tu-16, it had engines mounted inside the rear fuselage, fed by long intake ducts curving over the wing. The crew numbered three, with a navigator in a pointed, glazed nose.

Both the Tu-98 and Il-54 were cancelled in favour of the small Yak-28, but the Tupolev bureau developed the Tu-98 into the refined Tu-102, which was apparently intended to fill the light strike role as well as having potential as an interceptor. The Tu-102 is believed to have made its first flight in 1959, and differed from the Tu-98 in having a more sharply swept wing, adjustable half-cone inlets and podded main bogies.

In the event, the Tu-102 was to be adapted as the carrier for a new long-range air-to-air missile and its

The Tu-28P has had no direct Western equivalent, although aircraft such as the Grumman F-14 Tomcat and Panavia Tornado F.2 fill a similar patrol-interception role at a much more advanced technology standard. Note radar-homing AA-5 'Ash' missile on inboard pylon.

Tupolev Tu-28 Fiddler

Production-type Tu-28Ps were demonstrated for the first time at the Domodedovo air show in 1967, having entered service a few years earlier. The type may be replaced by the new 'Super MiG-25'.

powerful 'Big Nose' radar. The intended role of the eventual Tu-28P was to intercept Western subsonic bombers before they came close enough to launch long-range missiles such as the North American Hound Dog, Hawker Siddeley Blue Steel or Douglas Skybolt. This demanded considerable endurance at remote patrol points, and the answer was an aircraft of considerable size.

Development of the radar, avionics and AA-5 'Ash' missile (the largest air-to-air missile in the world until the appearance of the AA-6 'Acrid') appears to have run behind that of the airframe. The Tu-28s demonstrated at Tushino in 1961 carried only two AA-5s (both apparently infra-red homing), a very large ventral fairing and ventral fins.

Production deliveries are believed to have started in 1963-64, but it was not until 1967 that the production standard aircraft was observed, at the Domodedovo air display. Production Tu-28Ps carry two AA-5s under each wing, and are reported to be armed with a mix of semi-active radar and infra-red homing weapons. The ventral fairing and fins are absent. It is possible that the ventral blister was a 'mission pack' containing stores of avionics, designed for the Tu-102's original multi-role function and deleted when the type was assigned to interception. It is likely that pre-production Tu-102s, like the Tu-98, were powered by AL-7Fs; production aircraft, in this case, would almost certainly have the more powerful AL-21F, which may have been developed for the Tu-28.

The Tu-28 continues to fill a niche in the defensive cordon of the Soviet Union which cannot be catered for adequately by any other type, and it is likely to remain in service until the new air-defence system expected in the early 1980s becomes operational. The aircraft referred to by US sources as the 'Super MiG-25', the main air vehicle in the new system, is the only other two-seat Soviet fighter. It is also likely to match the range and loiter capability of the Tu-28P; the present MiG-25 lacks this by a large margin. The effectiveness of the Tu-28P depends on the degree to which it has been updated, but it is likely to fall well short of Western systems such as the AWG-9/Phoenix system carried by the Grumman F-14. Even operating in conjunction with the Tu-126 'Moss', the Tu-28P is unlikely to be effective against low-flying targets. However, its presence will still tend to force them down on to the deck, reducing penetration range; and rebuilding these impressive aircraft with new radar and weapons might be logical.

Specification

Type: two-seat long-range interceptor
Powerplant: two 24,500-lb (11000 kg) Lyulka AL-21F afterburning turbojets
Performance: maximum speed 1,200 mph (1900 km/h) Mach 1.8 at 36,000 ft (11000 m); maximum speed with four missiles 1,000 mph (1600 km/h), or Mach 1.5; service ceiling 60,000 ft (18000 m); range 2,000 miles (3200 km); tactical radius 800 miles (1300 km)
Weights: empty 40,000 lb (18000 kg); maximum take-off 85,000 lb (38500 kg)
Dimensions: span 65 ft (20 m); length 85 ft (26 m); height 23 ft (7 m); wing area 850 sq ft (80 m²)
Armament: four AA-5 'Ash' air-to-air missiles
Operators: USSR

Tupolev Tu-28 Fiddler

A fully armed Tu-28 'Fiddler' of the PVO air defence force. The conical tips of the AA-5 'Ash' air-to-air missiles on the outer pylons reveal that they are infra-red-homing types; inboard weapons are radar homers. The use of IR homing is surprising on a large and supposedly long-range weapon, since IR is essentially a short-range homing system. One wonders whether the IR weapons have some sort of additional mid-course guidance from the carrier aircraft, perhaps connected with the long and combersome 'towel-rail' HF antenna under the fuselage.

Tupolev Tu-95 Bear

History and notes

Unquestionably the most spectacular of contemporary warplanes, the vast Tupolev Tu-95 'Bear' remains in service with the DA and the AVMF (Soviet Naval Aviation) by virtue of its unmatched range. The Tupolev giants are the only turboprop combat aircraft in use, and the only swept-wing turboprop aircraft ever to see service. Their mighty propellers still defy conventional design wisdom, which states that the peak in propeller efficiency has been passed long before the speed of the aircraft is high enough to justify a swept wing.

The design of the Tu-95 is directly descended from that of the Boeing B-29, copied by Tupolev as the Tu-4 'Bull'. The refined Tu-80 development of the Tu-4 led to the much larger Tu-85, whose speed was inadequate to evade jet fighters. In view of the progress being made on turbine engines, it was decided to abandon the Tu-85 and develop a more advanced design using a similar fuselage.

Design of the Tu-95 started before 1952, in parallel with the Myasishchev M-4 'Bison'. The massive NK-12 turboprop was bench-tested at 12,000 hp (8952-kW) in 1953 and the first prototype Tu-95 flew in the following year. In flight tests without military equipment the Tu-95 attained a speed of 590 mph (950 km/h), equivalent to nearly Mach 0.9, an achievement matched by scarcely any other propeller aircraft, and certainly by none of its size.

The Tu-95 entered service in 1955 with the DA bomber force, and caused something of a panic in US defence circles; at that time most of the all-weather/night fighters in US service were still straight-winged, and would have had trouble intercepting the Soviet bomber. However, with the advent of the surface-to-air guided missiles and radar-controlled, missile-armed interceptors in the late 1950s, the Tu-95 became largely obsolete as a bomber. To maintain a credible deterrent, the massive AS-3 'Kangaroo' missile was developed, measuring 49 ft (15 m) from nose to tail and weighing nearly 10 tons.

About 50 of the DA's Tu-95s became 'Bear-Bs' with the AS-3 missile and a large nose radar, and the bomber force retains more than 100 Tu-95s. However, a major user of the aircraft is the AVMF, whose aircraft are apparently designated Tu-142. 'Bear-C' is apparently an MR type with the same radar. The 'Bear-E' is similar to the bomber, but equipped for Elint (electronic intelligence) and other reconnaissance duties. The 'Bear-F' is a more recent MR modification, with extended inner engine nacelles, and conversion of Tu-95s to this standard continues. The 'Bear-D' is a highly interesting variant, with a large ventral radar in a bulged radome. One theory is that the 'Bear-D' is a director for over-the-horizon surface-to-surface missiles such as the SS-N-3 and SS-N-12. Within these types there are many sub-variants, and no two AVMF Tu-142s

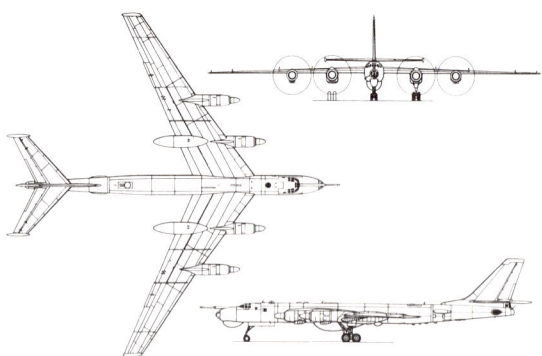

Tupolev Tu-142 'Bear-D'.

appear to be exactly alike. Recently, some aircraft have been seen with some or all defensive armament deleted. The 'Bear-F' has a small stores bay in place of the ventral turret.

It is possible that the last 'Bear-Bs' will not be retired until the mid-1980s. Equally, there is no sign of any aircraft which can match the Tu-95's superlative range and endurance and replace it in AVMF service, although the Tu-26 offers a close approach to its range performance. According to the US journal *Aviation Week*, a large subsonic aircraft is under development to replace Tu-95s in both these roles. For many years, the force has been dwindling due to accidents (several of the type have been lost on patrol) and even structural reconditioning can only delay the damage caused by vibration from the propulsion system. Apart from the AVMF and DA, the only operator of the Tu-95 has been Aeroflot: a rudimentary passenger and mail version, designated Tu-114D, operated some high-priority services in the early 1960s.

Specification

Type: strategic bomber, missile platform and maritime reconnaissance aircraft
Powerplant: four 15,000-shp (11190-kW) Kuznetsov NK-12MV turboprops
Performance: maximum speed 540 mph (870 km/h); economical cruising 465 mph (750 km/h); service ceiling 41,000 ft (12500 m); maximum range 11,000 miles (17500 km)
Weights: empty about 165,000 lb (about 75,000 kg); normal take-off 330,000 lb (150000 kg); maximum overload, 375,000 lb (170000 kg)
Dimensions: span 167 ft 8 in (51.1 m); length 155 ft 10 in (47.5 m); height 38 ft 8 in (11.78 m)
Armament: (original aircraft) six NR-23 23-mm cannon on dorsal semi-retractable barbette, ventral barbette and manned tail turret, plus a normal bomb load of 22,000 lb (10000 kg); 'Bear-B' converted to carry AS-3 'Kangaroo' stand-off weapon
Operator: USSR

Tupolev Tu-95 Bear

Tu-142 'Bear-D' reconnaissance aircraft as observed recently, with tail turret replaced by extended tailcone. It has been suggested that the tail houses a very long low-frequency wire antenna.

An AVMF Tu-142 'Bear-D' on one of the type's long over-ocean patrols. No replacement has yet emerged.

Tupolev Tu-95 Bear

Radar reconnaissance of the world's oceans, with passive antennae and the world's largest air-to-surface radar, is the task of the Tu-142.

Tupolev Tu-124 Cookpot

History and notes

After enjoying limited success in its designed role as an airliner, the Tupolev Tu-124 'Cookpot', a scaled-down version of the Tu-104, has remained in service as a VIP and government transport, for which its small size and relatively good field performance render it suitable.

The Tu-124 was designed in the late 1950s to meet an Aeroflot requirement for an Ilyushin Il-14 replacement, designed to carry 44 – 56 passengers and to operate from small and unprepared fields. The prototype flew in June 1960, and possessed the distinction of being the first airliner to be designed specifically for turbofan engines. The Tu-124's D-20P turbofans were also the first engines to carry the name of the Soloviev bureau, which since then has powered a number of Soviet transport types.

In general arrangement the Tu-124 is similar to the Tu-104, but smaller in all respects, with a narrower cabin cross-section. The undercarriage is considerably shorter than that of the Tu-104, to facilitate servicing without inspection platforms, and the wing-loading is lower. The wing is fitted with double-slotted trailing-edge flaps and over-wing spoilers for better short-field performance. Like the later Tu-134, the Tu-124 features a large door-type airbrake beneath the centre section, to steepen the glide-path and thus shorten the field length.

Initial production Tu-124s have 44 seats, but the later Tu-124V seats 56 in a high-density layout. Government and VIP versions are the 36-seat and Tu-124K and the 22-seat Tu-124K2.

Rather small in capacity for an economic jet airliner, the Tu-124 has seen service as a VIP transport. This aircraft carries Soviet air force markings.

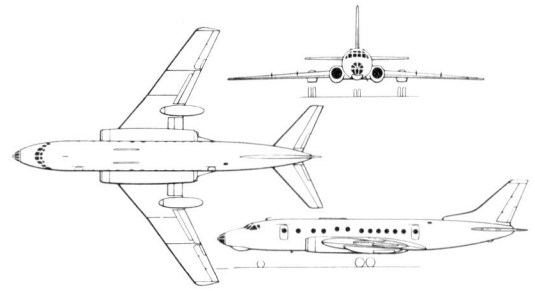

Tupolev Tu-124 'Cookpot'.

Specification

Type: twin-engined 44/56-seat airliner and government transport
Powerplant: two 12,000-lb (5400-kg) Soloviev D-20P turbofans
Performance: cruising speed Mach 0.82 or 540 mph (870 km/h); range with maximum payload of 13,200 lb (6000 kg) 775 miles (1250 km); maximum range with 30 – 35 passengers 1,300 miles (2100 km); service ceiling 38,400 ft (11700 m); take-off ground roll at maximum take-off weight 3,380 ft (1030 m); landing ground roll, 3,050 ft (930 m)
Weights: empty 50,485 lb (22900 kg); maximum payload 13,200 lb (6000 kg); normal take-off 80,500 lb (36500 kg); maximum take-off 82,500 lb (37500 kg)
Dimensions: span 83 ft 10 in (25.55 m); length 100 ft 4 in (30.58 m); wing area 1,285 sq ft (119.37 m²)
Operators: (governments of) Czecholovakia, East Germany, India, USSR

Tupolev Tu-126 Moss

History and notes

The existence of a Soviet equivalent to the Western Boeing E-3A Sentry airborne warning and control system (AWACS) was revealed in late 1969, by which time the type had probably been flying for at least two years. The fact that the type was not among those demonstrated at the 1967 Domodedovo air display may be significant: the Soviet Union would hardly have anything to gain from attempting to conceal so large and distinctive a weapon system while at the same time revealing so many smaller aircraft. It is therefore likely that the first flight of a development aircraft took place in late 1967, with the system becoming operational in 1970. In 1971 a single aircraft was detached with its crew to assist the Indian air force in the war with Pakistan, indicating that the type was operational by that time.

Carrying the designation Tu-126 in Soviet service, and codenamed 'Moss' by NATO, the Soviet AWACS resembles the Boeing aircraft in the location of its main radar in a saucer-shaped rotodome on a fuselage. The location is chosen to reduce the interference generated by the wing and propellers

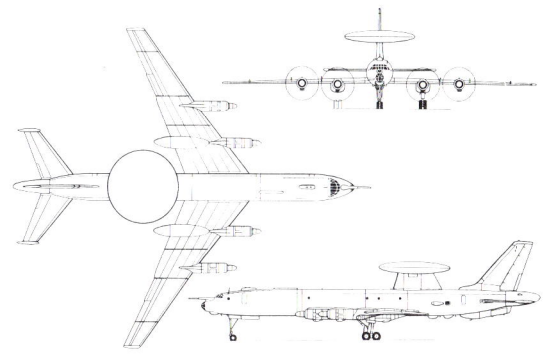

Tupolev Tu-126 'Moss'.

The PVO's Tu-126 early-warning aircraft may have been based on surplus Aeroflot Tu-114s.

The Tu-126 follows the US pattern in early warning aircraft, with a wide radar antenna in a saucer-shaped rotodome. 'Look-down' capability is thought to be limited.

Tupolev Tu-126 Moss

while minimizing the effects of the radome and its pylon on stability.

The Tu-126 is based on the airframe of the Tu-114 airliner, and it is probable that aircraft of this type have been converted from Tu-114s surplus to Aeroflot requirements. The advantages of the Tu-114 for this role include its roomy cabin (the comparable E-3A has a crew of 17, including systems operators) and its impressive endurance, especially at reduced patrol speeds. Less favourable aspects of the design probably include high vibration levels at cruising speed, providing a less-than-perfect environment for delicate electronic systems.

In addition to the main radar, the Tu-126 carries a considerable array of smaller aerials, enabling it to communicate with the fighter aircraft it controls and to interrrogate the IFF (identification, friend or foe) systems of radar contacts. Blister fairings around the rear fuselage presumably contain defensive and offensive electronic countermeasures (ECM) equipment.

The Tu-126 programme ran some eight years ahead of the Western AWACS development, and the US Department of Defense has a low opinion of its performance. According to the DoD, the Tu-126 system is 'ineffective' over land and 'only marginally effective' over water. If this unsubstantiated estimate is accurate, it would explain why only a small number of these aircraft have been seen in service: Western estimates are that fewer than 20 are in use.

The ability of the Tu-126 system to look-down on targets in the presence of high sea states or ground clutter depends on the technological standard of its

Compared with the Tu-95/142, the 'Moss' has a much longer and wider fuselage and extended-chord flaps.

radar and data-processing equipment, and it is thought that the Soviet Union has not progressed as far in these areas as the West. Moreover, the Tu-126 is the first airborne early warning (AEW) aircraft of any sort to enter service with the Soviet air forces. This contrasts with the 35 years of continuous US experience in the field. It would thus be surprising if the Tu-126 did fully match Western standards.

A more capable Soviet AWACS system is expected to be deployed in the early 1980s. It is expected to incorporate important advances in the areas of data processing and radar performance and to have overland look-down capability. A likely carrier aircraft for the new system is the Ilyushin Il-86 wide-body airliner, first flown in December 1976.

Specification
Type: airborne warning and control (AWACS) aircraft
Powerplant: four 15,000-shp (11900-kW) Kuznetsov NK-12MV turboprops
Performance: maximum speed at 33,000 ft (10000 m) 460 mph (740 km/h); long-endurance patrol speed 320 mph (520 km/h); service ceiling 33,000 ft (10000 m); endurance more than 20 hours
Weights: empty 200,000 lb (90000 kg); loaded 365,000 lb (165000 kg)
Dimensions: span 167 ft 8 in (51.1 m); length 188 ft (57.3 m); height 38 ft (11.6 m); wing area 3,350 sq ft (312 m^2)
Operator: USSR

Tupolev Tu-134 Crusty

History and notes

Originally designated Tu-124A, the Tupolev Tu-134 'Crusty' started life as a highly developed version of the Tu-124 incorporating the then-fashionable rear-engined layout. The Tu-134 retains the fuselage section, undercarriage layout and wing design philosophy of the Tu-124, but the later aircraft is substantially larger and heavier than its predecessor.

The Tu-134 made its first flight in 1963–64, being contemporary with the BAC One-Eleven and Douglas DC-9. As well as the revised arrangement, the new aircraft had more powerful Soloviev engines than those fitted to the Tu-124. (The designation D-30 is, however, something of a mystery: the Tu-134 powerplants have much more in common with the earlier D-20 than with the much larger and later Soloviev D-30K.)

The Tu-134 was followed into service in 1970 by the Tu-134A, with a fuselage stretched to 124 ft 2 in (37.7 m) and capacity for up to 80 passengers. Gross weight, payload and fuel capacity have been increased, and thrust reversers are fitted. Later Tu-134As were fitted with a solid nose containing weather radar, in place of the glazed nose which had been inherited from the Tu-104 and Tu-16 bomber.

Like the Tu-124, the Tu-134 features a ventral door-type speedbrake, but this has been wired shut on some aircraft because it closes too slowly for safety in case of a missed approach. Featuring a comparatively sharply-swept wing and no leading-edge devices, the Tu-134 has a high approach speed compared with Western types, and thus never completely replaced older turboprop transports in Aeroflot service. The Yakovlev Yak-42 has been expected to replace the Tu-134 in due course. The Tu-134D was a proposed 110-passenger version of the design, but it does not appear to have been proceeded with.

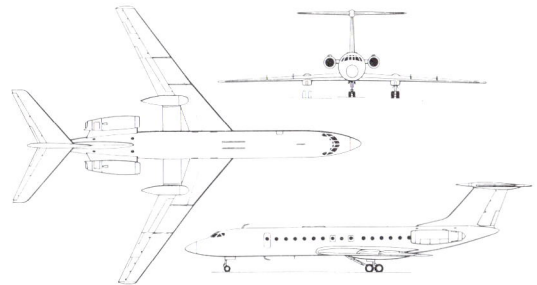

Tupolev Tu-134A 'Crusty'.

Specification

Type: airliner (72 seats), VIP and government transport
Powerplant: two 15,000-lb (6800-kg) Soloviev D-30 turbofans
Performance: Cruising speed 530 mph (849 km/h) at 36,000 ft (11000 m); range with maximum payload of 16,980 lb (7700 kg), 1,500 miles (2400 km); take-off field length to international standards 7,150 ft (2180 m); landing field length to international standards 6,730 ft (2050 m)
Weights: empty 60,500 lb (27500 kg); maximum landing 88,000 lb (40000 kg); maximum take-off 99,000 lb (45000 kg)
Dimensions: span 95 ft 2 in (29.0 m); length 114 ft 8 in (34.9 m); height 29 ft 7 in (9.0 m); wing area 1,370 sq ft (127 m^2)
Operators: Bulgaria, East Germany, Hungary, Poland

Hungary is one of the Warsaw Pact governments which uses the Tu-134 as a VIP transport.

Yakovlev Yak-11 Moose

History and notes

Although phased out by the Soviet Union and the more advanced Warsaw Pact forces, the Yakovlev Yak-11 'Moose' continues in service with some users. Designed as an advanced combat trainer, the Yak-11 is the last offshoot of the long line of Yakovlev fighters of the 1939–45 war; the wing platform, and the basic construction of the all-metal wing and metal-and-fabric covered fuselage are similar to the later Yak fighters.

The Yak-11 was flown in 1946 and entered service in the following year. Production in the Soviet Union totalled 3,850 aircraft, and the type was the first aircraft used by the expanding satellite air forces in the 1950s. In 1954 it was put into production in Czechoslovakia, as the C-11, and among the 707 examples of the type produced in Czechoslovakia were a number of C-11Us, a modified version of the type with a nosewheel landing gear and mainwheels mounted farther aft. The C-11U offered handling characteristics more representative of contemporary combat aircraft than the tailwheel version, but was heavier and of slightly lower performance.

Replacement of the Yak-11 in the basic trainer role started in 1963, but the type fulfilled a useful role as a transitional aircraft between the basic trainers of the time and the MiG-15UTI.

Specification

Type: two-seat advanced trainer
Powerplant: one 570-hp (425-kW) Shvetsov

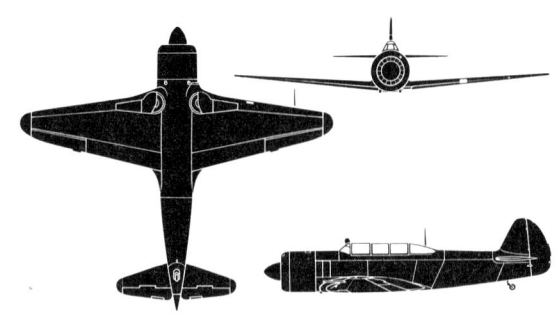

Yakovlev Yak-11 'Moose'.

ASh-21 seven-cylinder radial piston engine
Performance: maximum speed at sea level 263 mph (424 km/h); maximum speed at 7,380 ft (2250 m) 285 mph (460 km/h); ceiling 23,290 ft (7100 m); range 800 miles (1290 km)
Weights: empty 4,190 lb (1900 kg); normal take-off 5,290 lb (2400 kg)
Dimensions: span 30 ft 10 in (9.4 m); length 27 ft 11 in (8.5 m); height 10 ft 9 in (3.28 m); wing area 165.6 sq ft (15.4 m)
Armament: one 12.7-mm UBS machine-gun and two 110-lb (50-kg) practice bombs
Operators: Albania, Austria, Afghanistan, Bulgaria, China, Czechoslovakia, Egypt, Hungary, Poland, Romania, Syria, USSR, Yemen

Air forces as advanced as Czechoslovakia's CL have long since retired the Yak-11, but it soldiers on elsewhere.

Yakovlev Yak-18 Max

History and notes

The Yakovlev Yak-18 'Max' basic trainer has shown extraordinary longevity; itself a development of a pre-war design, the UT-2, it remained under active development into the 1970s and its probable replacement, the Yak-52, bears a close resemblance to its predecessor. The original Yak-18 flew in 1946, with the tailwheel undercarriage of its predecessor and the same 'helmet-type' cowling over the five cylinder M-11FR radial engine. The tricycle undercarriage of later versions was introduced on the Yak-18U of 1954, but the main production version was the Yak-18A, introduced in 1957, which added a more aerodynamically efficient NACA-type cowling and the much more powerful AI-14 engine. The aircraft is of metal construction with fabric covering, in typical Yakovlev style.

The first single-seat version of the Yak-18 was an unsuccessful prototype of 1946, but the concept was revived in 1959 with the first Yak-18P aerobatic aircraft. The prototype Yak-18P had the single cockpit in the aft position, while the initial production aircraft had a forward-set cockpit. The pilot was moved aft of the wing again in the Yak-18PM of 1965, which was strengthened to accept aerodynamic loadings of plus 9g to minus 6g, and it was this aircraft which started the run of Soviet success in international aerobatics. The Yak-18PS of 1970 reverted to the tailwheel landing gear of the first aircraft, to save weight and led to the development of the Yak-50.

The latest version of the Yak-18 is the four-seat Yak-18T, first seen in 1967 and recently reported to be entering service with the Soviet Union's state flying clubs. The wing span is increased by the installation of a wider centre-section, and a new cabin-type fuselage is fitted. The inwards-retracting landing gear is basically similar to that of the Yak-18PM.

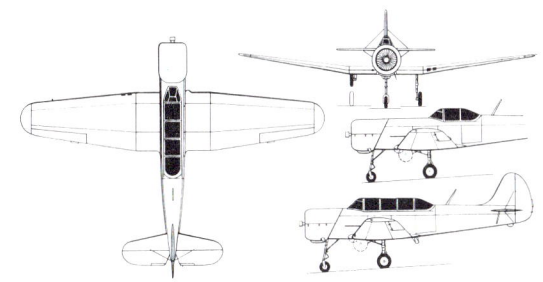

Yakovlev Yak-18A 'Max' and (inset) Yak-18PM.

About 6,700 Yak-18 trainers have been built, and the Yak-18T is still in production. It has been built in China as the BT-5.

Specification

Type: (Yak-18A) two-seat basic trainer; (Yak-18PM) single-seat aerobatic aircraft; (Yak-18T) four-seat liaison and training aircraft (specification for Yak-18A).
Powerplant: one 260-hp (194-kW) Ivchenko AI-14R nine-cylinder radial piston engine
Performance: maximum speed at sea level 163 mph (263 km/h); ceiling 16,600 ft (5060 m); range 440 miles (710 km)
Weights: empty 2,238 lb (1025 kg); normal take-off 2,900 lb (1316 kg); fuel load 210 lb (95 kg)
Dimensions: span 34 ft 9½ in (10.6 m); length 27 ft 5 in (8.354 m); wing area 182.9 sq ft (17 m²)
Operators: China, Czechoslovakia, East Germany, Egypt, Hungary, North Korea, Poland, Rumania, USSR

The Yak-18PM started the long line of successful Yakovlev aerobatic aircraft.

Yakovlev Yak-25RD Mandrake/Yak-27 Mangrove

History and notes

The original Yakovlev Yak-25 'Flashlight', flown in 1953, was a twin-engined tandem-seat night and all-weather interceptor, armed with cannon and later modified to carry air-to-air missiles. It had swept wings mounted in the mid position, and bicycle landing gear with small wing-tip outriggers. From this stemmed a prolific range of later tactical aircraft, many of which are still in service. Closest to the original, and possily even rebuilds of Yak-25s, are the Yak-25RD 'Mandrake' reconnaissance platforms, with a mid-high wing without sweep and having span increased from 36 ft (11 m) to just twice as much. Roughly in the class of the long-span Martin B-57 high-altitude platforms, this extremely high-flying machine was usually operated as a single-seater. In the 1970s surviving examples were being converted into radio-controlled targets and RPVs for electronic warfare.

The Yak-26 introduced a wing of greater strength, area and sweepback than the original, with many other changes, and was usually seen with a glazed nose and three seats. The -27 was a diverse family with the same wing but afterburning Tumansky RD-9B engines each rated at 8,820 lb (4000 kg). Most sub-types had a glazed nose and were reconnaissance platforms (NATO name 'Mangrove') though the -27P was a tandem-seat night fighter ('Flashlight-C'). Considerable numbers were built, and though all are thought to have been withdrawn from first-line service the majority appear still to be operational in second-line duties such as advanced

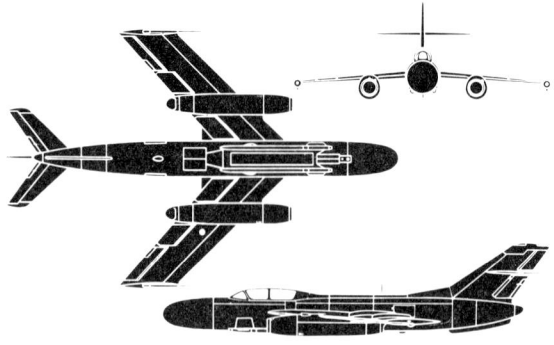

Yakovlev Yak-25RD.

trainers, trials platforms, engine test-beds, target tugs and as RPVs of various kinds. Recent photographs also suggest that some Yak-27s are active in the EW (electronic-warfare) role, with additional fuselage-mounted avionic installations.

Specification
Type: various (see text)
Powerplant: (27) two 8,820-lb (4000-kg) Tumansky RD-9B afterburning turbojets
Performance: maximum speed at altitude 686 mph (1104 km/h) (-25RD much slower); range very varied, but usually about 1,675 miles (2700 km)
Weights: (typical -27R) empty about 17,000 lb (8000 kg); maximum loaded 24,000 lb (10900 kg)
Dimensions: (-27R) span 38 ft 6 in (11.75 m); length 55 ft 0 in (16.75 m); height 14 ft 6 in (4.4 m)
Armament: today, none
Operators: USSR and possibly other Warsaw Pact air forces

The Soviet Union's 'U-2' was the far less sophisticated and less capable Yak-25RD 'Mandrake'. It did not enjoy its US counterpart's long service career.

Yakovlev Yak-28 Firebar/Brewer/Maestro

Soviet Air Force Yakovlev Yak-28P 'Firebar' two seat interceptor
of the IA-PVO Strany.

History and notes

Alexander Yakovlev's Yak-28 family of combat aircraft, similar in concept and performance to the
French Sud-Ouest Vautour series, continues to fill
an important role in the Soviet air arm, although the
numbers in service are declining. The last to be
retired will be the 'Brewer-E' ECM aircraft, with
some Yak-28P 'Firebar-Es' carrying on in less
strategically important areas of the Soviet
periphery.

The current Yak-28s are direct descendants of the
original Yak-25, developed from 1950 as the Soviet
Union's first all-weather jet fighter. The layout of
the Yak-25, with engines under the swept wings,
was conventional and followed wartime German
studies; it was one of the first aircraft to feature a
'zero-track tricycle' undercarriage, with a single
twin-wheel main unit on the centre of gravity and
single nose and outrigger wheels. Like the Mikoyan-
Gurevich MiG-19, the Yak-25 was initially powered
by Mikulin AM-5 engines, but most aircraft were fitted with the Tumansky RD-9. Developments of the
Yak-25 included the Yak-25RD 'Mandrake', Yak-26
and Yak-27 'Mangrove'.

The Yak-28 series bears little relationship to these
earlier aircraft, beyond a general similarity in con-
figurations. Initially, the Yak-28 seems to have been
developed as a transonic all-weather fighter using
two of the Tumansky R-11 turbojets developed for
the MiG-21, designed to carry a more effective radar
and missile than the Su-9. The Yak-28's wing is
more sharply swept than that of its predecessors
and is raised from the mid to the shoulder position.
The landing gear has a true bicycle layout, leaving
space for a large weapons bay between the main
units. On the Yak-28P interceptor this space is used
for fuel; the strike version carries stores in the internal bay, and drop tanks on underwing stations.

Deliveries of the Yak-28P 'Firebar' started in
1962, and the type is still widely used by the PVO
air-defence force. It offers considerably better endurance than the Sukhoi Su-15, which has similar
engines but is lighter and much faster. Later Yak-
28Ps, seen from 1967, have sharper and much
longer nose radomes and provision for AA-2 'Atoll'
short-range missiles on additional underwing
pylons.

Developed in parallel with the Yak-28P was a
glazed-nose strike version with a second crew
member seated ahead of the pilot and a bombing-

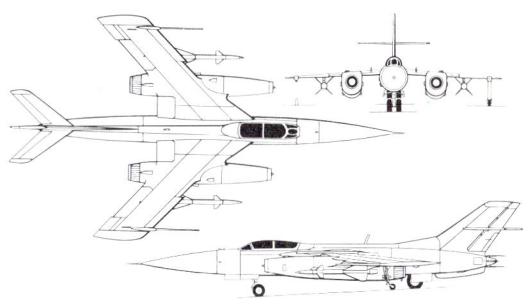

Yakovlev Yak-28P 'Firebar'.

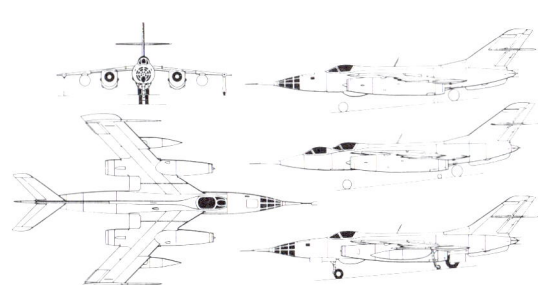

Yakovlev Yak-28 'Brewer-C' with (top side-view)
Yak-28 'Brewer-A' and (centre) Yak-28U 'Maestro'.

navigation radar aft of the nose landing gear.
Originally codenamed 'Firebar' by NATO, the type
was re-christened 'Brassard' when its bomber role
became obvious, and the reporting name was then
changed to 'Brewer' to avoid confusion with the
French Holste Broussard. Because the designations
'Firebar-A' and 'Firebar-B' has already been allotted, the 'Brewer' series appears to have started as
'Brewer-C'.

The 'Brewer-C' was used as a replacement for the
Ilyushin Il-28 in Soviet Frontal Aviation strike units,
but was not supplied to any aligned nations. The
presence of an internal weapons bay strongly suggests that its primary role was tactical nuclear
strike; the small cross-section of the fuselage limits
the load that can be carried internally, but the internal bay may have been necessary for the en-
vironmental control and arming of a nuclear
weapon. The Soviet Union's reluctance to supply the
aircraft to its allies is understandable if it is seen as

Yakovlev Yak-28 Firebar/Brewer/Maestro

basically a nuclear system. The closest Western equivalent was probably the early BAe (HS) Buccaneer S.1. The type is probably now used mainly in the 'Brewer-D' reconnaissance and 'Brewer-E' ECM versions, many 'Brewer-Cs' having been converted to this configuration. The 'Brewer-E' appears to carry active jamming equipment in the weapons bay for the support of strike formations. The other operational version of the Yak-28 series is the Yak-28U 'Maestro' conversion trainer, which like many Soviet trainers has separate cockpits for instructor and pupil.

Specification

Type: Yak-28 'Brewer-C' strike; 'Brewer-D' reconnaissance; 'Brewer-E' electronic countermeasures (ECM); Yak-28P 'Firebar-8' all-weather interceptor; Yak-28U 'Maestro' two-seat conversion trainer

Powerplant: two 13,000-lb (6000-kg) Tumansky R-11 afterburning turbojets

Performance: maximum speed at medium altitude 750 mph (1200 km/h) or Mach 1.13; maximum speed at sea level Mach 0.85; service ceiling 55,000 ft (17000 m)

Weights: empty 30,000 lb (13600 kg); maximum loaded 45,000-50,000 lb (20000-22000 kg)

Dimensions: span 42 ft 6 in (12.95 m); length (except late 'Firebar') 71 ft (21.65 m); length (late 'Firebar') 76 ft (23.17 m); height 13 ft (3.95 m)

Armament: ('Brewer-C') one 30-mm NR-30 cannon plus underwing bombs or rocket pods and 4,500 lb (2000 kg) of internal stores; ('Firebar C') two AA-3 'Anab' air-to-air missiles and, on some aircraft, two AA-2 'Atoll' air-to-air missiles

Operators: USSR

Yakovlev's Yak-28 'Brewer'—the glazed-nose version of the basic multi-role aircraft—continues to fill a limited role as a reconnaissance and electronic countermeasures platform.

Yakovlev Yak-28 Firebar/Brewer/Maestro

Yakovlev's transonic Yak-28P 'Firebar-B' interceptor is certainly dramatic in shape, and fills a niche between the Su-15 and Tu-28.

Yakovlev Yak-36 Forger

History and notes

In the late 1960s US reconnaissance satellites revealed that the Nikolayev shipyards on the Black Sea were starting construction of a warship far bigger than the 'Moskva' class ASW helicopter cruisers. As work progressed, it became clear that the new ship was to be a compound of missile cruiser and aircraft-carrier, with an open angled flight-deck over more than half its length. The new ship, *Kiev*, the first of its class, was obviously designed to carry V/STOL aircraft as well as helicopters, and Western observers waited with interest for the *Kiev*'s first voyage in international waters.

Some indication of progress in V/STOL technology in the Soviet Union had already been given. In the late 1950s, a group of Soviet engineers flew a VTOL test rig called the Turbolet, a simple wingless machine intended, like the similar Rolls-Royce Flying Bedstead, to explore the problems of zero-airspeed reaction control systems. Some years later, the Kolesov engine bureau began to study the design of specialized lift engines.

The Yakovlev bureau became involved in the study of V/STOL airframes, and two examples of a small research aircraft of Yakovlev design were demonstrated at the Domodedovo air display in 1967. Codenamed 'Freehand' by NATO, the type appeared to be crude in comparison with Western designs; the third-generation BAe Harrier was at that time undergoing flight tests before entering RAF service, while the 'Freehand' appeared little more advanced than the Bell X-14 of 1957. The basic layout was awkward, with two engines in the forward fuselage feeding rear vectoring nozzles, and

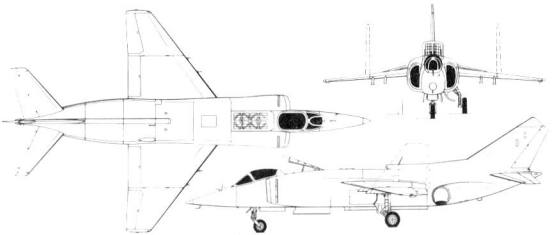

Yakovlev Yak-36 'Forger'.

the type clearly had little space for operational equipment. At the same time, a number of conventional aircraft fitted with lift-jets were demonstrated, showing that considerable progress had been made in this area. One of the 'Freehand' prototypes was reported to be used for sea trials aboard *Moskva*.

A considerable number of V/STOL prototypes appears to have been tested in the Soviet Union before the Yakolev Yak-36 'Forger' design was selected for large-scale evaluation. The configuration is unique, with only two rear vectoring nozzles on the lift-cruise engine and two lift jets forward, and imposes some basic limitations on the design. The most important is that the Yak-36 is apparently unable to make a short take-off. The short take-off is the standard operating mode for the Harrier, and permits a substantial increase in payload: the aircraft rolls forward with nozzles aft for 200 ft (60 m), the nozzles are rotated partially down and the aircraft lifts off with a combination of wing and engine lift (with the

The 'Forger-B' trainer version of the Yak-36 is even less aesthetically appealing than the basic fighter aircraft.

Yakovlev Yak-36 Forger

Three Yak-36s parked on the flight-deck of the Soviet carrier *Minsk*. The aircraft cannot fully exploit the carrier's angled flight-deck, because they are unable to make short or rolling take-offs.

'ski jump' ramp the gains are even greater). The Yak-36 cannot emulate this performance because the thrust of its lift jets has to be balanced by full vectoring of the rear nozzles, and is limited to what can be achieved with a vertical lift-off. Other drawbacks of the layout include a far higher risk of engine failure (more than tripled, because the lift engines are started twice as often as the cruise engine), this will usually result in loss of the aircraft because the Yak-36 cannot land with one engine out. Neither can the Yak-36 take advantage of an incidental benefit of the Harrier's V/STOL technique: the ability to use vectored thrust for air combat (Viffing).

Theoretical advantages of the 'Forger' layout include a cruise-matched main engine, but the improvement in efficiency is at least partly offset by the higher fuel consumption in transition. The 'Forger' is, however, notably stable in transition, and the smoothness of operational approaches to *Kiev* has led to speculation about precision ship-guidance. Other details include large cushion-augmentation strakes under the fuselage.

When *Kiev* sailed into the Mediterranean in the summer of 1976, details of the Yak-36 became quickly apparent. She carried a small trials unit of about 12 Yak-36s, including two or three 'Forger-B' trainers with an ungainly lengthened forward fuselage and a balancing 'stretch' aft. The 'Forger-A' single-seaters were apparently pre-production

aircraft, some being equipped with blow-in doors around the inlets and others lacking them. At the time of writing it appears that the aircraft embarked on *Minsk*, the second of the 'Kiev' class ships, are not greatly different from the *Kiev*'s aircraft; *Minsk* made her maiden voyage into the Mediterranean in early 1979. *Kharkov*, third of the class, was reported to be nearer commissioning in late 1979, with a fourth carrier under construction.

The avionic systems carried by the Yak-36 limit them to a clear-weather role; the only weapon-aiming system is apparently a small ranging radar in the extreme nose. Although the aircraft on *Kiev* carry AA-8 'Aphid' missiles and gun pods, the unit seems to be concerned mainly with operational trials of VTOL operating techniques and control systems.

In the absence of any consensus on what the Kiev-class ships are intended to do, it is difficult to define the role of the Yak-36. If it is intended for point air defence against, for example, Harpoon-carrying Lockheed P-3s, its present performance may be adequate and the main modification needed would be the addition of air-to-air radar; if it is regarded as a multi-role aircraft in the class of the BAe Sea Harrier, however, it will probably be necessary greatly to increase its payload and offensive capability. The Soviet Union almost certainly intends to develop a completely new aircraft which can exploit the angled flight-decks of the 'Kiev' class by means of a rolling take-off.

Yakovlev Yak-36 Forger

Yakovlev Yak-36 Forger

Left: One of the Kiev's complement of Yak-36s lifts off from the flight-deck. Louvred doors above the lift engine are open, as are the plain bomb-bay-type doors beneath the engines. The main powerplant exhausts through two simple swivelling nozzles.

Right: One of the virtues of the Yak-36 is the small space it occupies on the deck, thanks to its small span and folding wing. Numerous antennae and dielectrics are apparent on these aircraft, seen aboard the *Minsk*.

Below: One of the Kiev's aircraft approaches for a vertical landing. The louvred doors and the air inlets of the two lift engines can be clearly seen, and the flaps are lowered to help the aircraft decelerate. Western observers have been impressed by the stability of the Yak-36 on approach.

Yakovlev Yak-36 Forger

Specification

Type: light VTOL shipboard strike fighter

Powerplant: one 16,500-lb (7500-kg) class lift/cruise engine (possibly a relative of the Tumansky R-27/R-29 series) and two 5,500-lb (2500-kg) Kolesov lift jets

Performance: maximum speed at 36,000 ft (11000 m) 800 mph (1280 km/h) or Mach 1.2; maximum speed at sea level 650 mph (1050 km/h) or Mach 0.85; service ceiling 46,000 ft (14000 m); combat radius 150 miles (250 km)

Dimensions: span 23 ft (7.0 m); length 49 ft 2 in (15.0 m); height 10 ft 6 in (3.2 m); wing area 170 sq ft (15.8 m²)

Armament: four external pylons for up to 2,200 lb (1000 kg) of stores, including AA-8 'Aphid' air-to-air missiles and gun pods

Operator: USSR

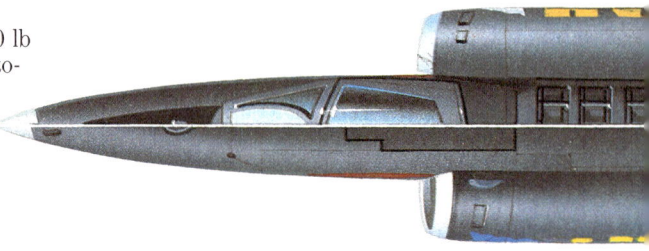

The Yak-36 is expected to be replaced by a more advanced aircraft which can exploit the angled-deck of the Soviet carriers by making a rolling take-off. Its already small wingspan can be further reduced by folding.

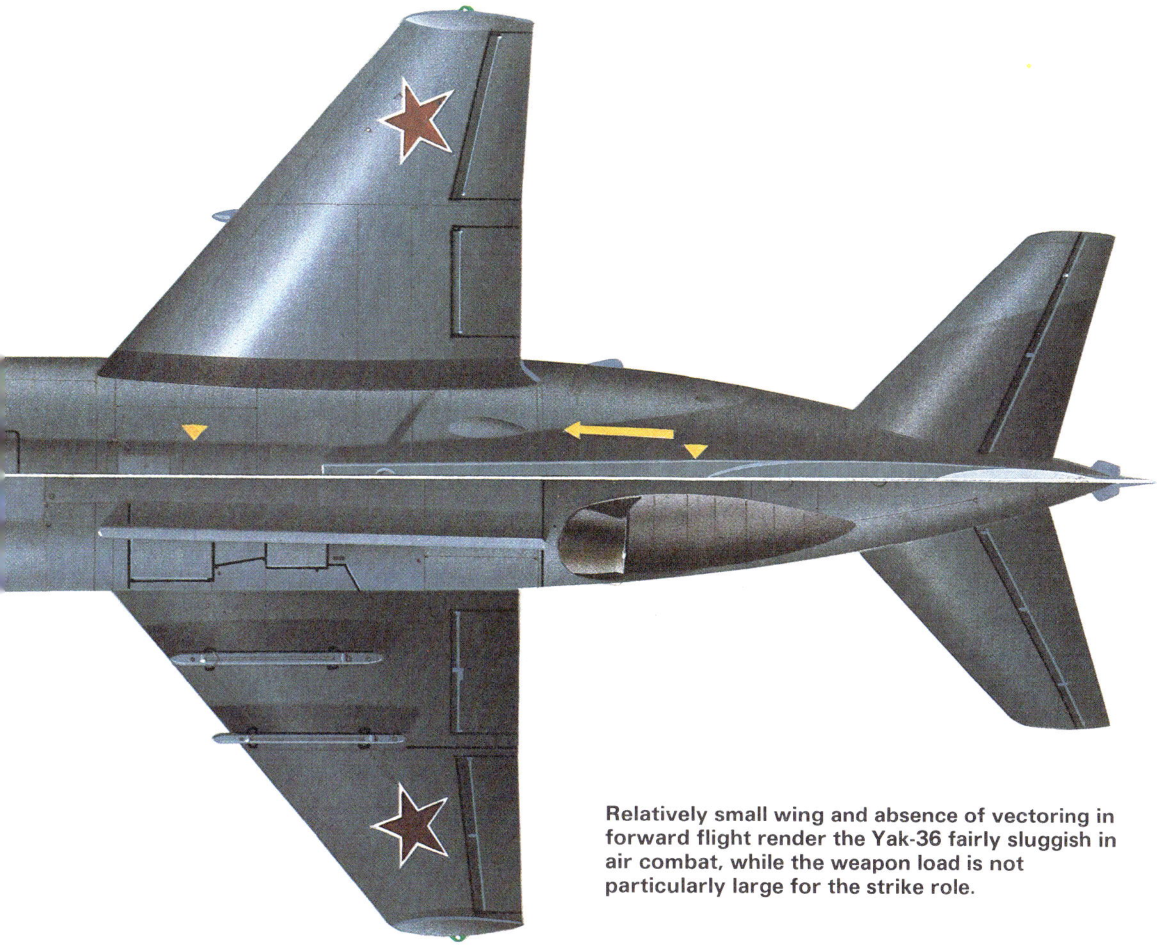

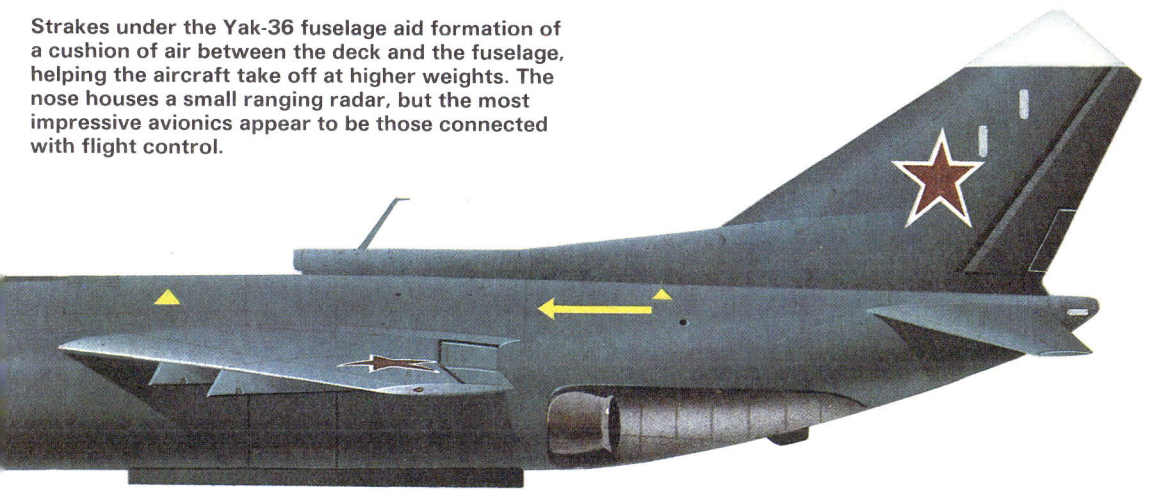

Relatively small wing and absence of vectoring in forward flight render the Yak-36 fairly sluggish in air combat, while the weapon load is not particularly large for the strike role.

Strakes under the Yak-36 fuselage aid formation of a cushion of air between the deck and the fuselage, helping the aircraft take off at higher weights. The nose houses a small ranging radar, but the most impressive avionics appear to be those connected with flight control.

Yakovlev Yak-40 Codling

History and notes

The Yakovlev Yak-40 'Codling' has been one of the Soviet Union's most successful commercial aircraft, and as the only small jet transport to emerge in the Soviet Union it fulfils a minor role as a VIP and government transport.

The design of the Yak-40 was started in 1964 to meet an Aeroflot requirement for a modern replacement for the unpressurized, piston-engined Lisunov Li-2, Ilyushin Il-12 and Il-14. For its first transport design, the Yakovlev bureau chose the unusual combination of jet engines and an unswept wing, the aircraft being optimised for good STOL airfield performance rather than speed. Location of the three engines at the rear of the fuselage, close to the centreline, also minimizes engine-out problems and makes the aircraft reasonably easy to fly. Manual controls are employed, and the aircraft has been designed with regard to ease of servicing at primitive fields. The high-aspect-ratio wing is fitted with simple Fowler-type flaps.

The first Yak-40 was flown in October 1966, and by September 1968 the first version was in service with Aeroflot. Later aircraft had greater payload and passenger capacity than the initial versions, and CSA took delivery of a convertible passenger/freight version of the aircraft. Considerable efforts have been made to export the Yak-40 to the West, and three aircraft of the type are operational in Italy. However, efforts to certificate the type in the UK and Canada have not been successful. The last of Aeroflots order for more than 800 Yak-40s was delivered in 1978.

Yakovlev's Yak-40 is the closest thing to an executive jet built in the Soviet Union, and as such is widely used for VIP transport.

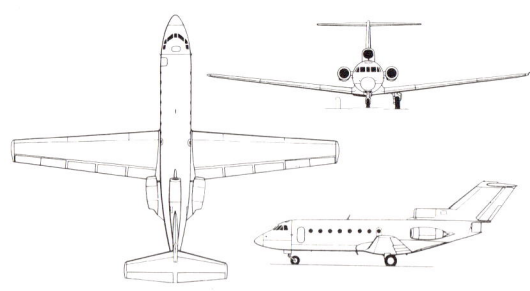

Yakovlev Yak-40 'Codling'.

Specification

Type: light 32-seat transport or VIP/communications aircraft

Powerplant: three 3,300 lb (1500 kg) Ivchenko AI-25 turbofans

Performance: maximum speed 345 mph (560 km/h) at 24,000 ft (7320 m); long-range cruising speed 290 mph (470 km/h); range with 3,750 lb (1700 kg) payload or 19 passengers 1,300 miles (2100 km); range with 30 passengers 900 miles (1450 km); take-off field length at sea level 3,540 ft (1076 m); landing field length 3,100 ft (945 m)

Weights: empty 22,630 lb (10263 kg); maximum take-off 35,280 lb (16000 kg); maximum landing 32,410 lb (14700 kg)

Dimensions: span 82 ft (25 m); length 66 ft 9 in (20.3 m); height 21 ft 4 in (6.5 m); wing area 753 sq ft (70 m²)

Operators: (airlines) Aeroflot, Avioligure, Balkan, Bulgarian, CSA, Vietnam; (governments) Malagay, Poland, probably USSR

Yakovlev Yak-50/52

History and notes

Whereas the Yak-18P series of aerobatic aircraft was developed from the original trainer, the Yakovlev Yak-52 trainer is a development of the Yak-50 aerobatic type. The Yak-52 is entering production in Romania, may be adopted by many Eastern bloc air forces as a replacement for the Yak-18.

Designed by Sergei Yakovlev and Y. Yankevitch as an improved aerobatic aircraft to succeed the Yak-18PM and Yak-18PS, the Yak-50 first competed at the 1976 world aerobatic championships Kiev. Design objectives included better manoeuvrability and inverted-flight characteristics than the Yak-18 series. As the new aircraft was designed to be a single-seater, it could be slightly smaller and lighter than the Yak-18; combined with a more powerful, fan-cooled version of the Yak-18's Ivchenko engine, this would markedly increase the power/weight ratio of the aircraft. Like the Yak-18PS, the Yak-50 has a rearwards-retracting tailwheel landing gear, although drawings of a version with a fixed, spatted gear have been published. The Yak-50 has a symmetrical aerofoil, for good inverted handling, and a variable-incidence tailplane.

The two-seat Yak-52 appeared in 1977. It is closely similar to the Yak-50 except in its undercarriage layout: the Yak-52 features a very basic semi-retractable tricycle gear, the wheels being completely exposed even when the legs are folded. The type is heavier and less agile than the single seater, and is stressed to lower 'g' levels (7g positive and 5g

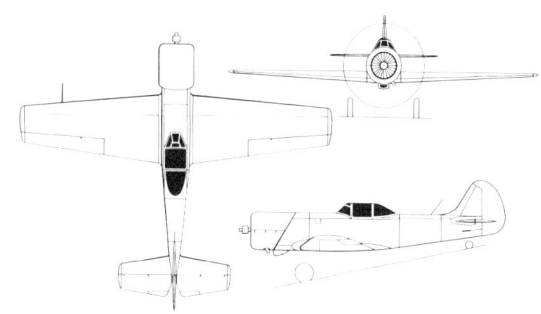

Yakovlev Yak-50.

negative), compared with 9g positive and 6g negative for the Yak-50).

The Yak-52 is being adopted by the DOSAAF, the network of state-run flying clubs in the Soviet Union which provides basic training for Soviet air force recruits and refresher training for reservists.

Specification

Type: (Yak-50) single-seat aerobatic aircraft; (Yak-52) two-seat trainer (specification for Yak-52)
Powerplant: one 360-hp (269-kW) Ivchenko/Vedeenev M-14P nine-cylinder radial engine.
Performance: maximum speed in level flight 175 mph (285 km/h); permissible diving speed 225 mph (360 km/h); ceiling 19,700 ft (6000 m); range 340 miles (550 km)
Weights: empty 2,200 lb (1000 kg); normal take-off 2,845 lb (1290 kg)
Dimensions: span 31 ft 2 in (9.5 m); length 25 ft 2 in (7.676 m); wing area 161.3 sq ft (15 m²)
Operators: USSR

Latest in the line of specialised aerobatic aircraft descended from the Yak-18, the Yak-50 is expected to be the forerunner of a new basic trainer.

INDEX

and see also the 'E'-series aircraft
export of Russian aircraft
  political significance of 20-23
  worldwide nature of 24-31

F

F-2: see MiG-15
F-4: see MiG-17 & see McDonnell Douglas aircraft
F-6: see MiG-19
F-7: see MiG-21
F-8: see MiG-21
F-14: see Grumman aircraft
F-15: see McDonnell Douglas aircraft
F-16: see General Dynamics aircraft
F-17: see Northrop aircraft
F-18: see McDonnell Douglas aircraft
F-86: see North American aircraft
F-104: see Lockheed aircraft
F-105: see Republic F-105 Thunderchief
F-106: see Convair F-106 Delta Dart
FA: see Soviet Air Force
FB-111: see General Dynamics aircraft
'Fagot': see MiG-15
Fairchild A-10 Thunderbolt II 14
'Faithless': see Mikoyan-Gurevich aircraft
'Farmer': see MiG-19
'Fencer': see Su-24
'Fiddler': see Tu-28
fighters:
  see MiG-15, MiG-17, MiG-19, MiG-21, MiG-23,
    MiG-25, Su-9, Su-11, Su-15, Tu-28 and Yak-28
'Firebar': see Yak-28
'Fishbed': see MiG-21
'Fishpot': see Su-9 & -11
'Fitter': see Su-7, -17, -20 & -22
'Flagon': see Su-15
'Flogger': see MiG-23 & -27
Focke-Wulf Ta 183 71
'Forger': see Yak-36
'Foxbat': see MiG-25
'Fresco': see MiG-17
Frontal Aviation: see Soviet Air Force

G

General Dynamics aircraft
  F-16 Fighting Falcon 9, 23
  FB-111 12, 159
Glushenkov: see powerplants
Grumman aircraft
  E-2 Hawkeye 11
  F-14 Tomcat 12, 159

H

'Halo': see Mi1 helicopters
'Hare': see Mi-1
'Harke': see Mi-10
'Harp': see Ka-25
Harrier: see BAe
'Haze': see Mi-14
helicopters:
  see Ka-25, Mi-1, Mi-2, Mi-4, Mi-6, Mi-8, Mi-10,
    Mi-14, Mi-24 V-3 Sokol
'Hind': see Mi-24
'Hip': see Mi-8
'Hook': see Mi-6
'Hoplite': see Mi-2
'Hormone': see Ka-25
'Hound': see Mi-4

I

I-350: see MiG-19
I-360: see MiG-19
Il-: see Ilyushin aircraft
Ilyushin aircraft
  Il-12 202
  Il-14 'Crate' 44, 47, 52, 186, 202
  Il-18 'Coot' 52, 53-54, 167
  Il-28 'Beagle' 55-58, 178, 193
  Il-38 'May' 8, 51, 59-62, 167
  Il-54 178
  Il-62 151
  Il-76 'Candid' 13, 15, 20, 39, 63-66
  Il-86 13, 15, 16
interdiction aircraft: see Su-24
Ivchenko: see powerplants

J

jet engines: see powerplants

K

Ka-: see Kamov helicopters
Kaman SH-2 Seasprite 67
Kamov helicopters
  Ka-8 66
  Ka-10 66
  Ka-15 66
  Ka-18 66
  Ka-25 'Hormone' 16, 66-70, 132
'Kangaroo': see missiles, air-to-surface
'Kelt': see missiles, air-to-surface
'Kennel': see missiles, air-to-surface
'Kerry': see missiles, air-to-surface
'Kingfish': see missiles, air-to-surface
'Kipper': see missiles, air-to-surface
'Kitchen': see missiles, air-to-surface
Klimov: see powerplants
Kolesov: see powerplants
Kuznetsov: see powerplants

L

LL-143: see Beriev aircraft
Li-2: see Lisuniv Li-2
Lightning: see BAe aircraft
Lisunov Li-2 'Cab' 44, 47, 52, 202
Lockheed aircraft
  A-11 108
  C-5 Galaxy 16, 43
  C-130 Hercules 36, 53
  C-141 StarLifter 43, 63
  EC-121 11
  Electra 53
  F-104 Starfighter 87, 100
  P-3 Orion 54, 59, 197
  SR-71 112
Lyulka: see powerplants

M

M-4: see Myasishchev aircraft
'Madge': see Be-6
'Maestro': see Yak-28
'Mail': see Be-12
'Mandrake': see Yak-25
'Mangrove': see Yak-27
maritime reconnaissance aircraft:
  see: Be-6, Be-12, Il-38, Tu-16, Tu-22, Tu-26, Tu-95

We are grateful to the following for supplying photographs
for this book:

Aviation Letter Photo Service 6, 22, 45, 63, 128, 202
Peter Steinemann 104, 105
Klaus Niska 18, 55, 56, 71, 87, 90, 125, 130, 131
Swedish Air Force via FLYGvapen NYTT 32, 175
Keystone Press Agency 75, 78, 92
Ministry of Defence 163, 183, 184
U.S. Navy 164
Mitsuo Shibata courtesy Air World 197, 199